MEL BAY PRESENTS
Early American Christmas Music

BY GLENN WILCOX

Cover Credit: W. Pote / H. Armstrong Roberts

© 1995 BY MEL BAY PUBLICATIONS, INC., PACIFIC, MO 63069.
ALL RIGHTS RESERVED. INTERNATIONAL COPYRIGHT SECURED. B.M.I. MADE AND PRINTED IN U.S.A.

CONTENTS

	Page
Introduction	4
Author's Notes	5
Alleluia Now We Sing	12
Angel Voice	14
Antwerp	18
Beautiful Star	24
Bethlehem	27
Bethlem	32
Birth of Christ	34
Boston	38
Braintree	40
Bristol	42
Child Jesus	44
Christmas	46
Christmas Anthem	49
Christmas Carol	52
Christmas Hymn	54
Clifton	56
Cookham	58
Courtney	60
Derrick	64
Eddington	68
Emanuel	70
Gabriel	73
Georgia	80
Glad Sound	82
Glad Tidings	86
Glorious Morn	88
Great Creator	90
Great Milton	92
Harborough	96
Harvard	100
Jamaica	102
Joyful Hope	104
Joyful News	106
Jubal	110
Judea	112
Lamb of God	115
Lancaster	120
London	122

Messenger	126
Milford	128
Milton	132
Mt. Ephraim	136
Nativity	138
New Hosanna	142
Oxford	146
Paxton	150
Randolph	152
Redeemer	154
Redemption	157
Rejoice	160
Sacred Day	164
Sark	167
Shining Star	170
Sing Alleluia	172
Somersett	176
Star	178
Star in the East	180
Wonder	184
Bibliography	186
Index of First Lines	187
Index of Authors, Composers and Compilers	188

INTRODUCTION

This volume is unusual in that everything in it has been published, but before this century. While a few items seem to be in the folk tradition, none of the music or words have been taken from oral sources. And, everything in here was obtained from some book published in America; the earliest one printed in the Colonies, the latest one when we were a nation of only forty-four states. The respective dates are 1761 and 1894.

Many early American composers believed that melodies did not belong to any individual, especially those they considered to be "common" tunes, and many of our tunes here may have had oral origins. So, each composer felt free to adapt a tune to his needs, which could mean setting different words, changing harmonic structure and accompanying voices, frequently embellishing the melody, and usually attaching a new title.

For these reasons, we prefer to say that all of our tunes here have been adapted from their source. This may mean as little as using one of the available alternate names (to keep from having a half-dozen each of Christmas, Christmas Carol, Christmas Hymn, etc.). It also means that words found to a given tune in one book may be set to a slight variant of that tune found in another book. We have modernized spelling and harmonic structure.

Most of these selections were taken from early American tunebooks. These are the oblong books, longer than they are high, which some call "end-openers." They are a fertile source of music which was sung and loved by generations of Americans. Well-known words can be found set to unknown melodies, which we hope will enhance your enjoyment of this collection.

We have attempted to recreate the best of the many variants in both words and music, which is a purely personal approach. The metronome markings are just suggestions, and are based on information printed in these early books. Certainly they are not meant to be restrictive to any performer.

Where we have not used the earliest source, for various reasons, we have tried to identify it as well as the source which we used.

We hope you will enjoy playing and singing these delightful songs, which evoke visions of a simpler lifestyle when such music was commonplace in the everyday life of most Americans.

Glenn Wilcox

AUTHOR'S NOTES

Alleluia Now We Sing

The first stanza of this traditional story is the only one speaking of the birth of the Christ. As this is a camp meeting style selection in which lyric improvisation was consistent in actual performance, we have chosen this traditional concept in creating additional couplets, all pertaining to the Christmas story. The *Sacred Harp*, compiled by composer White, is the source of melody and first verse.

Angel Voice

This was first printed in *Urania* by James Lyon, in 1761. The composer was a recent immigrant from Italy, who presented the first two secular concerts in Philadelphia early in 1757. George Washington purchased tickets and presumably attended the second one. The words are from the 1699 New Version of the English Metrical Psalter.

Antwerp

This is from the 1802 *Columbian Repository* of Holyoke and is said there "not before published." This was the most comprehensive oblong tunebook ever compiled and contains about 750 compositions. The words are part of the 97th Psalm paraphrase by Watts.

Beautiful Star

Both the words and music for this song apparently were published only one time, and that was in an 1894 compilation by Bertha Vella. The collection is eclectic and was designed primarily for use by young people attending Sunday schools, although many of the songs were included and just printed after having been tried in the public schools of Massachusetts.

Bethlehem

This well known work first appeared c. 1699 in an edition of the "New Version" of the English Psalter, of which Tate was one of the principal authors. Billings wrote one of the earliest American settings of these words, published in his 1778 *Singing Master's Assistant*.

Bethlem

This was adapted from the 1794 *Art of Singing, Part II,* by Andrew Law. The title, spelled as it is both on the page of the song and in the index, is but one of a half dozen titles for the same basic tune apparently written by Milgrove in 1769. The words are titled "The Nativity of Christ;" Watts based them on portions of the first and second chapters of Luke.

Birth of Christ

McCurry drew heavily on other shape note tunebooks for his own 1855 compilation, the *Social Harp,* but this composition is one of his own. The words are found in about a dozen settings in early 19th century American publications. They are part of "The Nativity of Christ" by Watts.

Boston

Billings frequently adapted or wrote new lyrics to his musical settings. He also showed this independent thinking in his unorthodox use of compositional techniques. These words were written and set to a tune named for his beloved native city.

Braintree

Our setting is from the *Columbian Repository* of Holyoke which gives as its source for this the *Harmonia Sacra*. This was a work compiled by Thomas Butts and printed in London about 1760. It was impossible to find a composer or an earlier printing at this time. The words were first published in 1782.

Bristol

Madan's famous *Lock Hospital Collection* of 1769 was reprinted on this side of the Atlantic because of its quality and popularity. Known by different names, this melody appears in the 1809 edition, which is our source. The words are one of the many hymns of Watts.

Child Jesus

This is an American translation and printing of a Scandinavian Christmas song. There is an earlier printing but our source is the Vella collection of 1894 which contains both secular and sacred songs.

Christmas

These familiar words are set to a much older tune, which was found in the 1840 *Knoxville Harmony*. Although the tune seems to be a good setting for the words, it has not achieved any recognition compared to the popularity of the words.

Christmas Anthem

Attribution of the words to Moore does not specify the person. Interestingly, earlier editions of the *Sacred Harp* have no composer named. It is only in the twentieth century reprints with their added comments that composer attribution is found.

Christmas Carol

This is another setting of these commonly recognized words. This tune is also from the Vella 1894 collection. The words and music appear to go well together, but over time, certainly this music has proven inferior to the words.

Christmas Hymn

The words are another version of Psalm 19 by Watts. The music is attributed to Stephenson, an English composer whose works were very popular and frequently printed in Colonial America. This is taken from the 1802 *Bridgewater Collection* by Bartholomew Brown.

Clifton

Our source for this is the 1833 *New Hampshire Collection* by Henry Moore. The words were written about 1735, and an early printing in America was in Jeremy Belknap's *Sacred Poetry* about 1800. Although there are other settings, this combination of words and music seems to have been the most common.

Cookham

Slight variants of this tune appear under a half-dozen names. The words are set to that many more tunes before 1850. The words themselves have an interesting history; apparently originated by Charles Wesley, they went through modifications by George Whitefield, Martin Madan, and even editors of a hymn collection in the late 18th century. At the moment, any composer seems lost in time.

Courtney

It is difficult to comprehend verse of this quality coming from the pen of the great John Milton. However, two sources tell why; all verses after verse one are by other named but unlocated and unknown individuals. The first verse only seems worthy of Milton, which may explain why it stands alone with the music in several printings. No composer has been found at this time. This tune is from the 1821 edition of the *Templi Carmina*.

Derrick

These words were first published posthumously in 1755, but they have never achieved the popularity of other Christmas lyrics. This is another melody for which no composer can be found; this version is from the 1854 *Southern Harmony* by William Walker.

Eddington

These words by Watts reflect the birth of Christ, but also encompass part of Revelation 21. This melody is found in several editions of the *Templi Carmina*, with this version coming from the 9th edition of 1824. The composer is not known.

Emanuel

The only early appearance of both words and music seems to be in the 1781 *Psalm Singer's Amusement*. Billings certainly wrote the music, and in the absence of other appearances, the lyrics also are attributed to him. Later printings, especially in shape note tunebooks, frequently do not acknowledge either author or composer.

Gabriel

The earliest known appearance of both words and music is in an 1801 *Collection of Hymns* which Richards compiled. There seems to be no question about his writing the words; but not enough is known about him to attribute the music to him. So, at this time, the composer remains unknown.

Georgia

This seems to be the only American setting of these words except for the jumbled 1774 book by Bayley. The author remains unknown, but the music is unquestionably that of Kimball and is found in his respected 1793 *Rural Harmony*.

Glad Sound

This is the second setting of these words by Moore in his 1832 *New Hampshire Collection*. For this music he does not give a composer, nor does he claim it to be original. At this time, no composer is known. First printing of the words seems to have been the posthumous 1755 collection of works by Doddridge.

Glad Tidings

At this time, no information has been found concerning author and composer, nor have additional works by either of them been located. Their joint effort is in the 1894 *Song and Study* by Vella.

Glorious Morn

Several sources use this hymn in various settings, but show only the first stanza. There seems to have been only one publication of additional verses, in an 1858 Alabama hymn book, after their initial printing in Williams' 1768 collection of hymns published in England. Information on the composer is as scarce as printing of the lyrics.

Great Creator

The first appearance in print of these words was 1659, but it was a century later before the tune of the setting was written. Our source is the 4th edition of the *Universal Psalmodist* by Williams, which appeared in 1770. No composer is known and Williams does not claim authorship.

Great Milton

These words seem to have been printed for the first time in the 1801 *Collection of Hymns* which Richards compiled and to which he contributed original words. Here they are set to a melody in Vol. II of the *American Harmony*. Aaron Williams is given as the author-compiler, which he was of the earlier English editions. However, given the prefatory statements by printer Bayley about various but not always specified additions and deletions, the composer still remains uncertain.

Harborough

This combination of words and music was assembled no later than 1769, when it appeared in the original English edition of the *Lock Hospital Collection*. Our source is the 1809 American edition of the same work.

Harvard

Both composer and author (who also was a well-known composer) were recognized for their production of religious music. We have a fortunate combination of words, first printed in Gabriel's 1878 *Sunday School Songs,* with music first appearing in the 1840 *Massachusetts Collection.*

Jamaica

Billings apparently liked a first line by Watts, but not the rest of the hymn, so he appropriated that first line and wrote the remainder of these words. This melody is in his 1781 *Psalm Singer's Amusement,* which is our source.

Joyful Hope

This is a second setting of these words which Madan used in his 1769 *Lock Hospital Collection*. Again we use the 1809 American edition which is identical to the English version.

Joyful News

These words, almost universally known, are part of the paraphrase of Psalm 98 by Watts. Our setting is adapted from the *Union Harmony* of 1796 which Holden wrote and compiled. He gave credit to the composer.

Jubal

This is one of his own compositions which Webb included in his 1840 *Massachusetts Collection,* which is our source. No author has been found, but this is among the earliest appearance of the words.

Judea

By the time of their first printing in 1734, these words may have been established as traditional lyrics. One of the earliest American settings is by Billings in his 1778 *Singing Master's Assistant.* He did not use the traditional melody but composed his own music.

Lamb of God

Paul Revere engraved the remarkable *Collection of the Best Psalm Tunes,* published by Josiah Flagg in 1764. There seem to be few printings of this in 18th century American works. Composer Williams was British, but the words may be by an American; at this time no author has been found.

Lancaster

Both words and music have deep roots in folk tradition, and our examples are just one of many variants found for both of them. We have used the 1848 first edition of the *Harp of Columbia* as our source.

London

Holyoke had a more comprehensive musical outlook than many of his contemporaries, as can be shown by the eclectic contents throughout his great tune book. This is taken from his 1802 *Columbian Repository.*

Messenger

Daniel Bayley, a Massachusetts printer, published pirated editions of Williams and Tans'ur. In his own words in the Advertisement (Preface) to the 1774 printing of the *American Harmony,* Vol. II, which is our source, he acknowledges deletion of much work by these two masters, and the addition of "sundry" works by various authors. He gives few attributions, and both words and music remain anonymous at this time.

Milford

One of the very rare settings of these words is to be found in *Select Harmony*, the 1779 compilation of Andrew Law. In his introductory material, he states that all known composers are named, and he obviously knew the composer of this work. As with most tune book compilers, he was much less careful with lyric attribution. The words remain anonymous.

Milton

Perhaps first printing of the tune is in Walker's *Southern Harmony.* This was the most popular tunebook ever printed, selling over 600,000 copies in just a few years. We attribute the setting to Walker as there seems to be no earlier source. The words are frequently found, like the tune, in variant forms. The complex rhyme scheme seems to demand a specific author, but as yet no one has been determined.

Mt. Ephraim

The first American printing of this tune seems to have been in the *Christian Harmony* of 1794, by Andrew Law, who chose from the *Sixteen Hymns* Milgrove published in 1769. The words are from part one of Psalm 19 by Watts.

Nativity

Probably the best known setting of these words is by Handel in the *Messiah*; the common source for both settings is Isaiah 9:6, a virtually identical passage. Our setting is from the *Massachusetts Collection* compiled by Webb and published in 1840.

New Hosanna

An unknown author was modified by an unknown editor, and these words are the result. The original first line was "Awake, arise and hail the morn." This is adapted from the 1859 *Sacred Harp,* although most editions contain it or a variant of it.

Oxford

These words were first published in 1760 in Vol. 1 of a collection of devotional poems by Steele. They are under the heading of "The Incarnation," and refer to the gospel according to John 1:14. The setting used here is of a much younger tune which is taken from the 1859 *Sacred Harp*.

Paxton

There are several printed sources for this tune about 1835, but none of these name a composer, which may indicate an undiscovered common folk source from which these publications derived. Of course, the words are well known in a different musical setting. Our source is the *Southern Harmony*.

Randolph

The words used as the first stanza are actually the seventh stanza of a nine stanza hymn by Watts on the Nativity, based on Luke chapters 1 and 2. Our source, the 1802 *Bridgewater Collection* by Brown, says "never before published," which certainly means the music, but may also mean the combination of these words and the music.

Redeemer

Both words and music seem to have unknown origins in Europe, and have continued in popularity since being transplanted to America. The first English publication of this setting seems to have been in 1750. Our source, which may be the first American printing, is the 1818 *Kentucky Harmonist* by Samuel Metcalf.

Redemption

Apparently the earliest appearance of this tune is in the 1816 *Kentucky Harmony* by Davisson, but each early appearance seems to be a variant. It thus is difficult to establish the authentic version. However, all share the same lyrics with occasional insignificant differences. The author remains unknown.

Rejoice

Our melody is adapted from the *Sacred Harp,* one of several settings of these words to various tunes. Watts is the established author, but composer Breedlove remains elusive, although he is a frequent contributor to mid-century tune books.

Sacred Day

It is unfortunate that he was not a first rank musician, for Tans'ur had a disproportionate effect on the writers and compilers of tunebooks, due to the easy availability of his theoretical works and compositions in America. The first appearance of this melody is in his 1760 *New Harmony of Sion.* This also may be the first appearance of the words which apparently were written before 1751 but not printed as poetry until 1763.

Sark

The source for this is the 1857 *Hesperian Harp* by William Hauser, M.D., who apparently was a competent musician and composer. Any professional relationship between Dr. Hauser and Dr. Miller is unknown. The lyrics are the ones in common usage which were modified from author Charles Wesley.

Shining Star

At this time, nothing has been found concerning E.B. Smith, both author and composer. No literary or musical works attributed to him have been found except for this contribution which is in the 1894 Vella collection.

Sing Alleluia

Gabriel, both author and composer of this lilting song, published it in his 1878 *Sunday School Songs*. Known as a competent and prolific hymnist and tune-writer, he remained active during the first third of this century.

Somersett

Watts was a favorite hymn writer for many earlier composers, as is partially attested by this additional set of words. Holyoke first combined these words with his music in his 1791 *Harmonia Americana*. However, we use his 1802 *Columbian Repository* as our source.

Star

Heber was a prolific writer of hymns, but they were not published until after his untimely death, which may have been due in part to the relatively primitive conditions he endured as an Anglican missionary to the Indian sub-continent. The *Southern Harmony* is our source, but the composer remains unknown.

Star in the East

This is one of the family of "Star" tunes, each of which is a variant. They are similar enough to permit a certain interchange of lyrics, if the poetic and musical meters agree. One of the earliest printings is in the 1833 *Christian Lyre* by Joshua Leavitt.

Wonder

There are at least four members of the Munson family active around 1800, any one of whom might be the composer. The author also remains unknown, and additional stanzas have not been located.

ALLELUIA NOW WE SING

First verse traditional
Additional verses GCW

Benjamin F. White

1) Christ was born in Bethlehem,
    And in a manger lay.

2) Wise men came to worship Him,
    Led by his eastern star.

3) Shepherds heard the heavenly host
    Sing praises unto God.

4) Peace on earth, good will to man,
    Resounded through the sky.

5) Let us join the heavenly throng,
    And praise Him with our song.

6) Christ was born in Bethlehem,
    And in a manger lay.

7) Alleluia now we sing,
    For Christ the new born King.

ANGEL VOICE

Nahum Tate John Palma

14

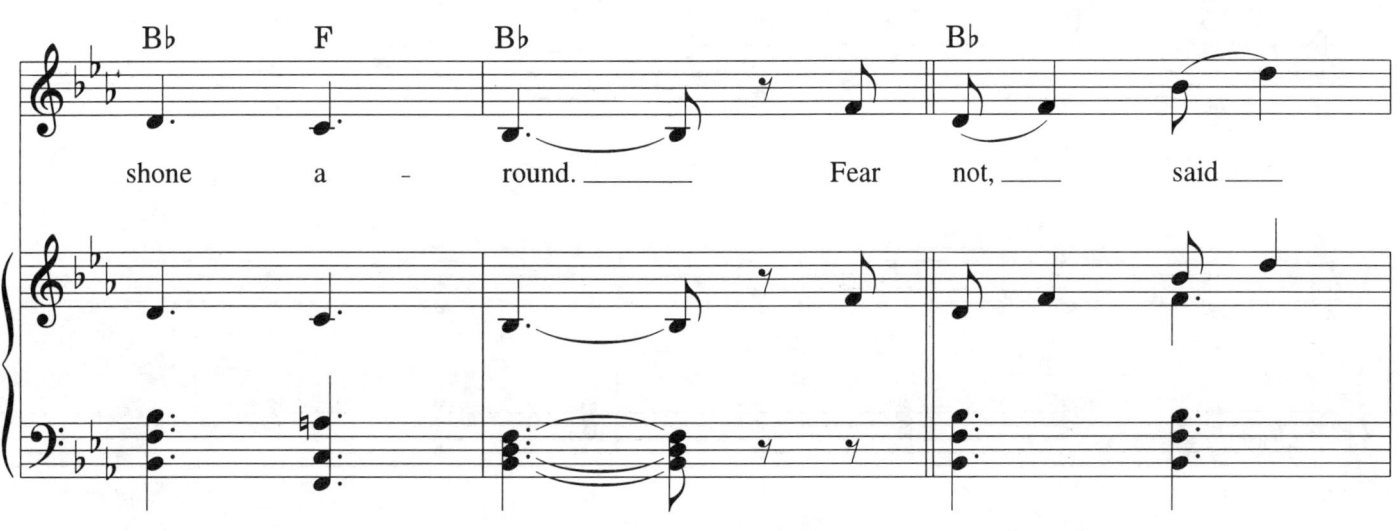

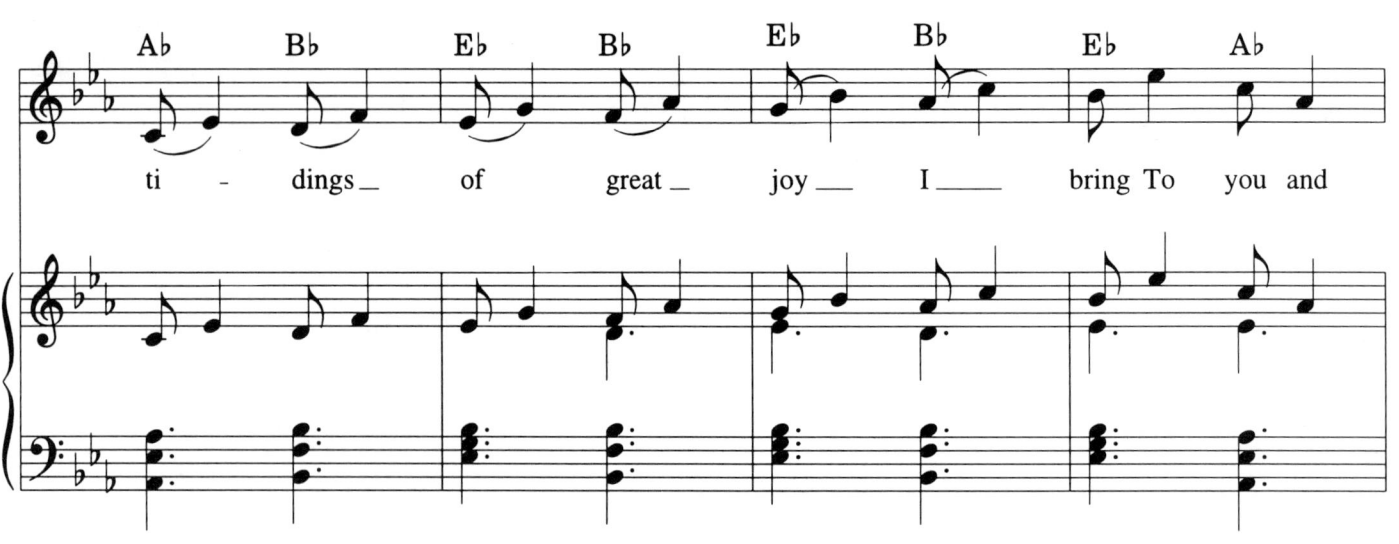
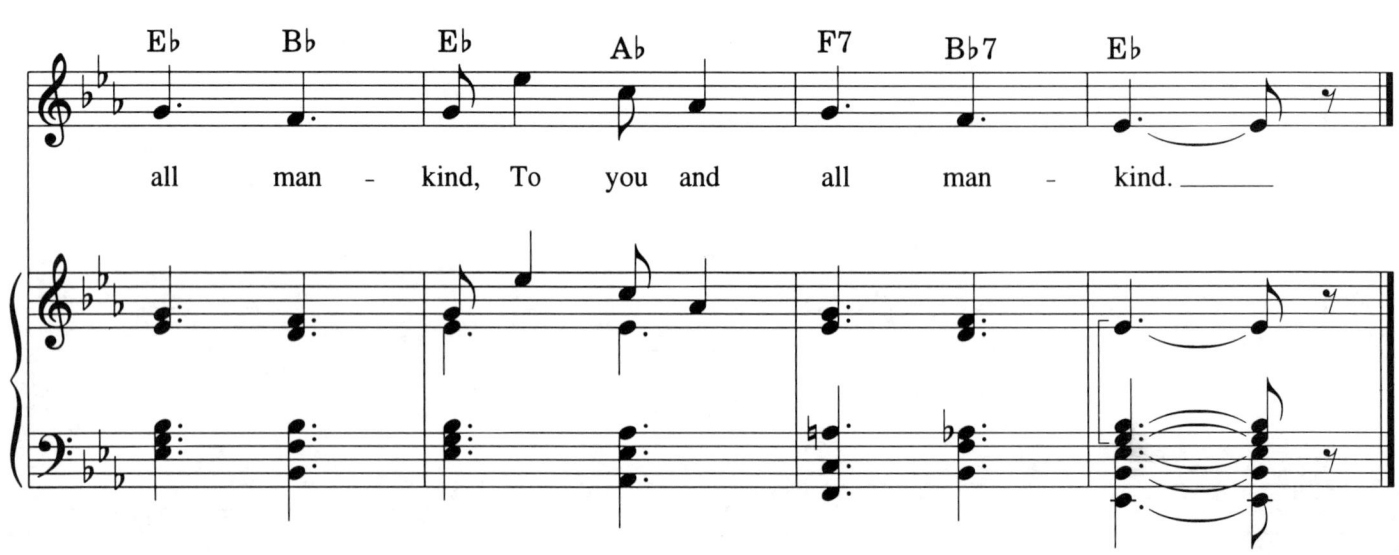

1) While shepherds watched their flocks by night,
   All seated on the ground,
   The angel of the Lord came down,
   And glory shone around.

2) Fear not, said he, for mighty dread
   Had seized their troubled mind;
   Glad tidings of great joy I bring
   To you and all mankind.

3) To you in David's town this day
   Is born of David's line,
   The Savior who is Christ the Lord,
   And this shall be the sign:

4) The heavenly babe you there shall find,
   To human view displayed,
   All meanly wrapped in swaddling bands,
   And in a manger laid.

5) Thus spake the seraph, and forthwith
   Appeared a heavenly throng
   Of angels praising God, who thus
   Addressed their joyful song:

6) All glory be to God on high,
   And to the earth be peace;
   Good will henceforth from heaven to men
   Begin and never cease.

ANTWERP

Isaac Watts
Samuel A. Holyoke

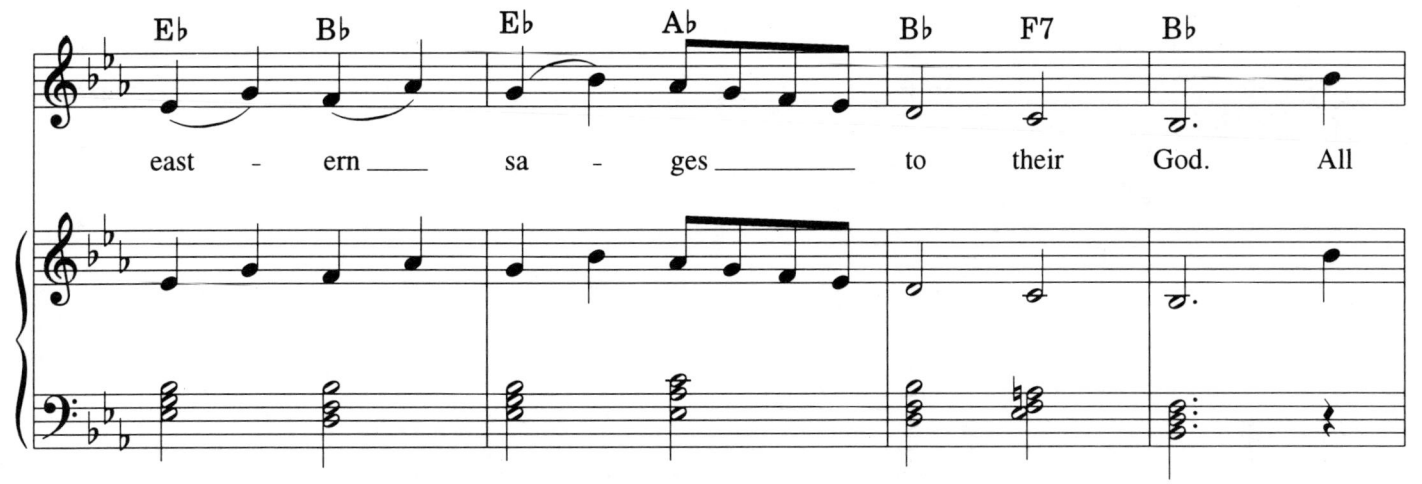
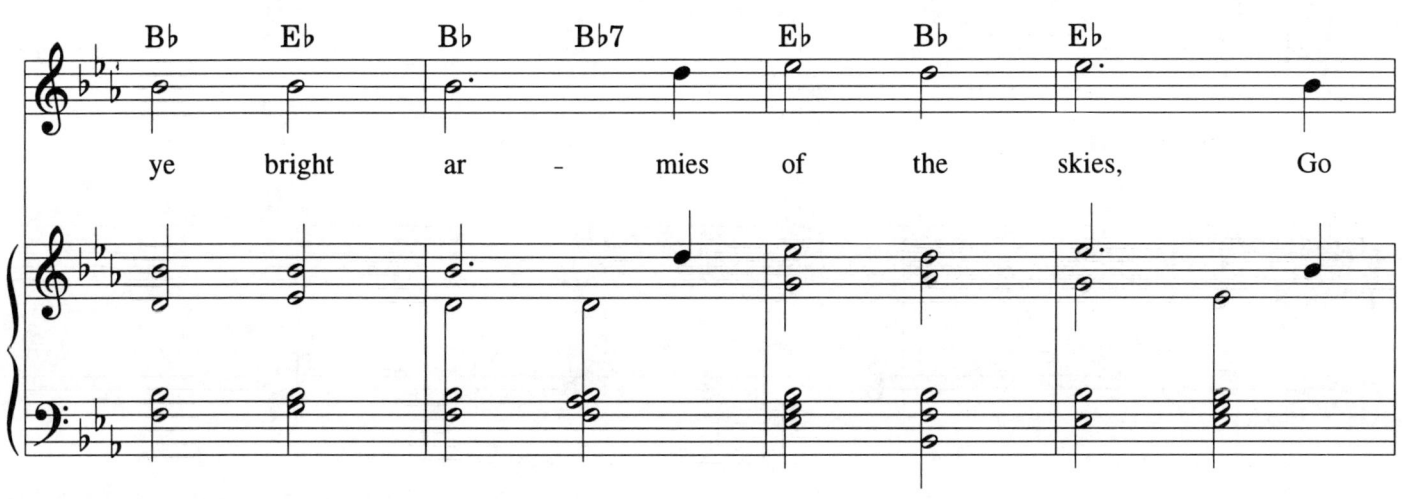

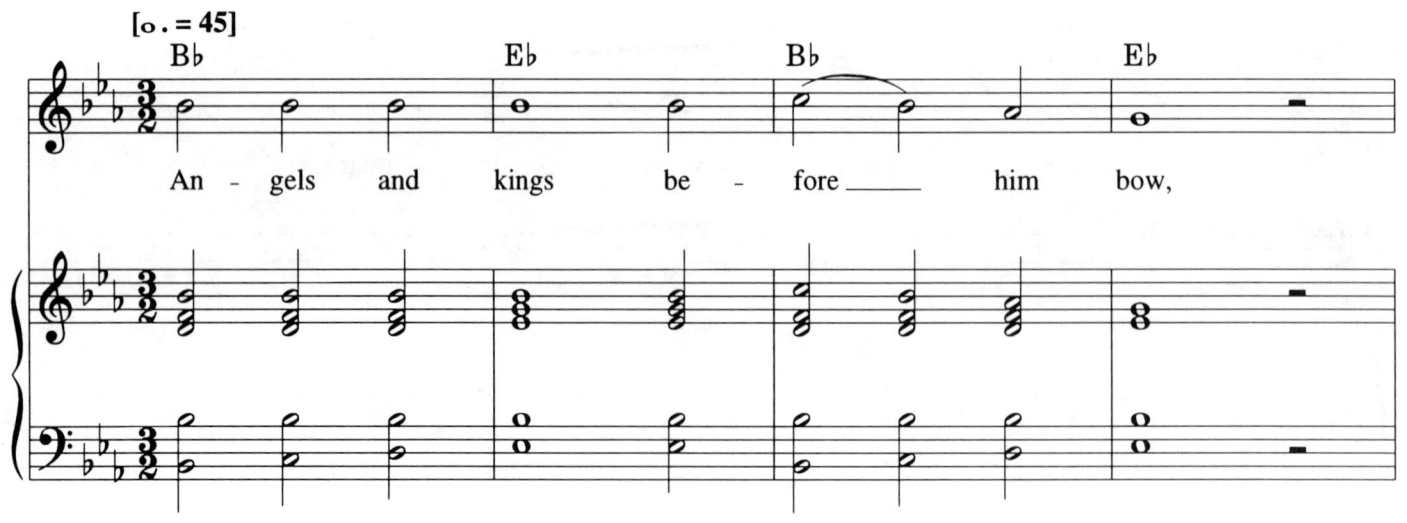
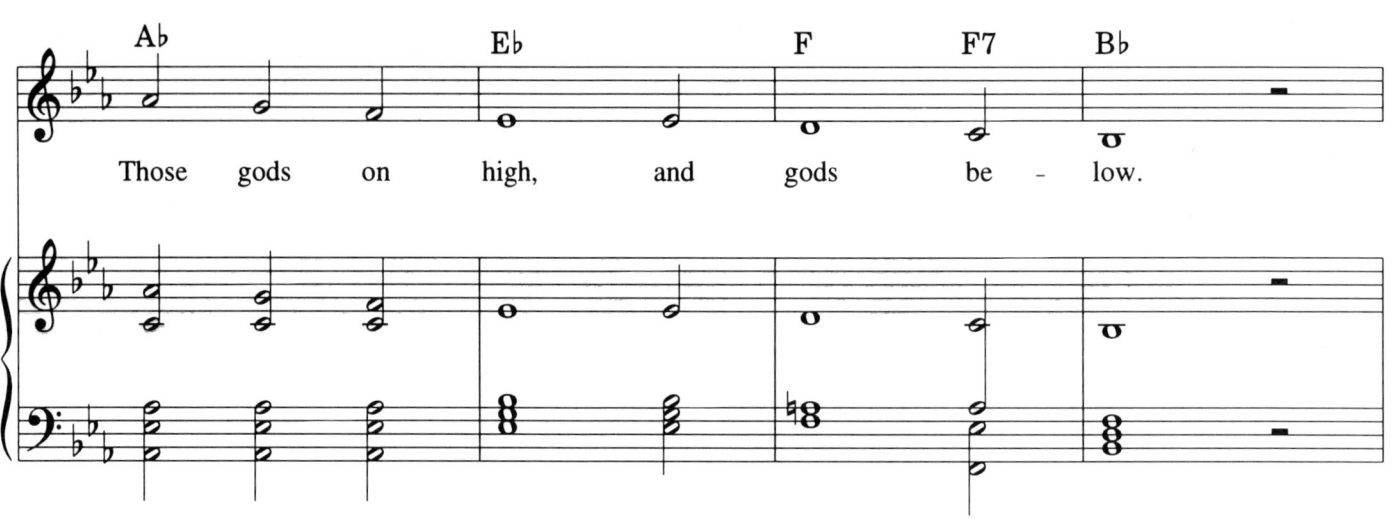
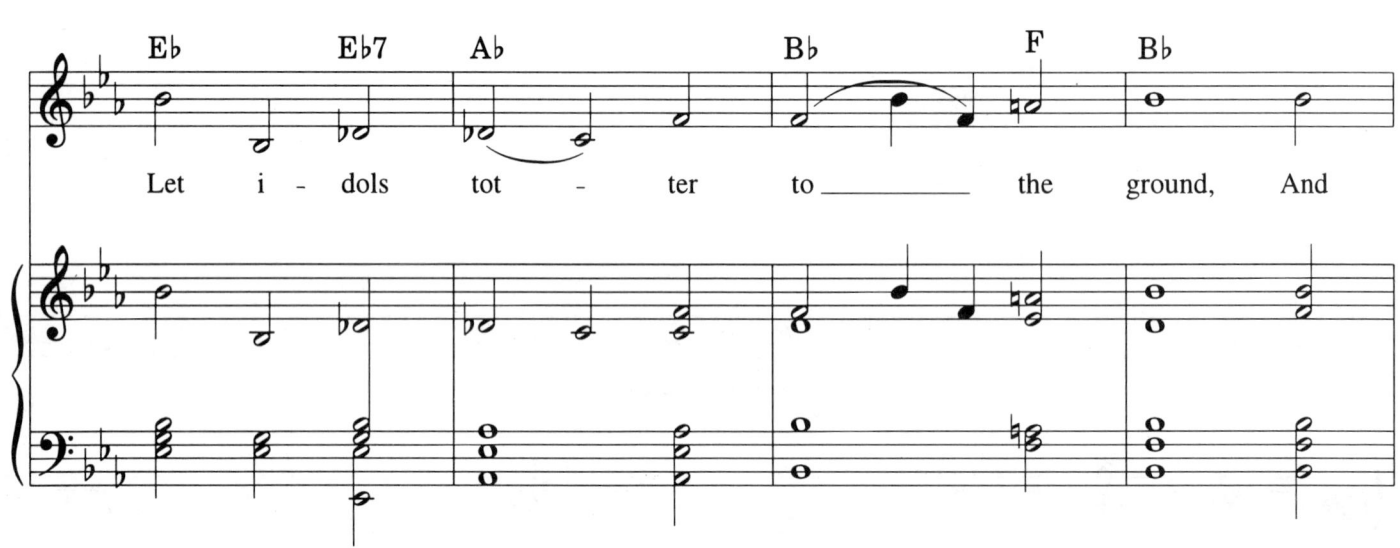

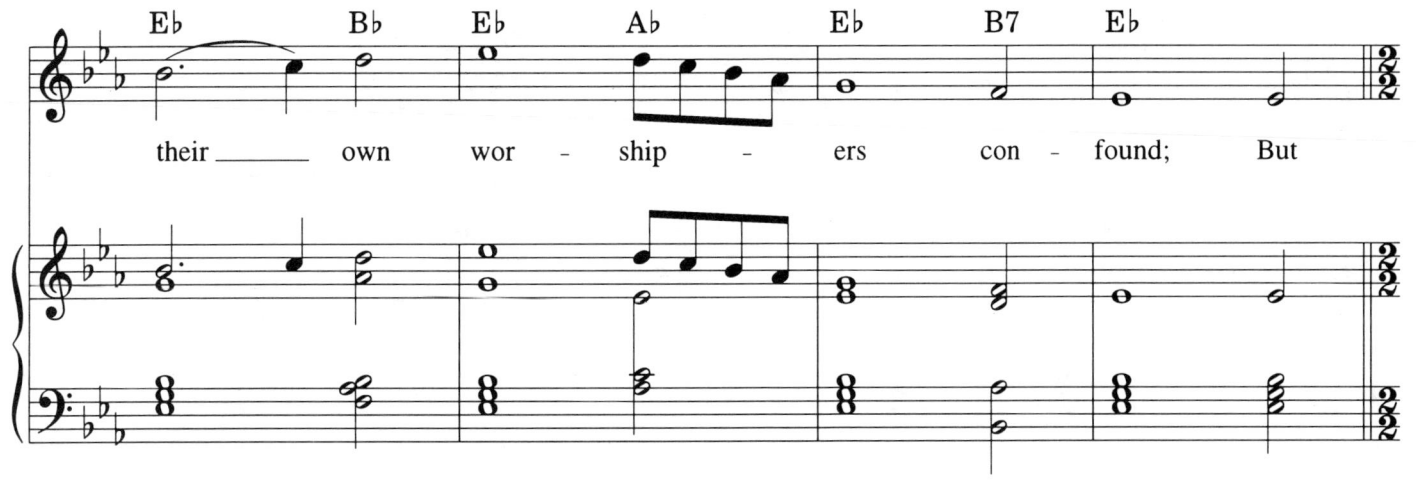
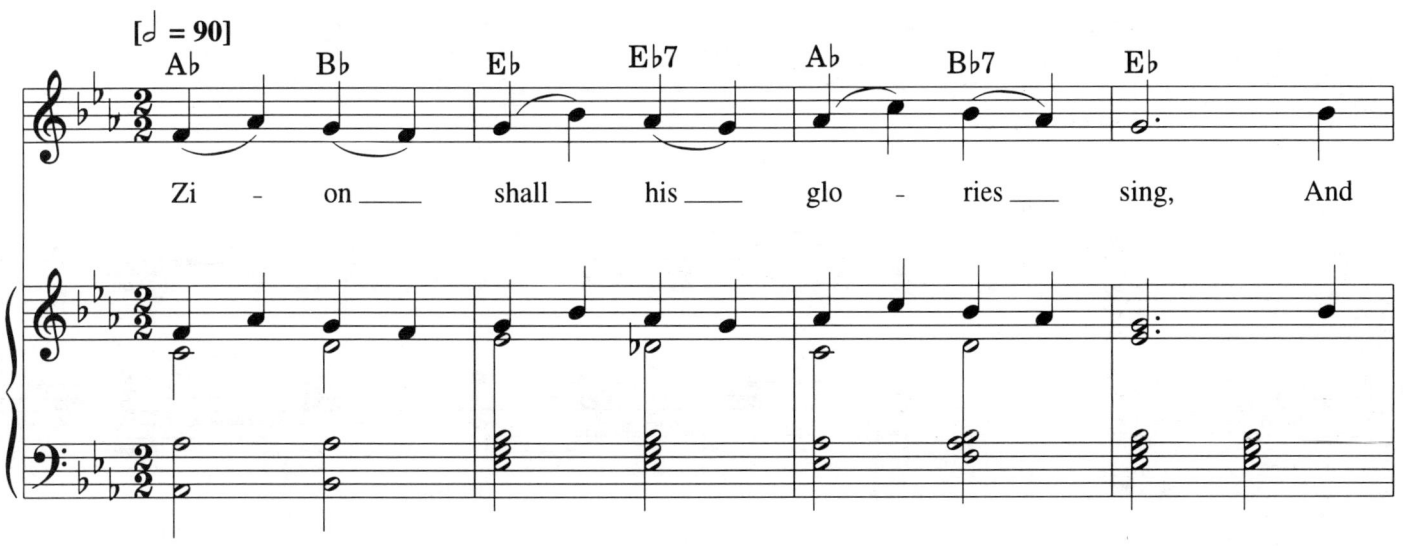

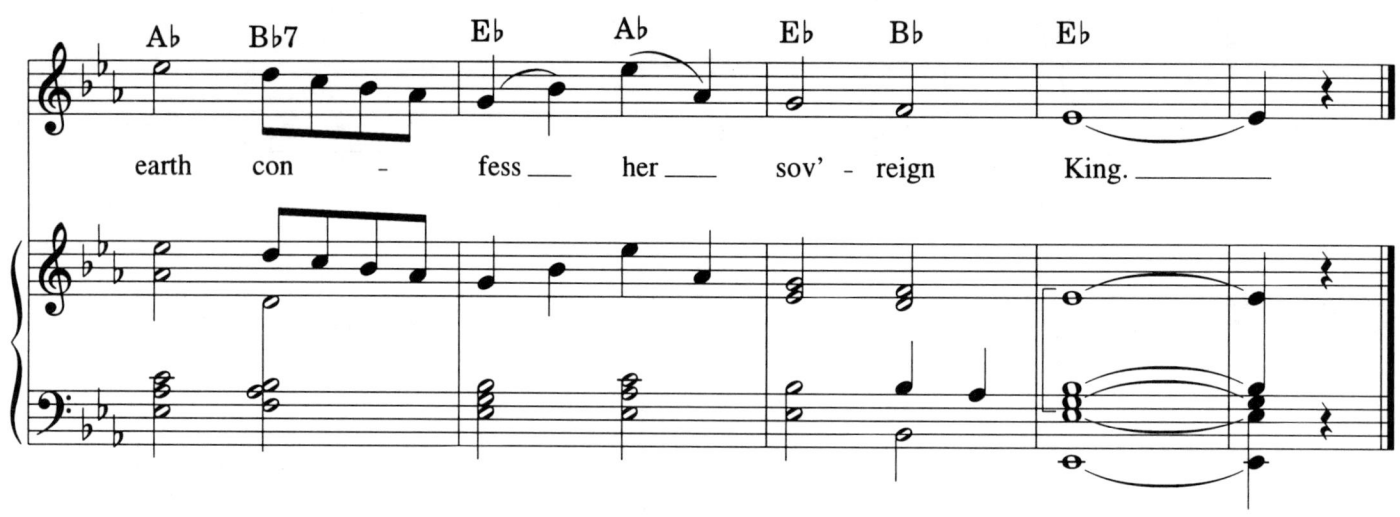

1) The Lord is come, the heavens proclaim
   His birth; the nations learn His name;
   An unknown star directs the road
   Of eastern sages to their God.

2) All ye bright armies of the skies,
   Go worship where the Saviour lies;
   Angels and kings before him bow,
   Those gods on high, and gods below.

3) Let idols totter to the ground,
   And their own worshippers confound;
   But Zion shall his glories sing,
   And earth confess her sov'reign King.

"The Christmas Tree," by F. A. Chapman.

BEAUTIFUL STAR

1) List to the beautiful story
    Of Bethlehem's wonderful star,
  Shining in radiant glory,
    Over the heavens afar.

Chorus: Wonderful star, Glorious star!
    Guiding the wise men who came from afar,
  Softly thy light shines through the night,
    Bethlehem's beautiful, beautiful star.

2) All through their journey so lonely
    The pilgrims that came from the east,
  Followed this guiding light only,
    Till the long wandering ceased.

3) Seeking the Savior so holy,
    Who came to be Israel's King,
  Soon to His cradle so lowly,
    Gold, myrrh, and frankincense bring.

4) Jesus, thou star of the morning,
    Though I'm but a child in thy sight,
  Turning from sin at thy warning,
    Gladly I follow thy light.

BETHLEHEM

Nahum Tate   William Billings

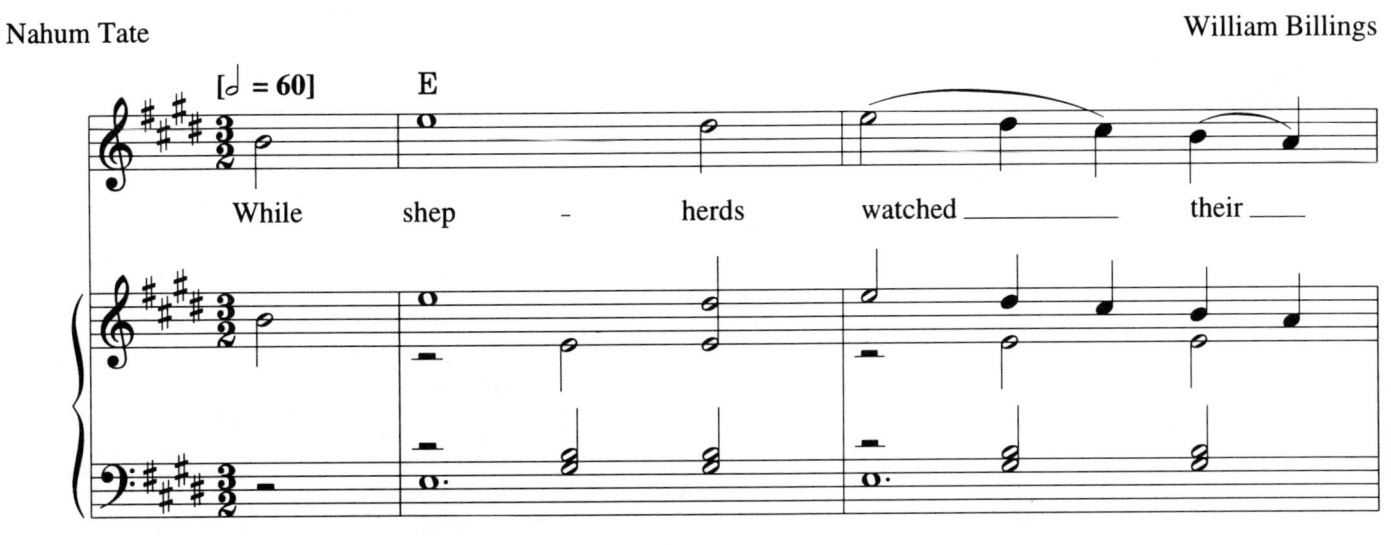
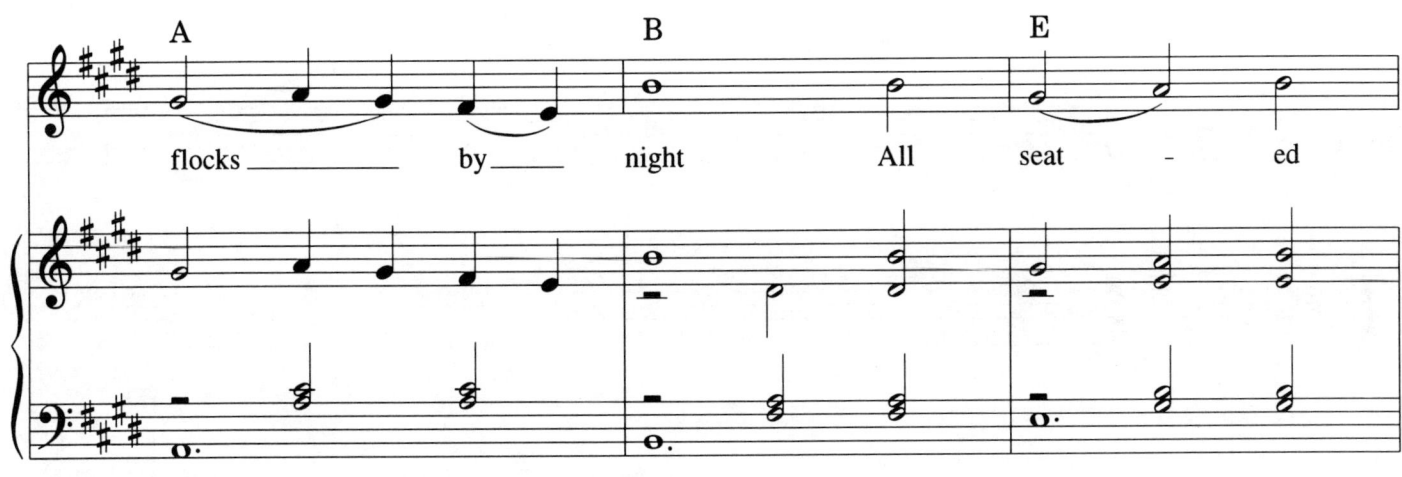
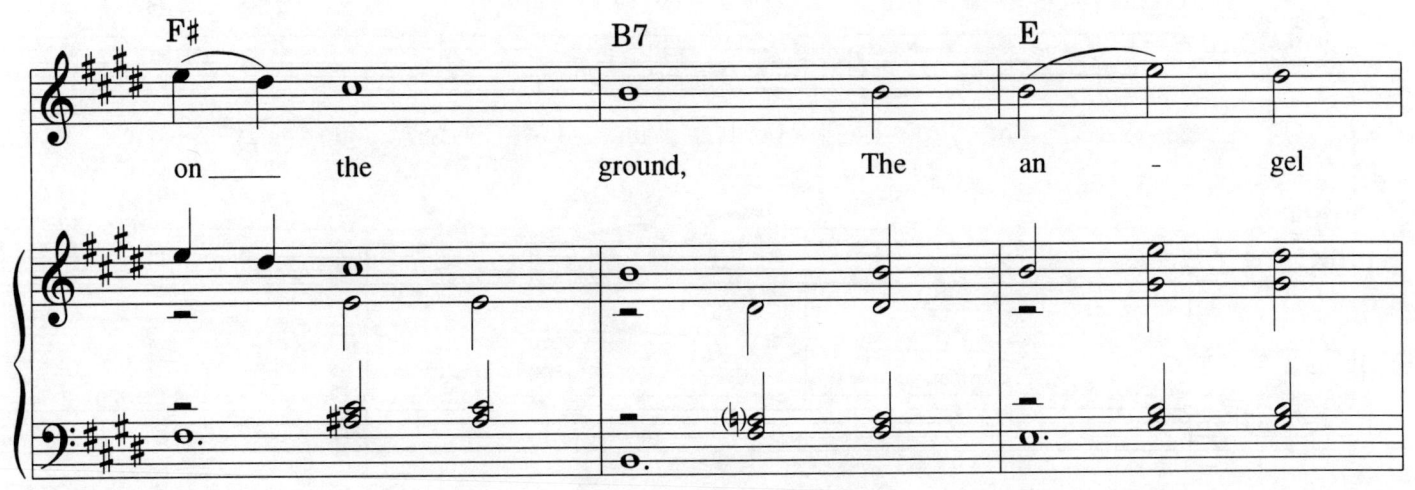

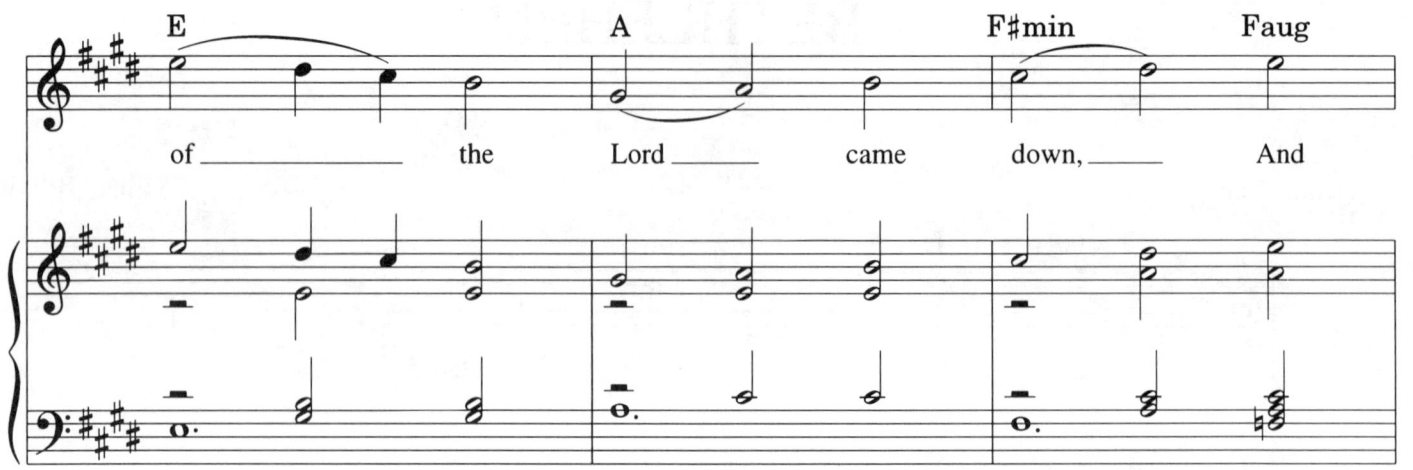
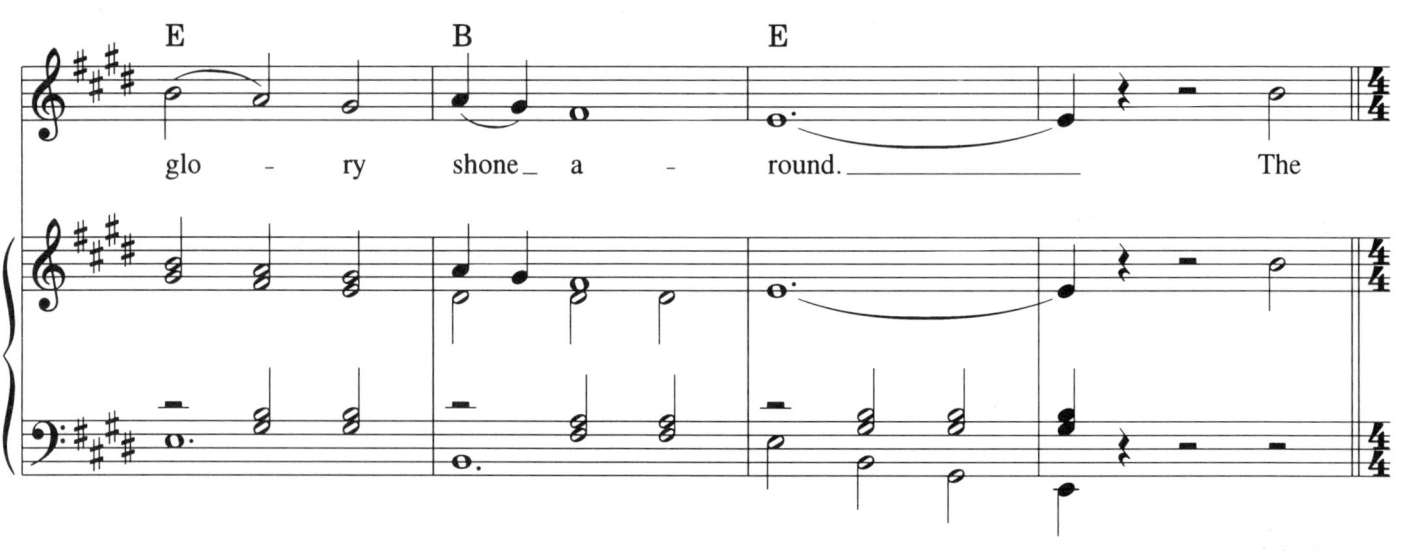

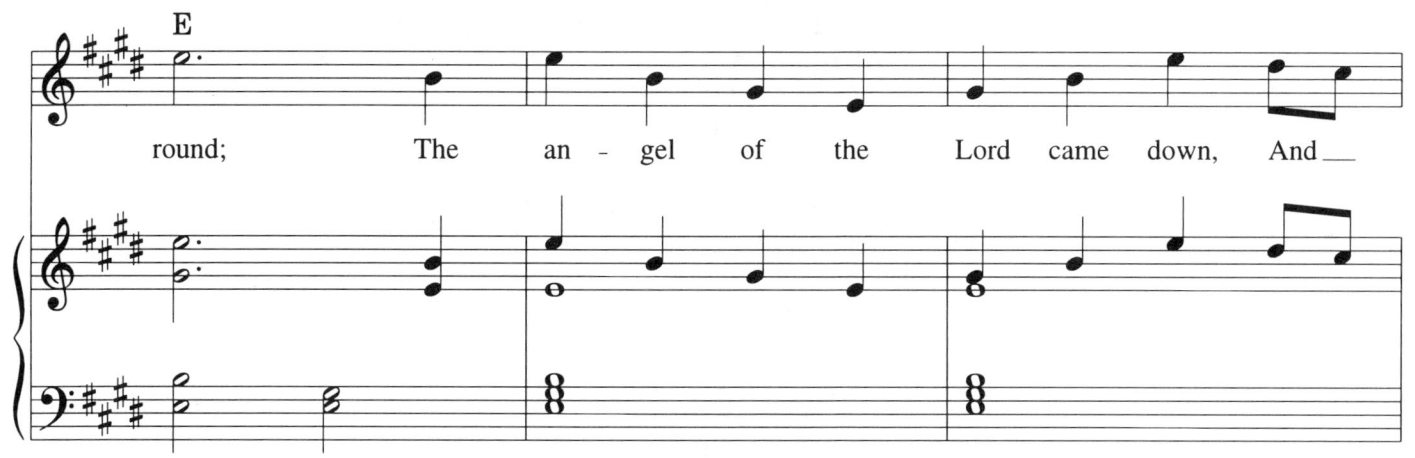
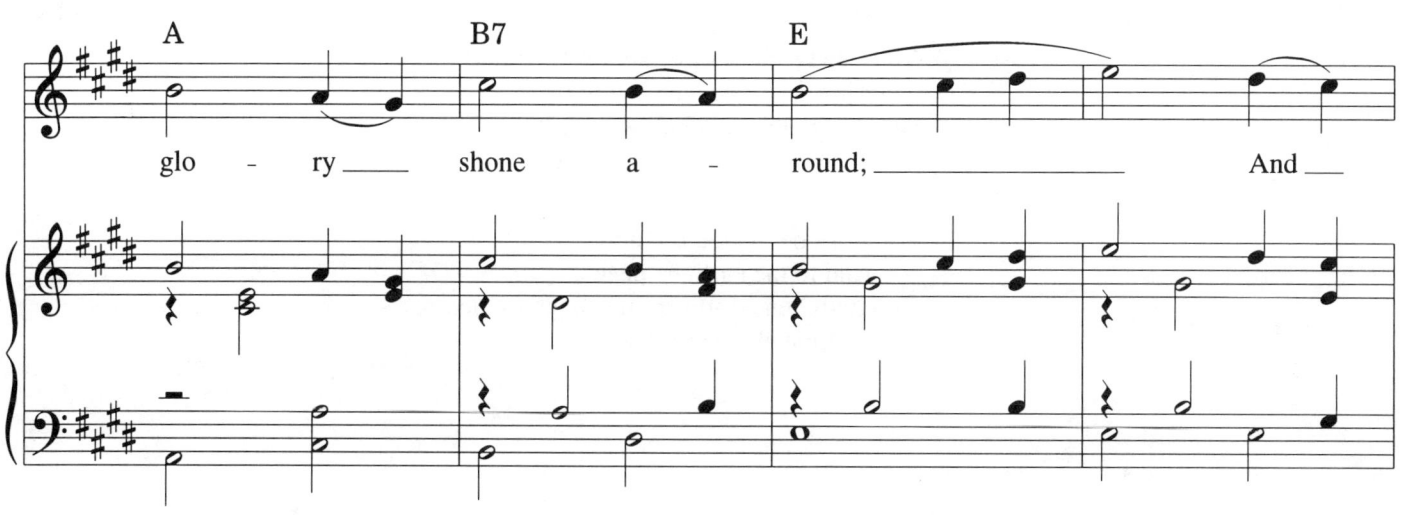
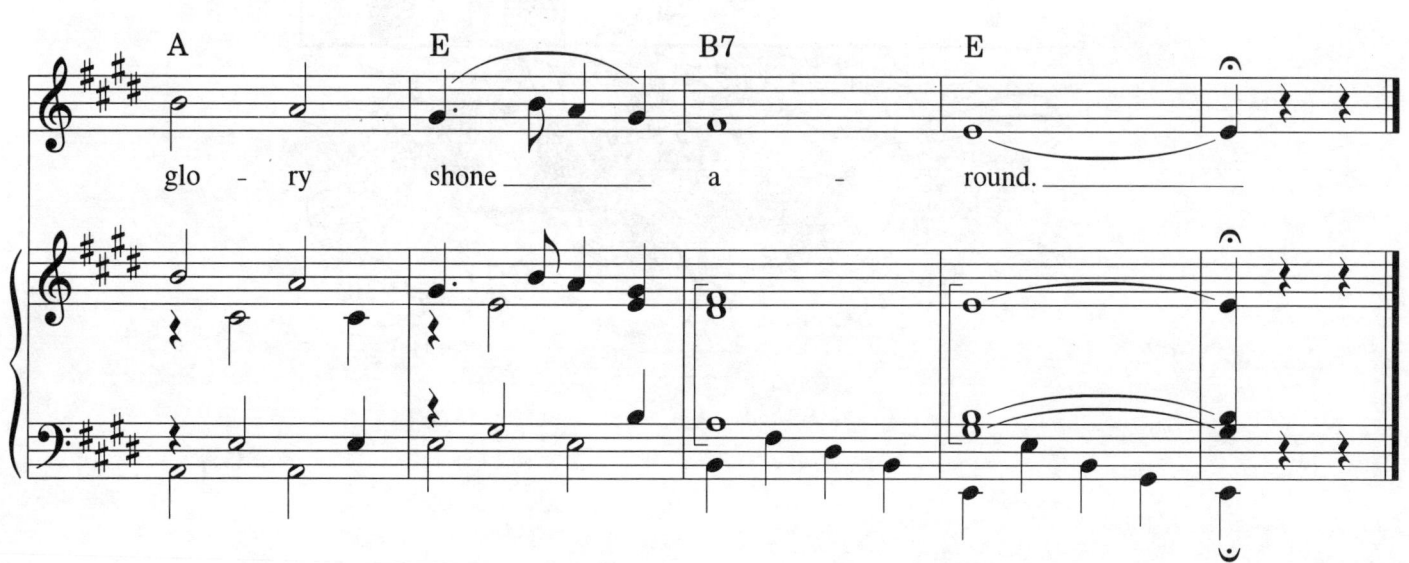

1) While shepherds watched their flocks by night
    All seated on the ground,
  The angel of the Lord came down,
    And glory shone around.

2) Fear not, said he, for mighty dread
    Had seized their troubled mind;
  Glad tidings of great joy I bring
    To you and all mankind.

3) To you in David's town this day
    Is born of David's line,
  The Savior who is Christ the Lord,
    And this shall be the sign:

4) The heavenly babe you there shall find,
    To human view displayed,
  All meanly wrapped in swaddling bands,
    And in a manger laid.

5) Thus spake the seraph, and forthwith
    Appeared a heavenly throng
  Of angels praising God, who thus
    Addressed their joyful song:

6) All glory be to God on high,
    And to the earth be peace;
  Goodwill henceforth from heaven to men
    Begin and never cease.

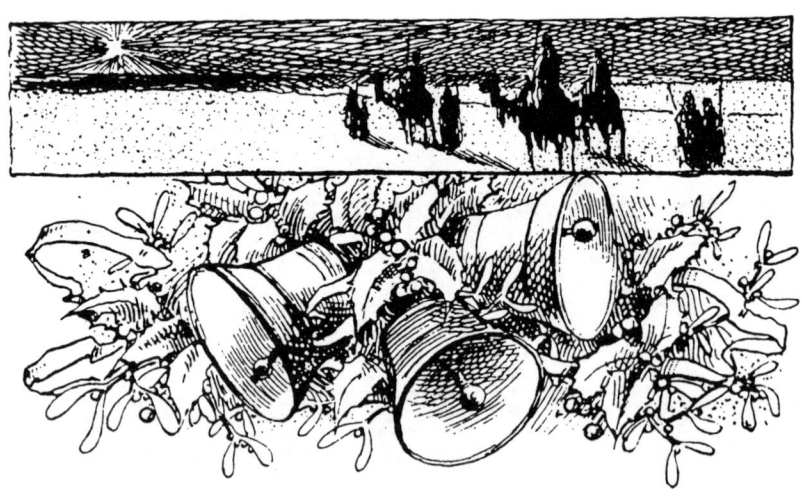

"Gathering Christmas Greens." An illustration from c. 1876.

BETHLEM

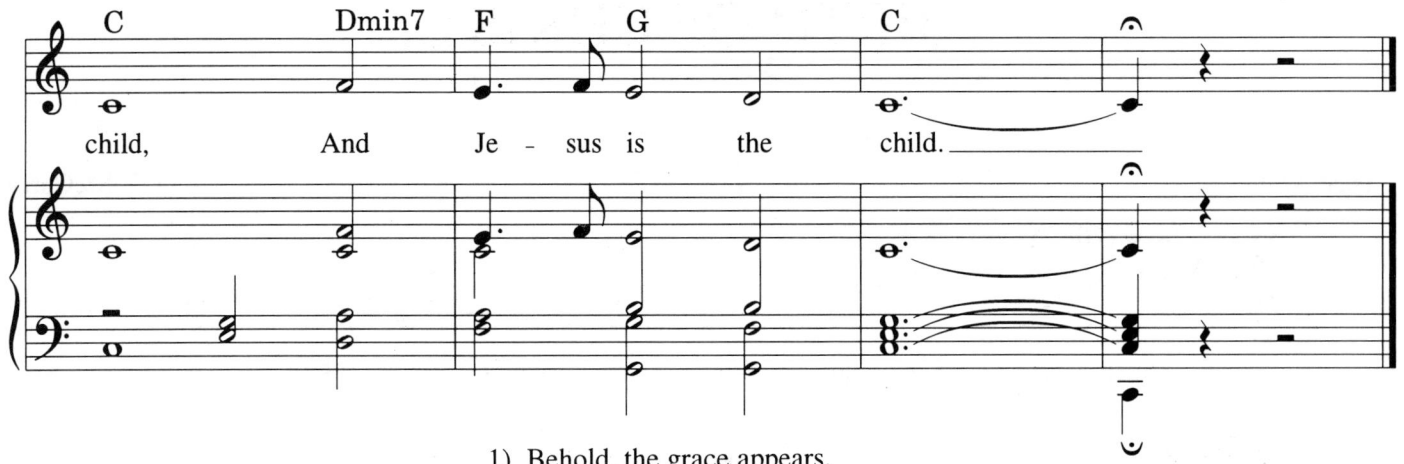

1) Behold, the grace appears,
   The promise is fulfilled;
     Mary, the righteous virgin, bears,
   And Jesus is the child.

2) [The Lord, the highest God,
   Calls him his only Son;
     He bids him rule the lands abroad,
   And gives him David's throne.

3) O'er Jacob shall he reign
   With a peculiar sway;
     The nations shall his grace obtain
   His kingdom ne'er decay.]

4) To bring the glorious news,
   A heav'nly form appears;
     He tells the shepherds of their joys,
   And banishes their fears.

5) "Go, humble swains," said he,
   "To David's city fly;
     The promised infant, born to-day,
   Doth in a manger lie."

6) "With looks and hearts serene
   Go visit Christ your king;"
     And straight a flaming troop was seen;
   The shepherds heard them sing.

7) Glory to God on high!
   And heavenly peace on earth,
     Good-will to men, to angels joy,
   At the Redeemer's birth!

8) [In worship so divine
   Let saints employ their tongues;
     With the celestial hosts we join,
   And loud repeat their songs:

9) Glory to God on high,
   And heavenly peace on earth,
     Good-will to men, to angels joy,
   At our Redeemer's birth!]

BIRTH OF CHRIST

Isaac Watts | John G. McCurry

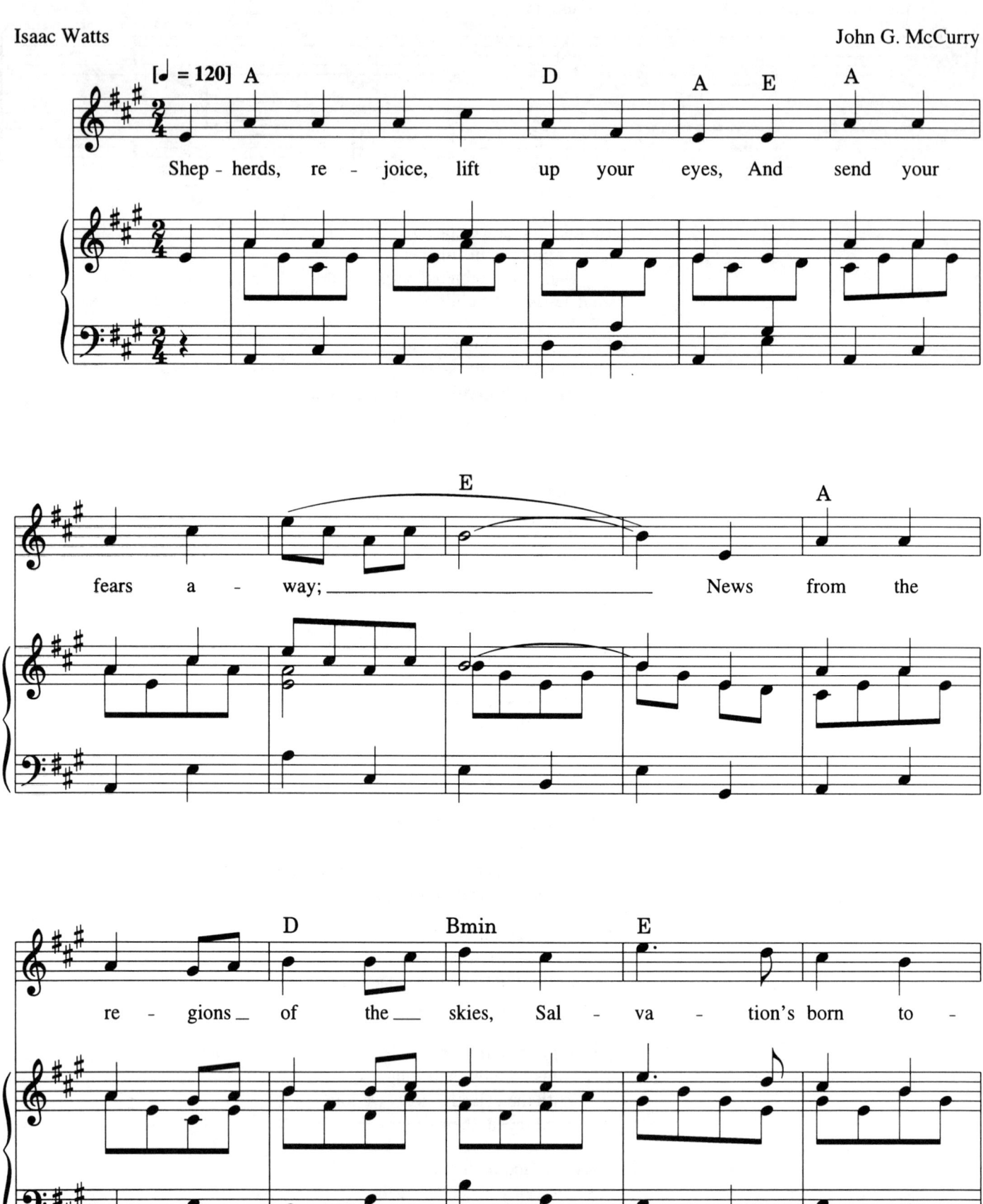

1) Shepherds, rejoice, lift up your eyes,
    And send your fears away;
  News from the regions of the skies,
    Salvation's born today.

  Jesus, the God whom angels fear,
    Comes down to dwell with you,
  Today he makes His entrance here,
    But not as monarchs do.

2) No gold, nor purple swaddling bands,
    No royal shining things;
  A manger for His cradle stands,
    And holds the King of Kings.

  Go, shepherds, where the infant lies,
    And see his humble throne;
  With tears of joy in all your eyes,
    Go, shepherds, kiss the Son.

3) Thus Gabriel sang, and strait around,
    The heavenly armies throng,
  They tune their harps to lofty sound,
    And thus conclude the song:

  Glory to God that reigns above,
    Let peace surround the earth;
  Mortals shall know their maker's love,
    At their Redeemer's birth.

4) Lord! and shall angels have their songs,
    And men no tunes to raise?
  O may we lose these useless tongues
    When they forget to praise.

  Glory to God that reigns above,
    That pities us forlorn;
  We join to sing our Maker's love
    For there's a Savior born.

"Winter Sports—Coasting in the Country." by Granville Perkins.
From *Harper's Weekly*, Feb. 17, 1877.

BOSTON

William Billings   William Billings

Me-thinks I see a heav'n-ly host Of an-gels on the wing; Me-thinks I hear their cheer-ful notes, So mer-ri-ly they sing. Let all your fears be

Methinks I see a heav'nly host
    Of angels on the wing;
Methinks I hear their cheerful notes,
    So merrily they sing.

Let all your fears be banished hence,
    Glad tidings we proclaim;
For there's a Savior born today,
    And Jesus is his name.

BRAINTREE

Samuel Medley

Attributed to *Harmonia Sacra*

Mortals, awake, with angels join, And chant the solemn lay; Joy, love, and gratitude combine To hail th'auspicious day.

40

1) Mortals, awake, with angels join,
　　　And chant the solemn lay;
　Joy, love, and gratitude combine
　　　To hail th'auspicious day.

2) In heaven the rapturous song began,
　　　And sweet seraphic fire
　Through all the shining legions ran,
　　　And strung and tuned the lyre.

3) Swift through the vast expanse it flew,
　　　And loud the echo rolled;
　The theme, the song, the joy was new;
　　　'Twas more than heaven could hold.

4) Down through the portals of the sky,
　　　Th'impetuous torrent ran;
　And angels flew with eager joy
　　　To bear the news to man.

5) Hark, the cherubic armies shout!
　　　And glory leads the song;
　Goodwill and peace are heard throughout
　　　Th'harmonious heavenly throng.

6) With joy the chorus we'll repeat,
　　　Glory to God on high;
　Goodwill and peace are now complete,
　　　Jesus is born to die.

7) Hail, Prince of life, forever hail,
　　　Redeemer, brother, friend;
　Though earth and time and life should fail,
　　　Thy praise shall never end.

BRISTOL

Isaac Watts
Martin Madan

Lo, what a glorious sight appears To our believing eyes! To our believing eyes! The earth and sea are passed away, And the old

1) Lo, what a glorious sight appears
    To our believing eyes!
  The earth and sea are passed away,
    And the old rolling skies.

2) From the third heaven where God resides,
    That holy, happy place,
  The new Jerusalem comes down
    Adorned with shining grace.

3) Attending angels shout for joy,
    And the bright armies sing,
  Mortals, behold the sacred seat
    Of your descending King.

4) The God of glory down to men
    Removes his blest abode,
  Men the dear objects of his grace,
    And he the loving God.

5) His own soft hand shall wipe the tears
    From every weeping eye,
  And pains, and groans, and griefs, and fears,
    And death itself shall die.

6) How long, dear Saviour, O how long,
    Shall this bright hour delay!
  Fly swifter round, ye wheels of time,
    And bring the welcome day.

CHILD JESUS

H. C. Andersen

Niels W. Gade

Child Jesus came from heav'n-ly height, To make us pure and ho-ly. On bed of straw, on Christ-mas night, He lay in man-ger low-ly; The star smiled down from

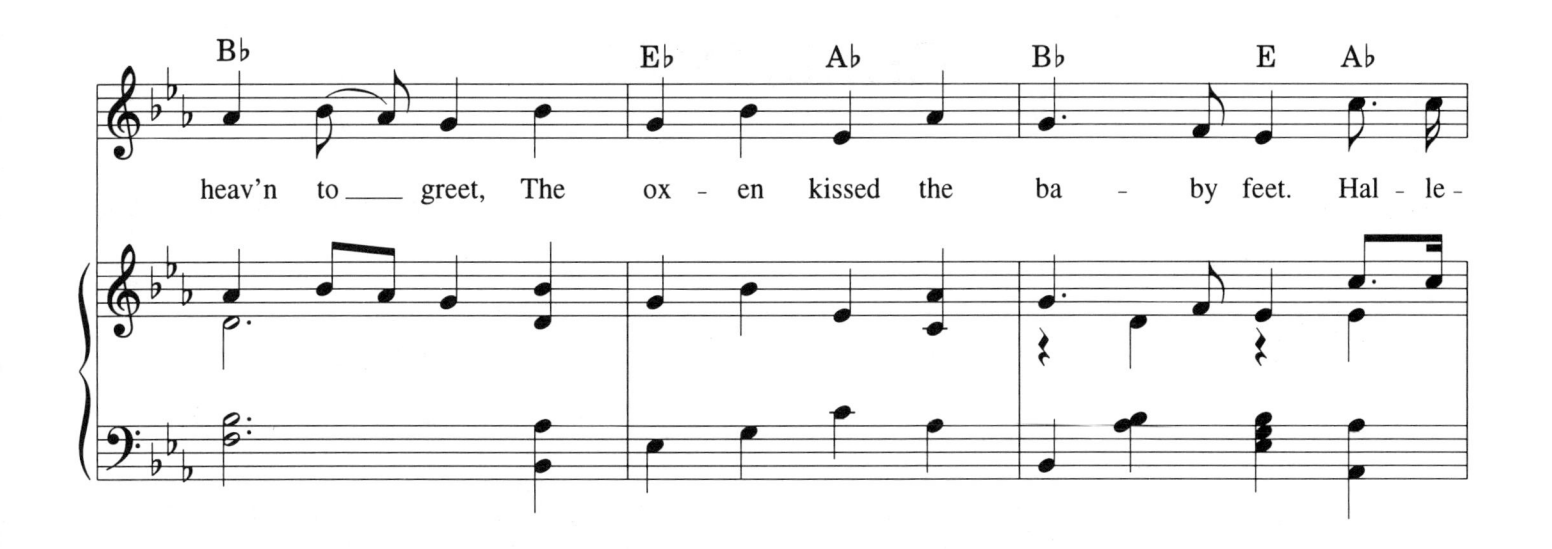

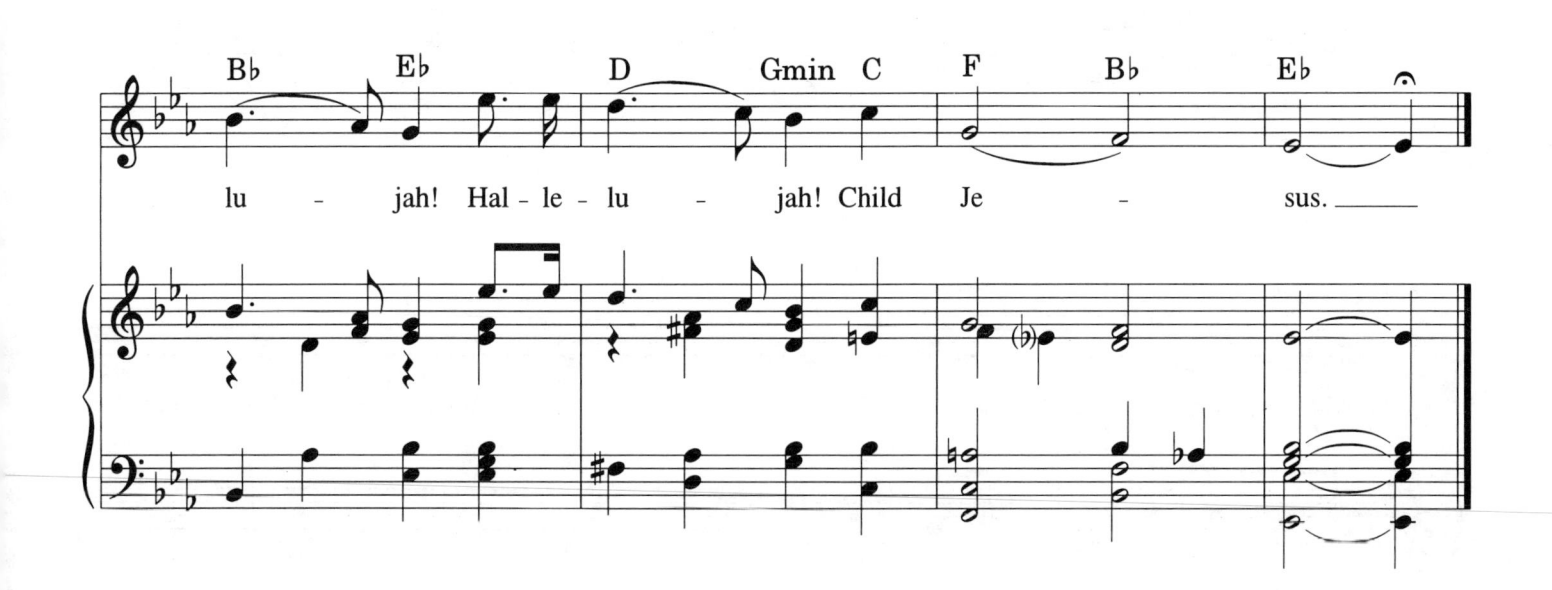

1) Child Jesus came from heav'nly height,
   To make us pure and holy.
On bed of straw, on Christmas night,
   He lay in manger lowly;
The star smiled down from heav'n to greet,
   The oxen kissed the baby feet.
Hallelujah! Hallelujah!
   Child Jesus.

2) All sorrow and all care lay down,
   And praise the Lord of heaven:
A child is born in David's town,
   To us a son is given;
Like children, let us kneel before
   The holy Christ child and adore.
Hallelujah! Hallelujah!
   Child Jesus.

CHRISTMAS

Phillips Brooks
Attributed to Abraham Wood

O little town of Bethlehem, How still we see thee lie! Above thy deep and dreamless sleep The silent stars go by: Yet in thy dark streets shineth The everlasting Light; The hopes and fears of all the years Are met in thee tonight.

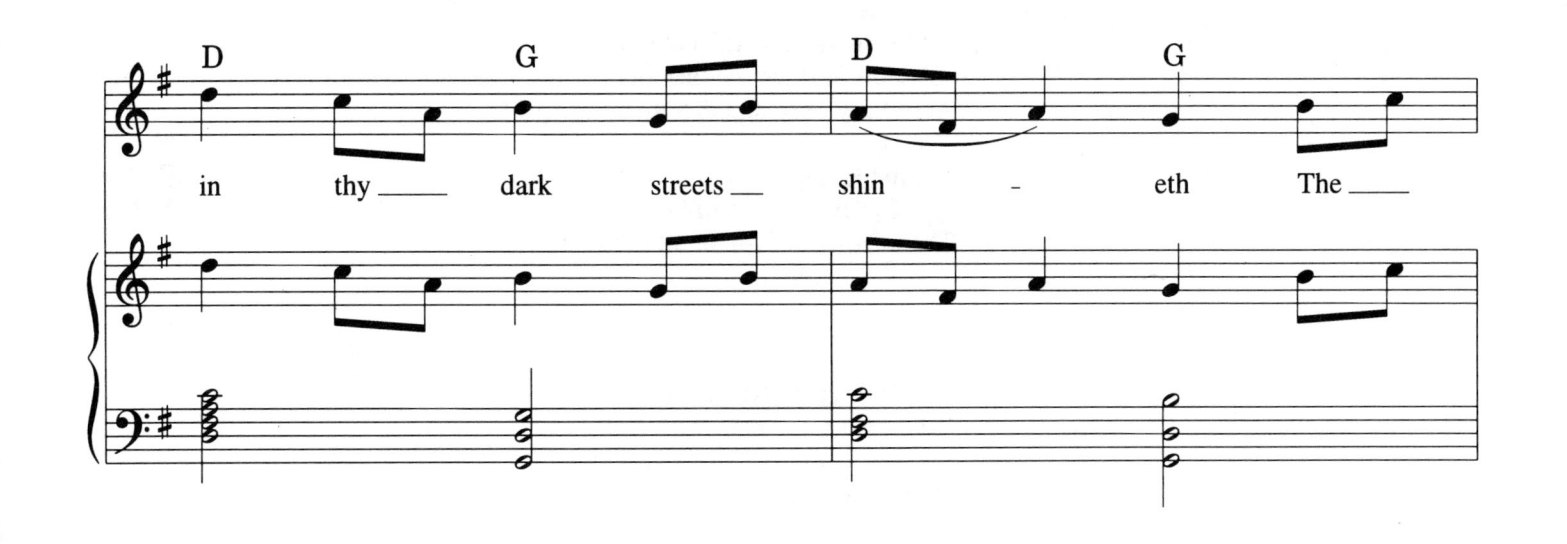

1) O little town of Bethlehem,
      How still we see thee lie!
   Above thy deep and dreamless sleep
      The silent stars go by:
   Yet in thy dark streets shineth
      The everlasting Light;
   The hopes and fears of all the years
      Are met in thee to-night.

2) For Christ is born of Mary;
      And, gathered all above,
   While mortals sleep, the angels keep
      Their watch of wondering love.
   O morning stars together
      Proclaim the holy birth,
   And praises sing to God the King,
      And peace to men on earth.

3) How silently, how silently,
      The wondrous gift is given!
   So God imparts to human hearts
      The blessings of his heaven.
   No ear may hear his coming;
      But in this world of sin,
   Where meek souls will receive him, still
      The dear Christ enters in.

4) O holy Child of Bethlehem,
      Descend to us, we pray;
   Cast out our sin, and enter in;
      Be born in us to-day.
   We hear the Christmas angels
      The great glad tidings tell;
   O come to us, abide with us,
      Our Lord Emmanuel.

CHRISTMAS ANTHEM

Moore
James Denson

O how charming, O how charming, Are the radiant bands of music, music, music, music. O how charming, are the radiant bands of music

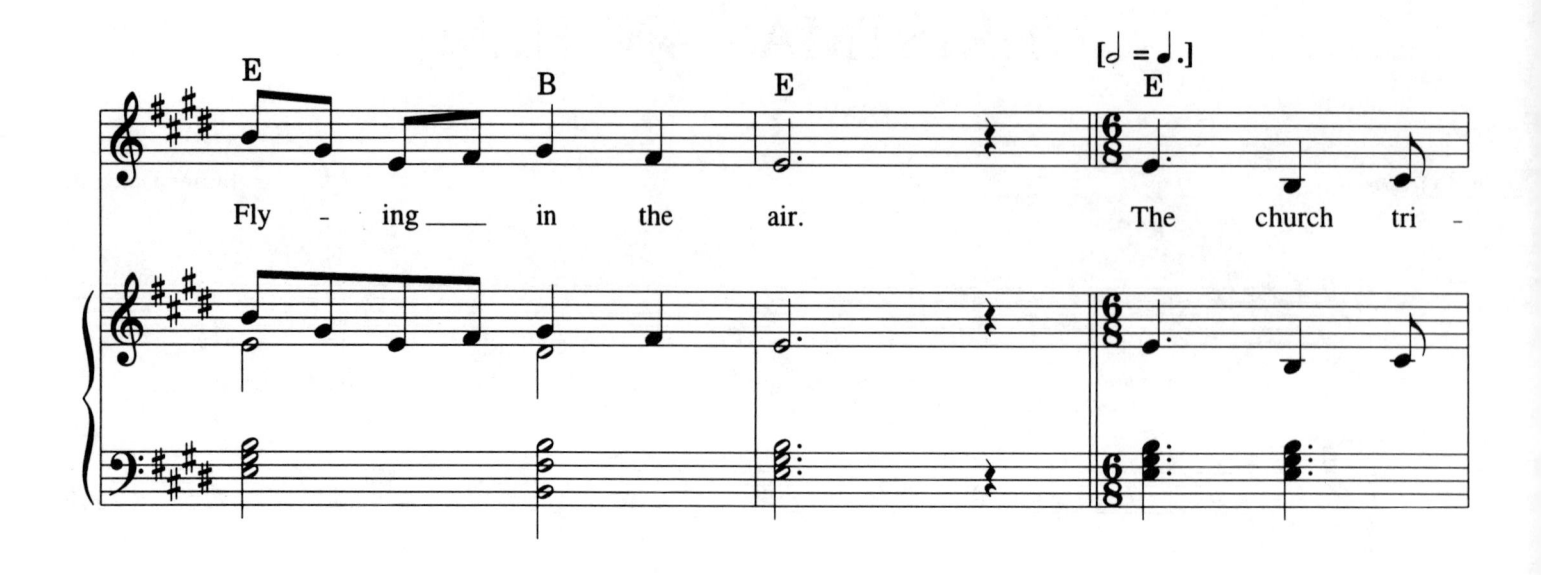

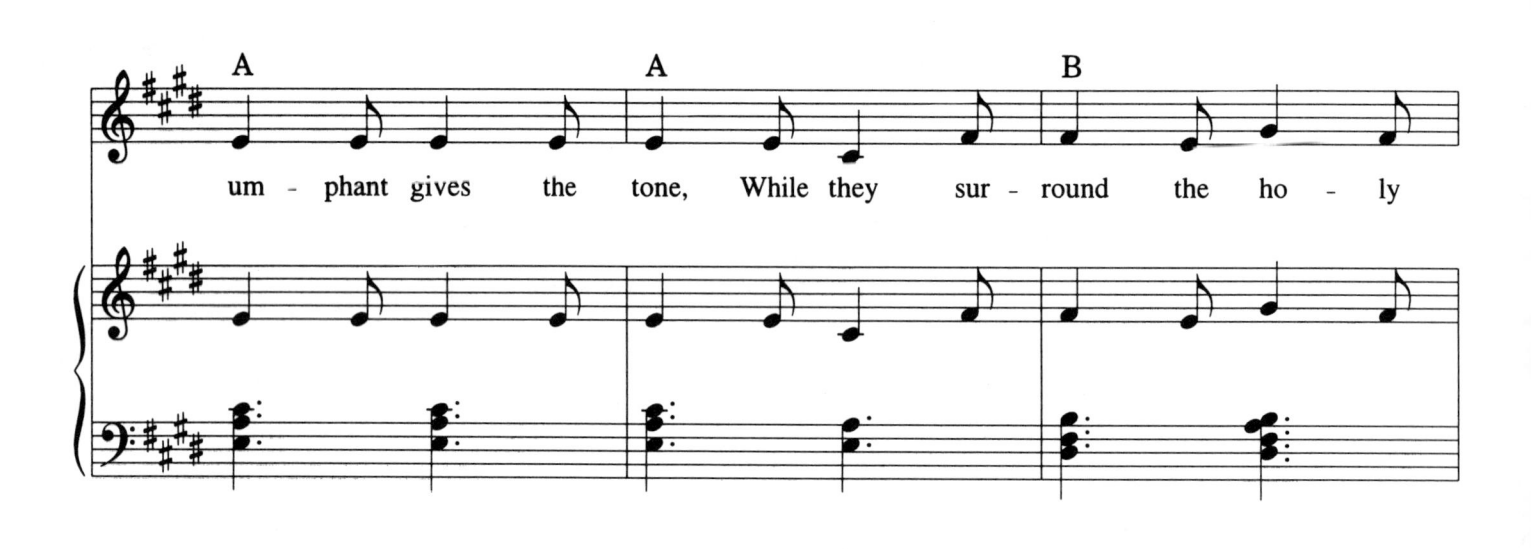

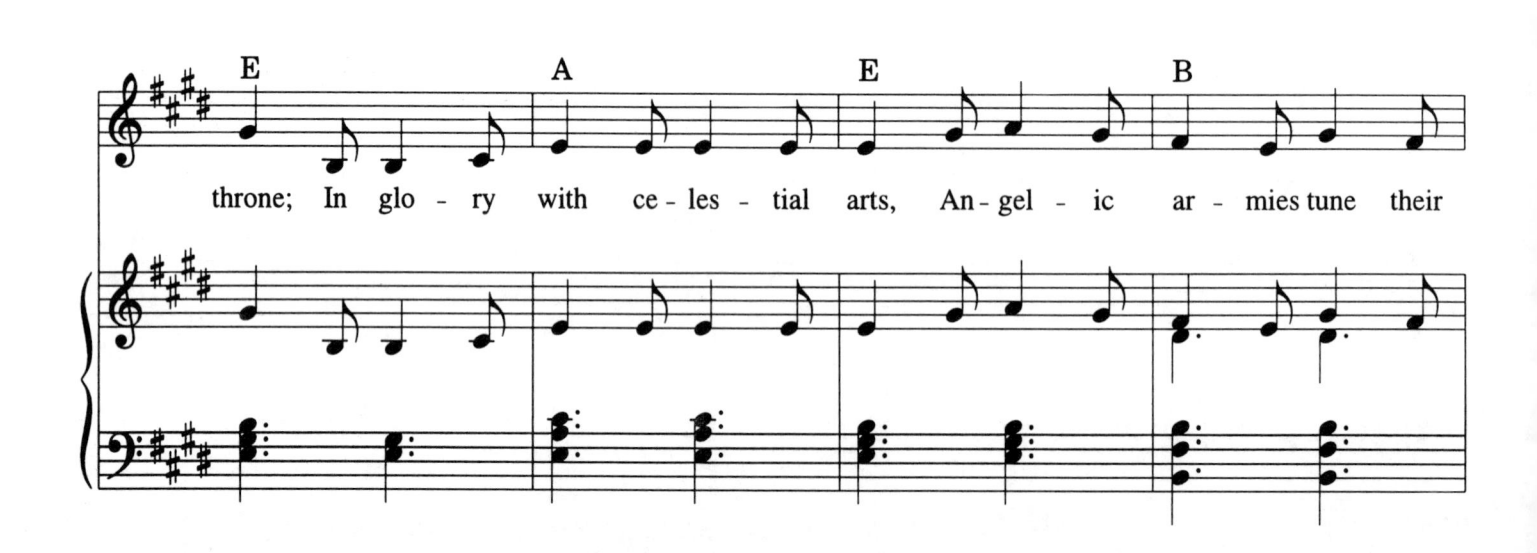

Fly - ing ____ in the air. The church tri - um - phant gives the tone, While they sur - round the ho - ly throne; In glo - ry with ce - les - tial arts, An - gel - ic ar - mies tune their

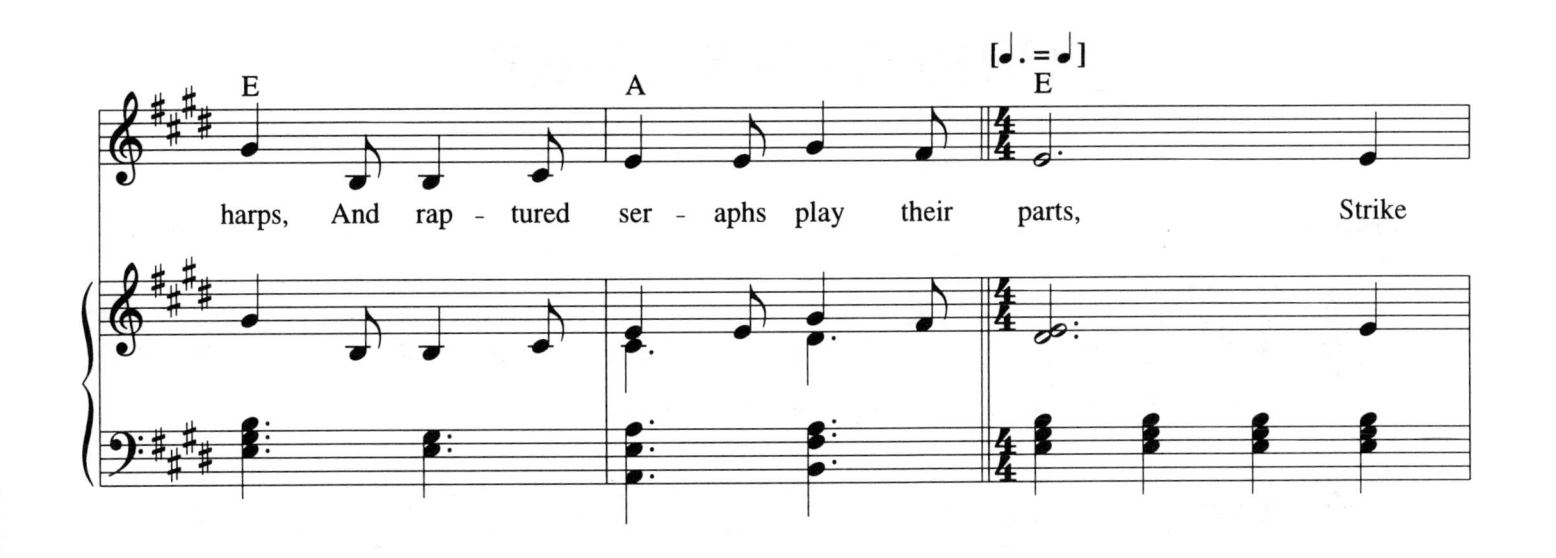

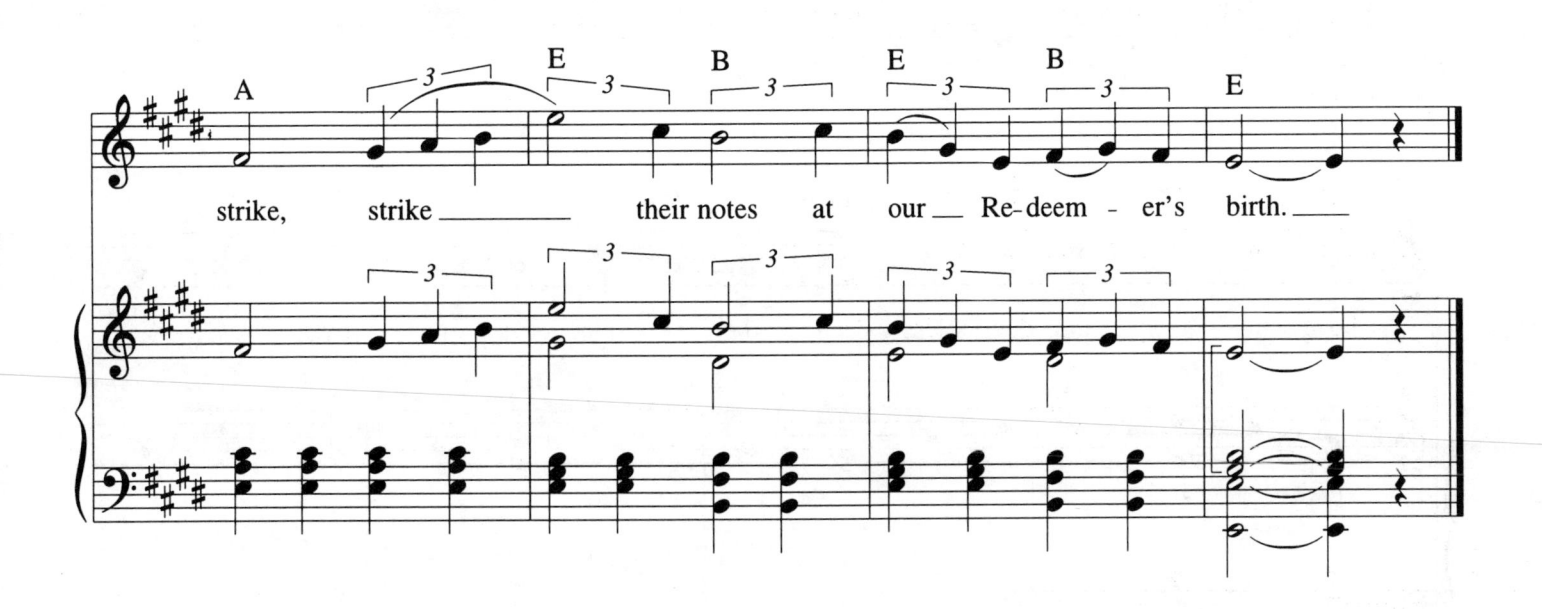

O how charming, O how charming,
Are the radiant bands of music
Flying in the air.

The church triumphant gives the tone,
While they surround the holy throne;
In glory with celestial arts,
Angelic armies tune their harps,

And rapured seraphs play their parts,
Strike their notes at our Redeemer's birth.

CHRISTMAS CAROL

Phillips Brooks   E. A. Wales

O little town of Bethlehem, How still we see thee lie! Above thy deep and dreamless sleep The silent stars go by: Yet in thy dark streets shineth The everlasting Light; The

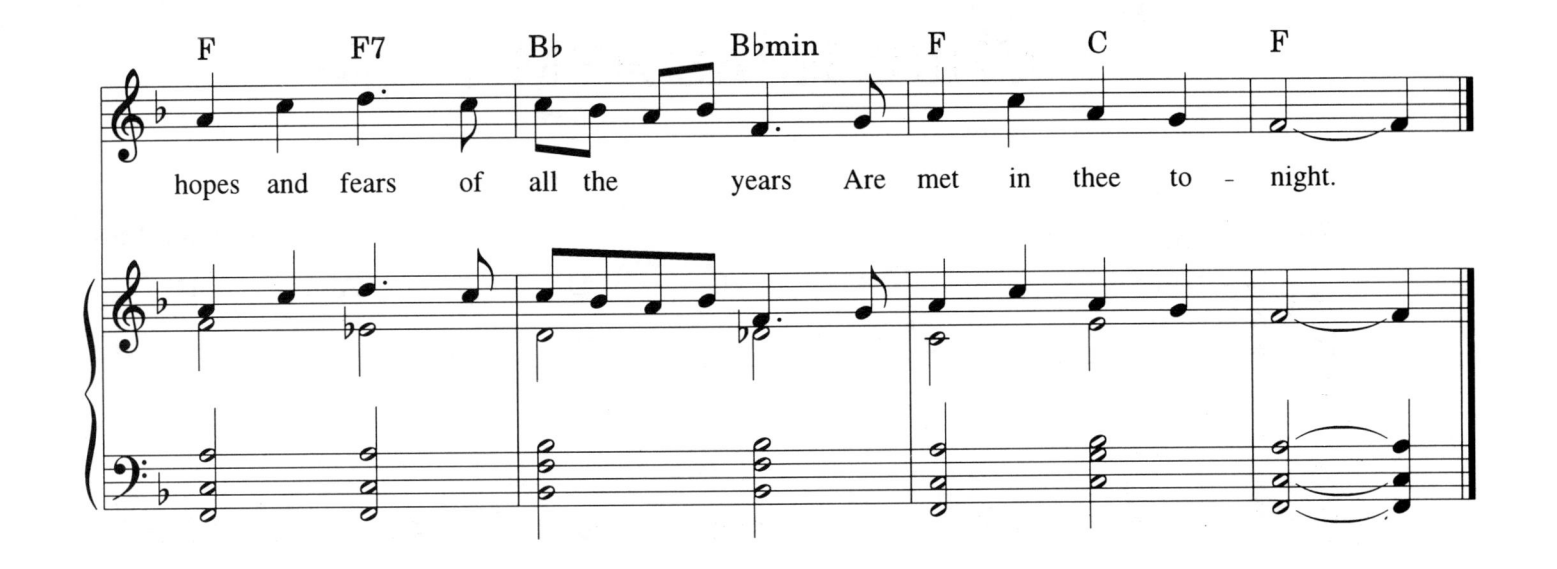

1) O little town of Bethlehem,
   How still we see thee lie!
   Above thy deep and dreamless sleep
   The silent stars go by:
   Yet in thy dark streets shineth
   The everlasting Light;
   The hopes and fears of all the years
   Are met in thee to - night.

2) For Christ is born of Mary;
   And, gathered all above,
   While mortals sleep, the angels keep
   Their watch of wondering love.
   O morning stars together
   Proclaim the holy birth,
   And praises sing to God the King,
   And peace to men on earth.

3) How silently, how silently,
   The wondrous gift is given!
   So God imparts to human hearts
   The blessings of his heaven.
   No ear may hear his coming;
   But in this world of sin,
   Where meek souls will receive him, still
   The dear Christ enters in.

4) O holy Child of Bethlehem,
   Descend to us, we pray;
   Cast out our sin, and enter in;
   Be born in us to - day.
   We hear the Christmas angels
   The great glad tidings tell;
   O come to us, abide with us,
   Our Lord Emmanuel.

CHRISTMAS HYMN

Isaac Watts
Joseph Stephenson

The heav'ns de-clare thy glo-ry, Lord, In ev-'ry star thy wis-dom shines; But when our eyes be-hold thy word, We read thy name in fair-er lines.

54

1) The heavens declare thy glory, Lord,
   In every star thy wisdom shines;
   But when our eyes behold thy word,
   We read thy name in fairer lines.

2) The rolling sun, the changing light,
   And nights and days thy power confess;
   But the blest volume thou hast writ
   Reveals thy justice and thy grace.

3) Sun, moon, and stars convey thy praise
   Round the whole earth, and never stand;
   So when thy truth began its race,
   It touched and glanced on every land.

4) Nor shall thy spreading gospel rest,
   Till through the world thy truth has run;
   Till Christ has all the nations blest
   That see the light, or feel the sun.

5) Great God of righteousness, arise,
   Bless the dark world with heavenly light;
   Thy gospel makes the simple wise,
   Thy laws are pure, thy judgments right.

6) Thy noblest wonders here we view
   In souls renewed and sins forgiven;
   Lord, cleanse my sins, my soul renew,
   And make thy word my guide to heaven.

CLIFTON

Philip Doddridge

William Arnold

Hark the glad sound! the Savior comes, The Savior promised long; Let ev'ry heart prepare him room, And ev'ry voice a song, And ev'ry voice a song.

1) Hark the glad sound! the Savior comes,
   The Savior promised long;
   Let ev'ry heart prepare him room,
   And ev'ry voice a song.

2) On Him the Spirit, largely poured,
   Exerts its sacred fire;
   Wisdom and might, and zeal, and love,
   His holy breast inspire.

3) He comes the prisoners to release,
   In Satan's bondage held;
   The gates of brass before Him burst,
   The iron fetters yield.

4) He comes from thickest film of vice,
   To clear the mental ray:
   And on the eyes oppressed with night,
   To pour celestial day.

5) He comes the broken heart to bind,
   The bleeding soul to cure;
   And with the treasures of his grace,
   T'enrich the humble poor.

6) His silver trumpets publish loud
   The jubilee of the Lord;
   Our debts are all remitted now,
   Our heritage restored!

7) Our glad hosannas, Prince of Peace,
   Thy welcome shall proclaim;
   And heaven's eternal arches ring
   With Thy beloved name.

COOKHAM

Charles Wesley

Unknown

Hark, the her - ald an - gels sing Glo - ry to the new - born king, Peace on earth and mer - cy mild; God and sin - ners rec - on - ciled.

1) Hark, the herald angels sing
   Glory to the new-born King,
   Peace on earth and mercy mild;
   God and sinners reconciled.

2) Christ, by highest heaven adored,
   Christ, the everlasting Lord,
   Late in time behold Him come,
   Offspring of a virgin's womb.

3) Veiled in flesh the Godhead see;
   Hail th'incarnate Deity!
   Pleased as man with men t'appear,
   Jesus our Immanuel here.

4) Hail the heaven-born Prince of Peace,
   Hail the Sun of Righteousness!
   Light and life to all he brings,
   Risen with healing in his wings.

5) Mild he lays his glory by,
   Born that man no more may die;
   Born to raise the sons of earth,
   Born to give them second birth.

6) Come, Desire of Nations, come,
   Fix in us thy humble home;
   Rise, the woman's conquering seed,
   Bruise in us the serpent's head.

7) Adam's likeness now efface,
   Stamp thine image in its place:
   Second Adam from above,
   Reinstate us in thy love.

8) Now ye saints, lift up your eyes!
   Now to glory see him rise,
   In long triumph, up the sky,
   Up to waiting worlds on high.

9) Praise him, all ye heavenly choirs!
   Praise, and sweep your golden lyres!
   Shout, O earth, in rapt'rous song,
   Let the strains be sweet and strong!

COURTNEY

John Milton
Unknown

No war or bat-tle's sound Was heard the world a-round; No hos-tile chiefs to fu-rious com-bat ran; But peace-ful was the night In which the Prince of _____ light, _____ His reign _____ of peace _____ up-on the earth be-gan, His reign of peace up-on the earth be-gan. _____

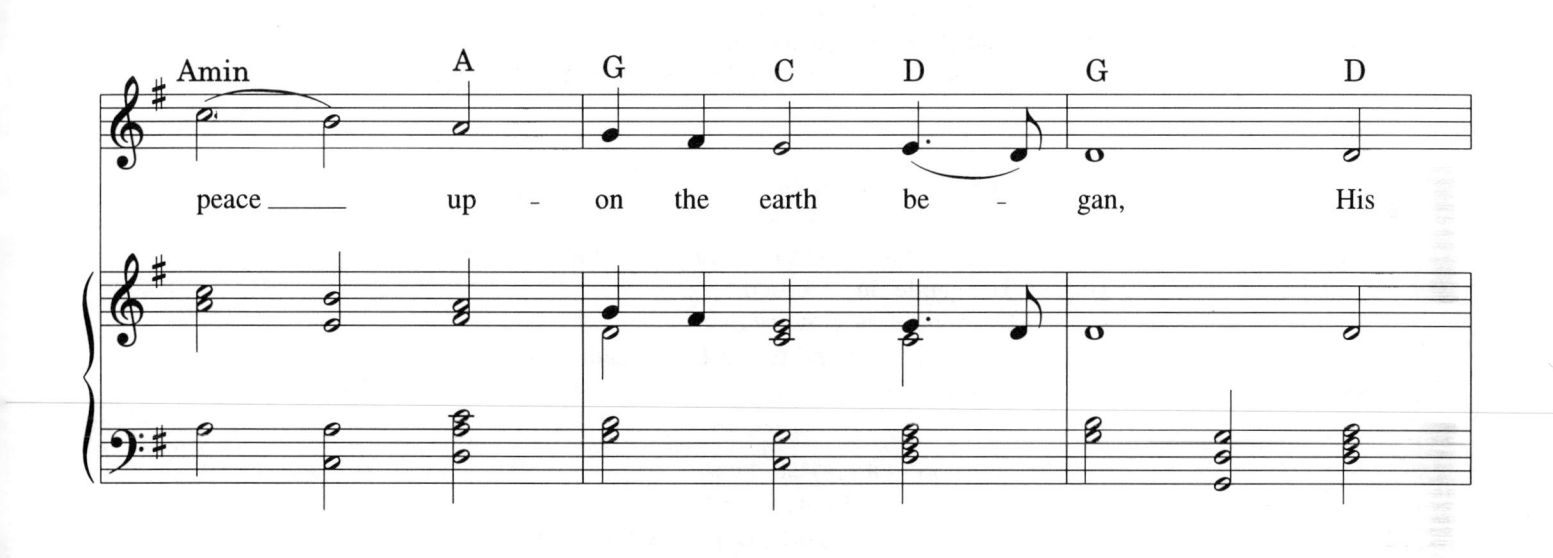

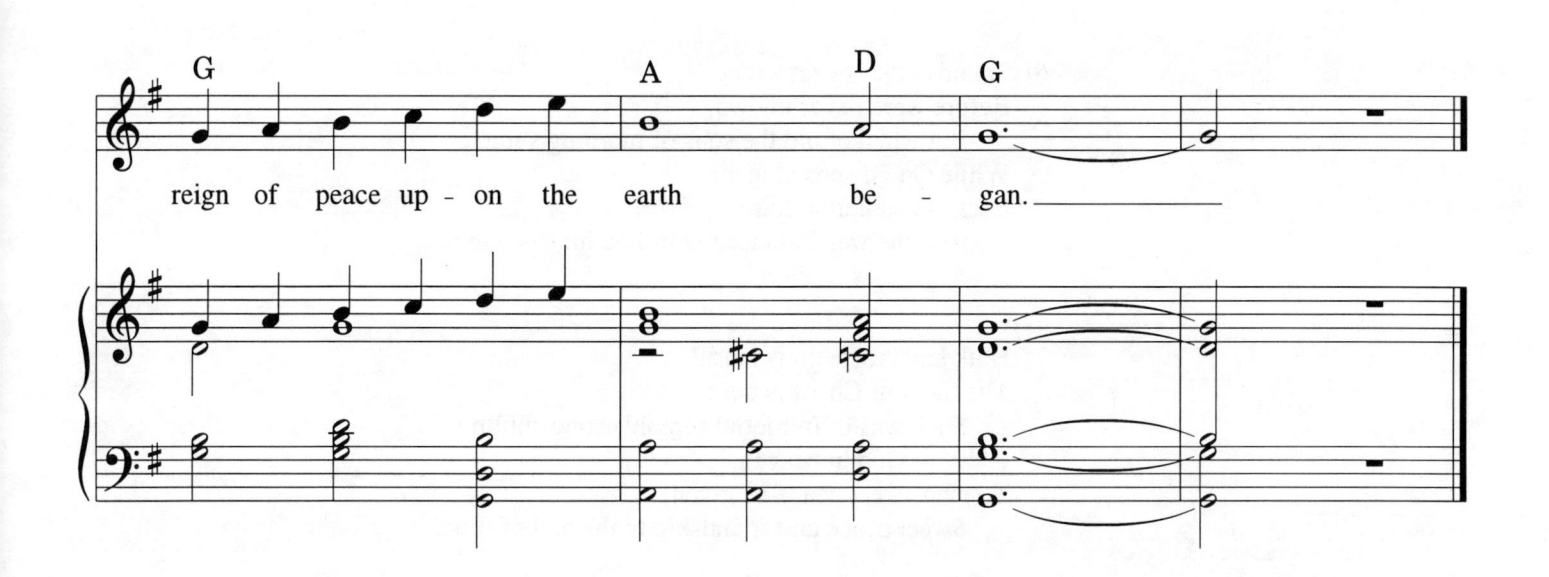

1) No war or battle's sound
    Was heard the world around;
        No hostile chiefs to furious combat ran;
    But peaceful was the night
    In which the Prince of light,
        His reign of peace upon the earth began.

2) No conq'ror's sword he bore,
    Nor war-like armor wore,
        Nor haughty passions roused to contest wild;
    In peace and love he came,
    And gentle was his reign,
        Which o'er the earth he spread by influence mild.

3) Unwilling kings obey'd,
    And sheath'd the battle blade,
        And called the bloody legions from the field;
    In silent awe they wait,
    And close the warrior's gate,
        Nor know to whom their homage thus they yield.

4) The shepherds on the lawn,
    Before the point of dawn,
        In social circle sat, while all around
    The gentle fleecy brood,
    Or cropp'd the flow'ry food
        Or slept, or sported on the verdant ground.

5) When lo! with ravish'd ears,
    Each swain delighted hears
        Sweet music, offspring of no mortal hand;
    Divinely warbled voice,
    Answering the stringed noise,
        With blissful rapture charm'd the list'ning band.

6) Sounds of so sweet a tone
    Before were never known,
        But when of old the sons of morning sung
    While God disposed in air
    Each constellation fair,
        And the well balanced world on hinges hung.

7) Hail, hail Auspicious morn!
    The Saviour Christ is born;
        Such was th'immortal seraph's song sublime
    Glory to God in heaven;
    To man sweet peace be given,
        Sweet peace and friendship to the end of time!

"Hurrah for the Pudding!" From *Little Folks*, c. 1870.

DERRICK

Philip Doddridge
Unknown

High let us swell our tuneful notes, And join th'angelic throng, For angels no such love have known To wake a cheerful song.

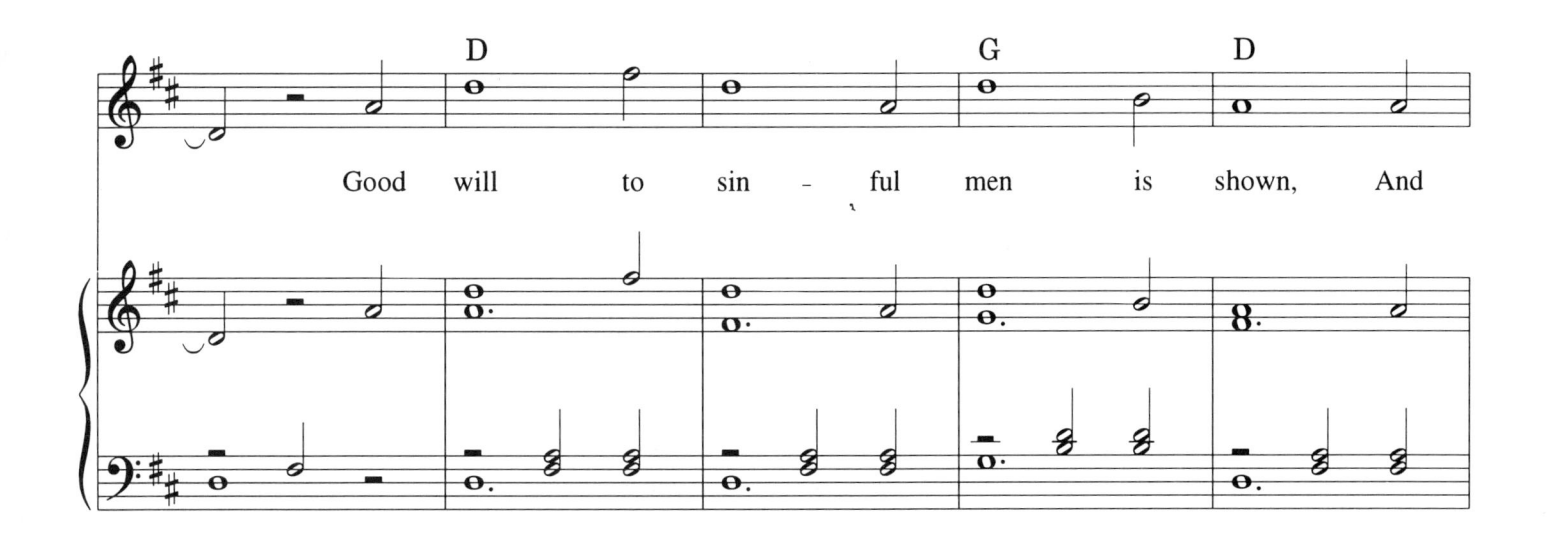

Good will to sinful men is shown, And peace on earth is giv'n: For lo, th'incarnate Saviour comes With grace and truth from heav'n.

65

1) High let us swell our tuneful notes,
    And join th'angelic throng,
For angels no such love have known
    To wake a cheerful song.

2) Good will to sinful men is shown,
    And peace on earth is giv'n:
For lo, th'incarnate Saviour comes
    With grace and truth from heaven.

3) Justice and peace with sweet accord
    His rising beams adorn;
Let heaven and earth in concert join:
    To us a Child is born!

4) Glory to God! in highest strains,
    In highest worlds be paid;
His glory by our lips proclaim'd,
    And by our lives display'd.

5) When shall we reach those happy realms,
    Where Christ exalted reigns!
And learn of the celestial choir
    Their own immortal strains!

6) High let us swell our tuneful notes,
    And join th'angelic song
For such a theme does less to them,
    Than to the saints belong.

"The Children's Corner at the Centennial—Exhibition of Dolls and Toys,"
by Theodore R. Davis, 1877.

EDDINGTON

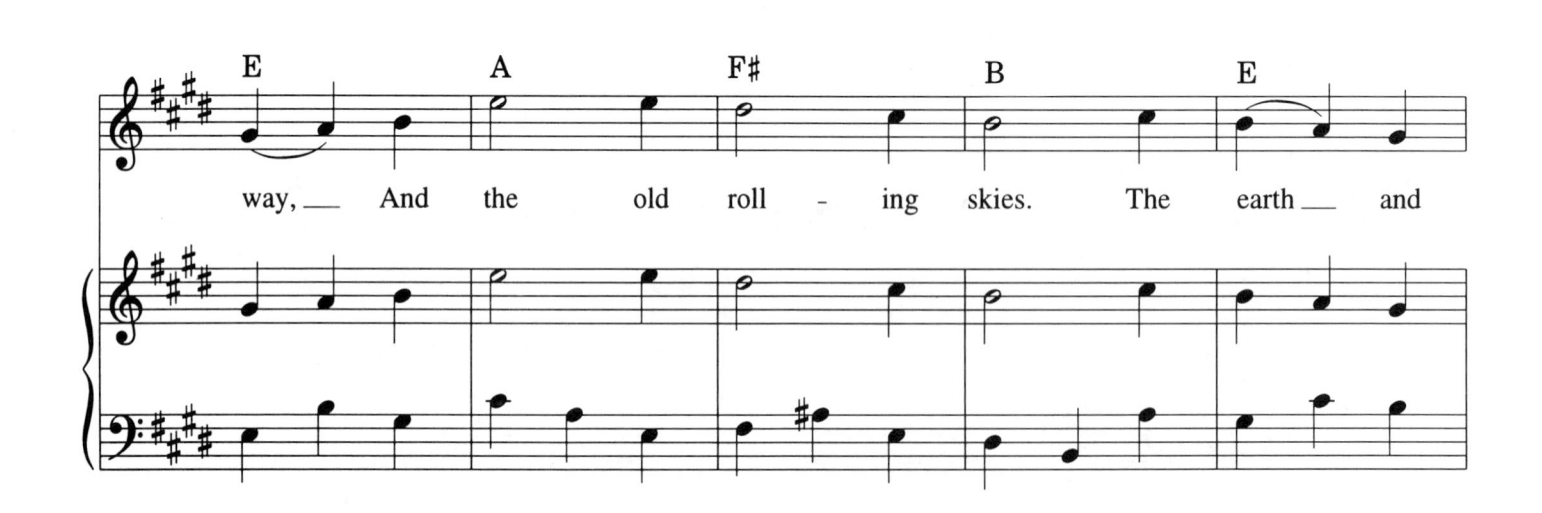

Isaac Watts
Unknown

Lo, what a glorious sight appears To our believing eyes! The earth and sea are passed away, And the old rolling skies. The earth and

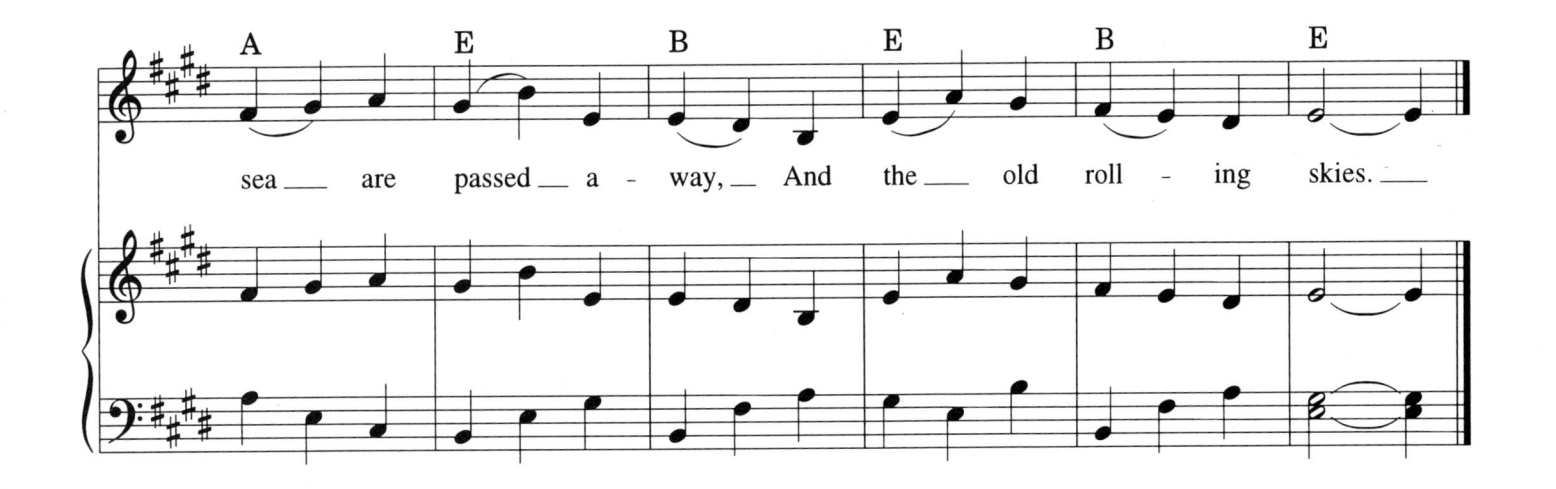

1) Lo, what a glorious sight appears
   To our believing eyes!
  The earth and sea are passed away,
   And the old rolling skies.

2) From the third heaven where God resides,
   That holy, happy place,
  The new Jerusalem comes down
   Adorned with shining grace.

3) Attending angels shout for joy,
   And the bright armies sing,
  Mortals, behold the sacred seat
   Of your descending King.

4) The God of glory down to men
   Removes his blest abode,
  Men the dear objects of his grace,
   And he the loving God.

5) His own soft hand shall wipe the tears
   From every weeping eye,
  And pains, and groans, and griefs, and fears,
   And death itself shall die.

6) How long, dear Saviour, O how long,
   Shall this bright hour delay!
  Fly swifter round, ye wheels of time,
   And bring the welcome day.

EMANUEL

Traditional
William Billings

As shep-herds in Jew-ry were guard-ing their sheep, Pro-mis-c'ous-ly seat-ed, es-trang-ed from sleep; An an-gel from heav-en pre-sent-ed to view, And thus he ac-cost-ed the trem-bling few. Dis-

Chorus
♩. = 60
F♯min
B
pel all your sor - rows, and ban - ish your fears, For
E
B
E
Je - sus your Sav - ior in Jew - ry ap - pears; Dis - pel all your sor - rows and
B
E
A
B
E
ban - ish your fears, For Je - sus your Sav - ior in Jew - ry ap - pears.

1) As shepherds in Jewry were guarding their sheep,
   Promisc'ously seated, estranged from sleep;
   An angel from heaven presented to view,
   And thus he accosted the trembling few.

Chorus: Dispel all your sorrows, and banish your fears,
   For Jesus your Savior in Jewry appears.

2) Tho' Adam the first in rebellion was found,
   Forbidden to tarry on hallowed ground;
   Yet Adam the second appears to retrieve
   The loss you sustained by the devil and Eve.

Chorus: Then shepherds, be tranquil, this instant arise,
   Go visit your Savior and see where he lies.

3) A token I leave you whereby you may find,
   This heavenly stranger, this friend to mankind;
   A manger's his cradle, a stall his abode,
   The oxen are near him and blow on your God.

Chorus: Then shepherds be humble, be meek and lie low,
   For Jesus your Savior's abundantly so.

4) This wondrous story scarce cooled on the ear,
   When thousands of angels in glory appear;
   They join in the concert and this was the theme:
   All glory to God and goodwill toward men.

Chorus: Then shepherds strike in, join your voice to the choir,
   And catch a few sparks of celestial fire.

5) Hosanna! the angels in ecstasy cry,
   Hosanna! the wondering shepherds reply;
   Salvation, redemption are centered in one,
   All glory to God for the birth of his Son.

Chorus: Then shepherds adieu, we commend you to God,
   Go visit the Son in his humble abode.

6) To Bethlehem city the shepherds repaired,
   For full confirmation of what they had heard;
   They entered the stable with aspect so mild,
   And there they beheld both the mother and child.

Chorus: Then make proclamation, divulge it abroad,
   That gentle and simple may hear of the Lord.

GABRIEL

George Richards
Unknown

[♩ = 80]

Th'Al-might-y spake, and Ga-briel sped Up-borne on wings of light; Je-ho-vah's glo-ry round him spread, And changed to day the night.

Slightly faster

Swift down to earth th'arch-an - gel flew From

God's e-ter-nal throne; His shin-ing robe of rain-bow hue The stars, moon, sun out-shone.

A tempo [♩ = 80]

Ten thou-sand thou-sand left the sky To catch sal-va-tion's sound; One note of peace was heard on high, Glad ti - dings rolled a - round.

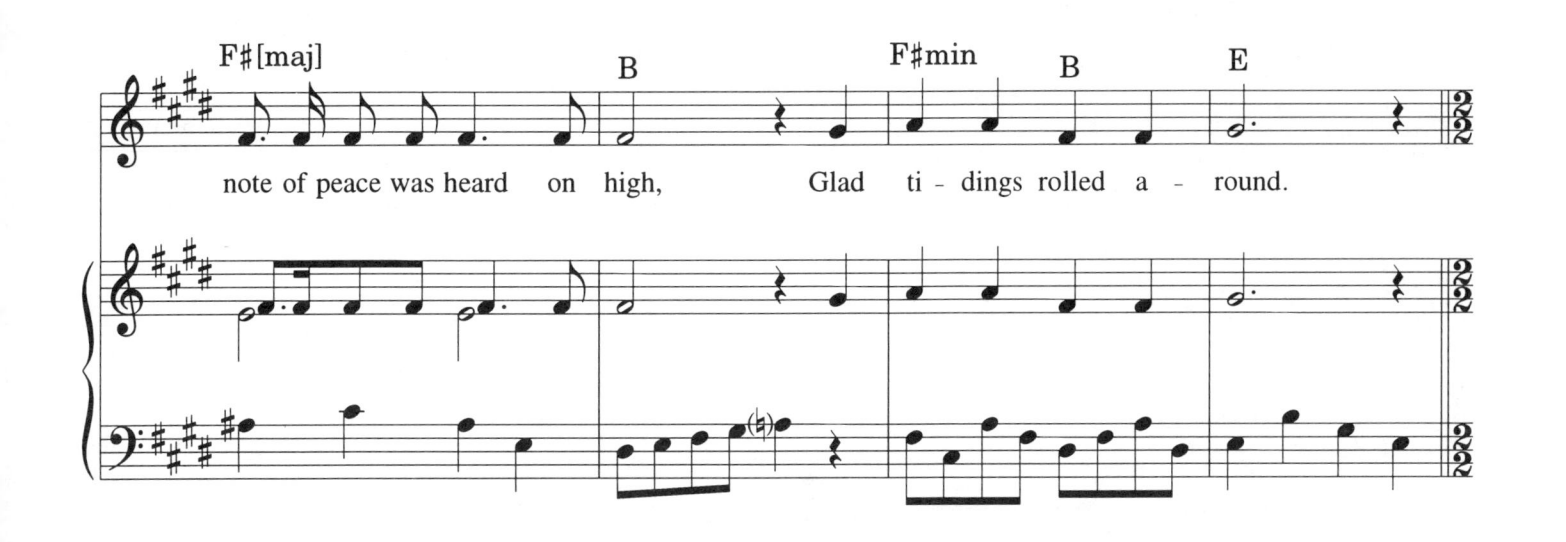

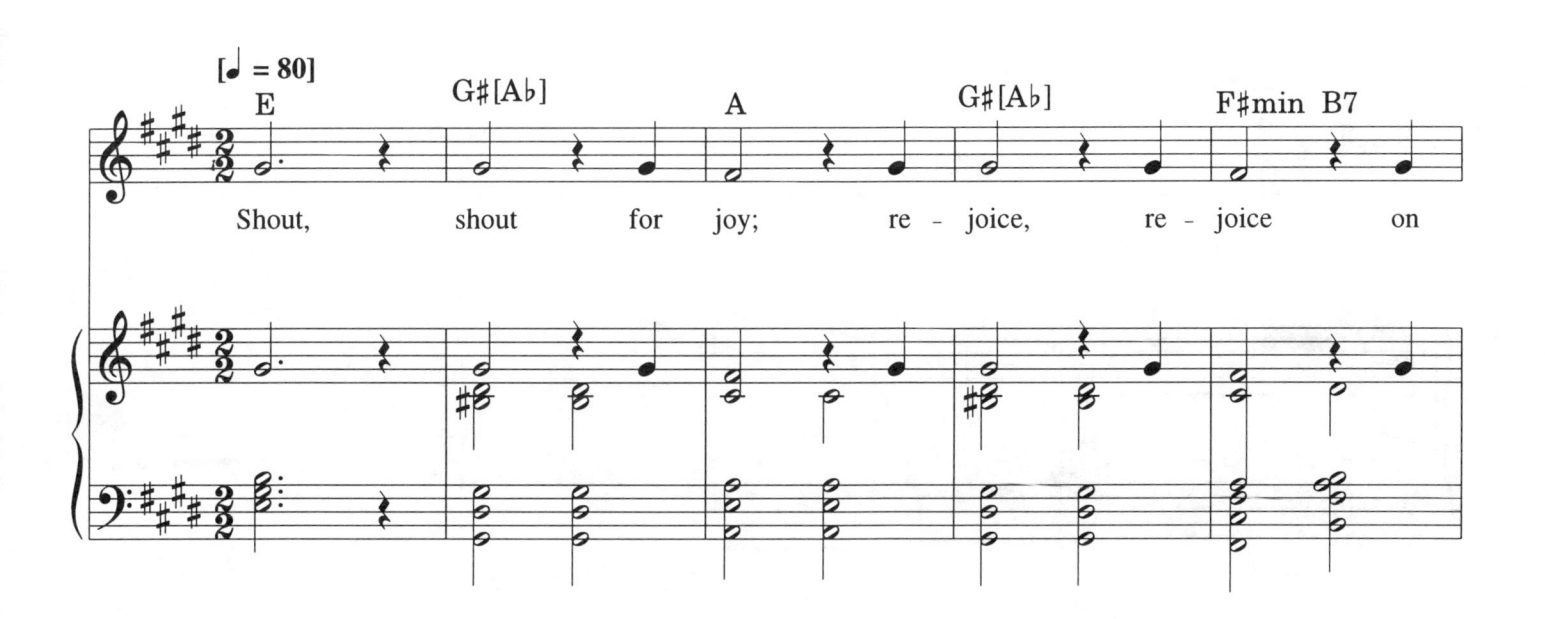

Shout, shout for joy; re - joice, re - joice on earth; All hail this glo - rious morn; Re - joice, re - joice in

E F♯ B E B E
Je - sus' birth; To - day are na - tions born. From
[♩ = 80]
A E A B
Zi-on's hills to worlds a - bove, Re-e-cho back the strain; And
E B E B E F♯ B
gold-en harps at-tuned to love, Thus sweep E - phra - tah's_ plain. He

comes, He comes, the Sav-ior God; Good - will, Peace, peace, joy for men; Glad tid-ings shout to all a-broad; A - men, A - men, A - men, A - men.

1) Th'Almighty spake, and Gabriel sped
    Upborne on wings of light;
   Jehovah's glory round him spread,
    And changed to day the night.

2) Swift down to earth th'archangel flew
    From God's eternal throne;
   His shining robe of rainbow hue
    The stars, moon, sun outshone.

3) Ten thousand thousand left the sky
    To catch salvation's sound;
   One note of peace was heard on high,
    Glad tidings rolled around.

4) Shout, shout for joy; rejoice on earth;
    All hail this glorious morn;
   Rejoice, rejoice in Jesus' birth;
    Today are nations born.

5) From Zion's hills to worlds above,
    Reecho back the strain;
   And golden harps attuned to love,
    Thus sweep Ephratah's plain.

6) He comes, He comes, the Savior God;
    Goodwill, peace, joy for men;
   Glad tidings shout to all abroad;
    Amen, Amen, Amen.

"The Old Homestead—Going Home for the Holidays," by Granville Perkins.
From *Harper's Weekly*, Dec. 25, 1875.

GEORGIA

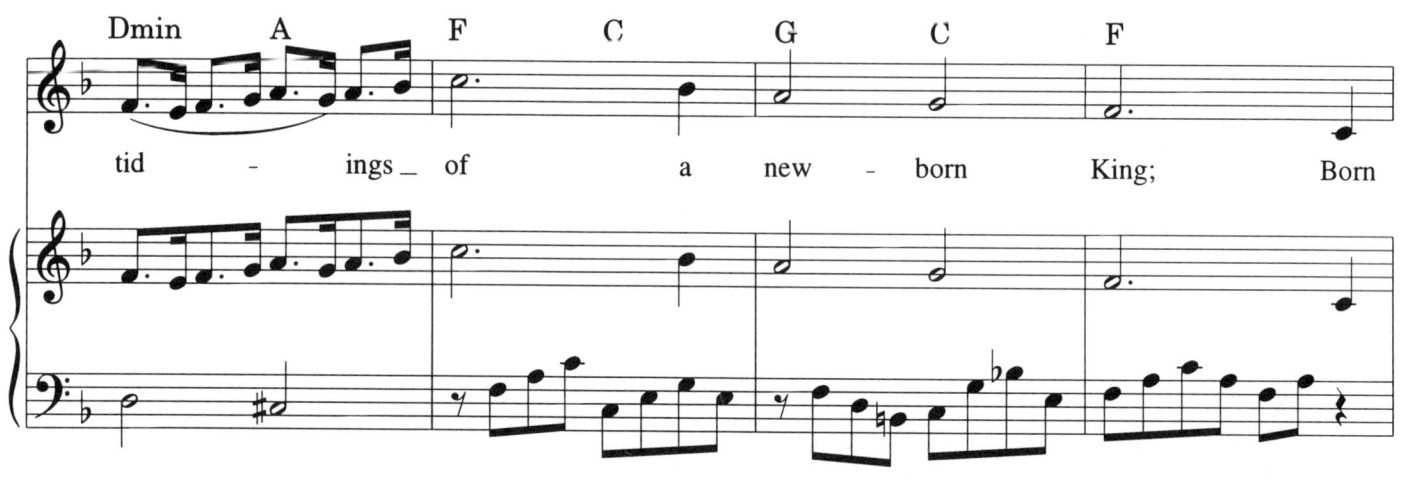

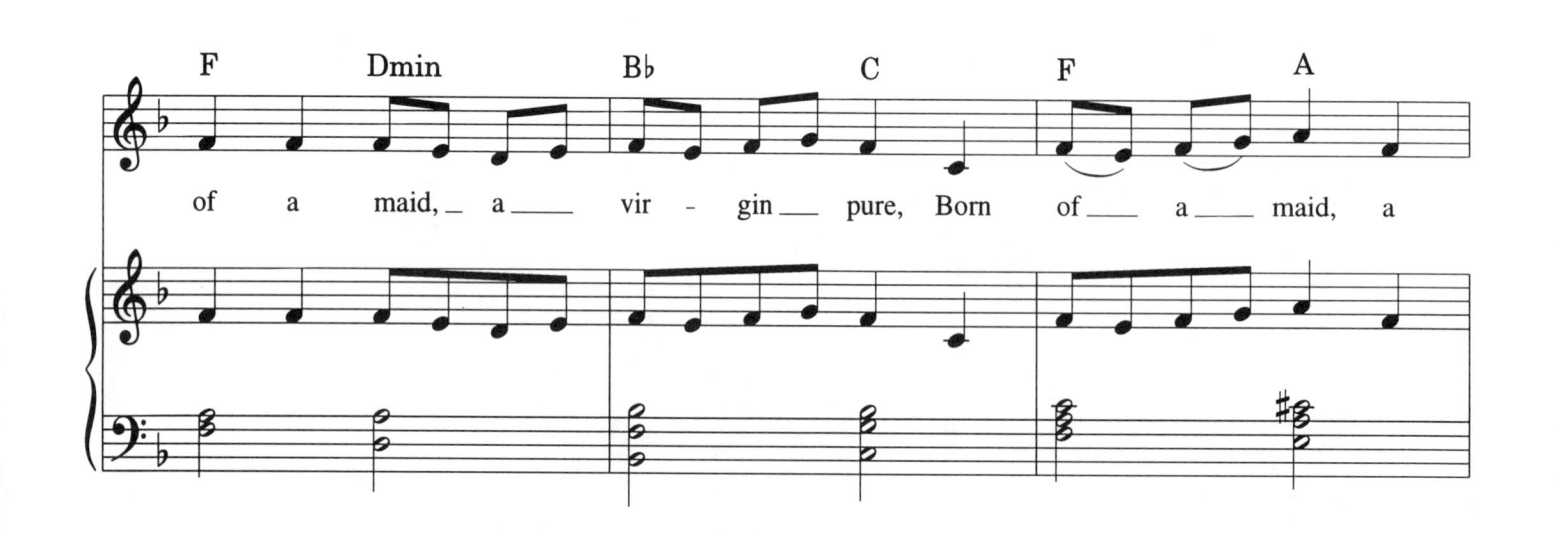

Unknown
Jacob Kimball

Hark! Hark! Hark, what news the angels bring, Glad tidings of a new-born King; Born of a maid, a virgin pure, Born of a maid, a

Dmin F7 B♭ F Gmin C
vir - gin __ pure, Born with - out sin from guilt se - -
G C F Gmin C
cure. Born of a maid, __ a ___ vir - gin pure, _ Born _
F B♭ C F
with - out sin __ from guilt se - - cure.

GLAD SOUND

Philip Doddridge
Unknown

[♩ = 80]

Hark! the glad sound! the Savior comes, The Savior promised long; Let ev'ry heart prepare him room, Let *ev' - ry heart pre - pare him room, And ev' - ry voice a song, And ev' - ry voice a song.*

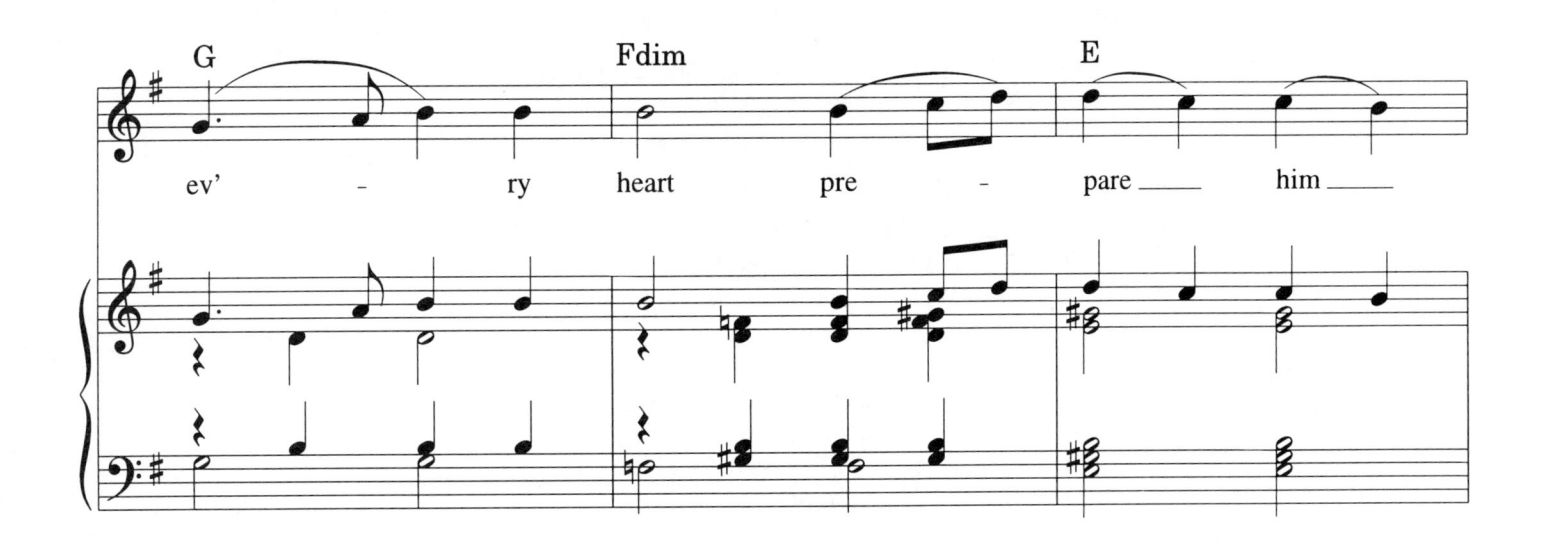

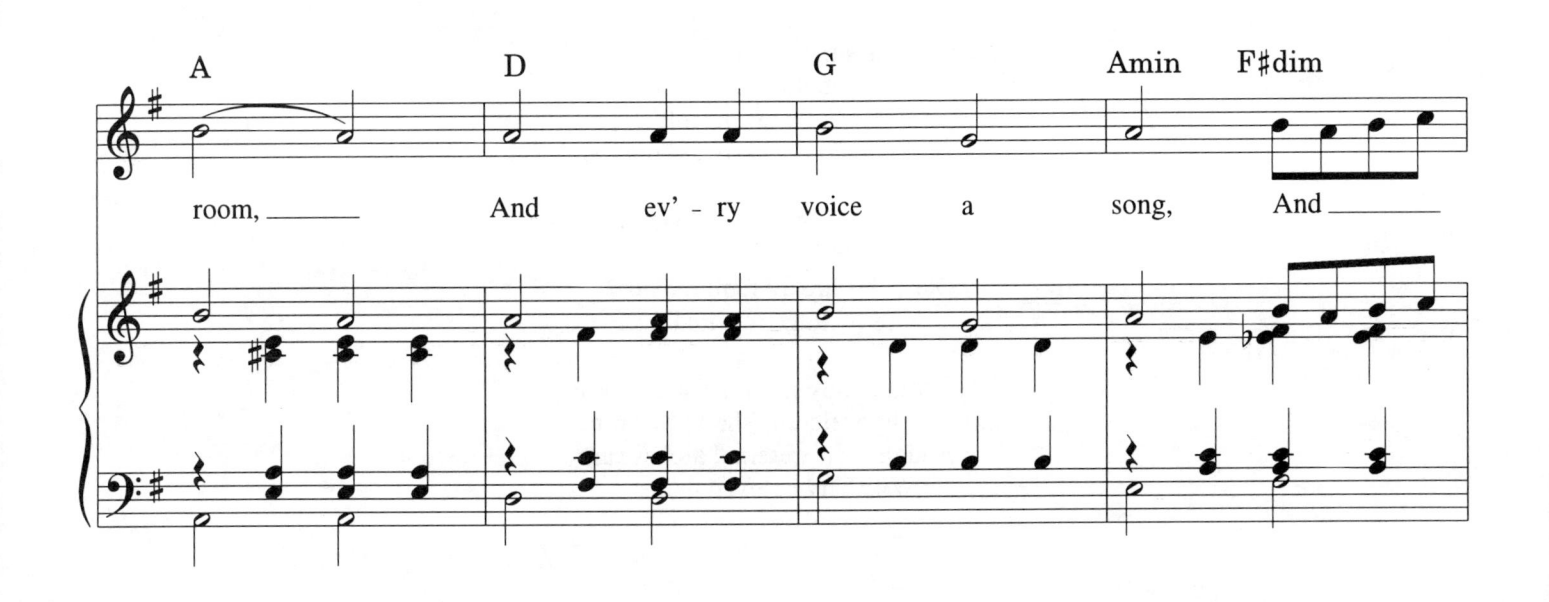

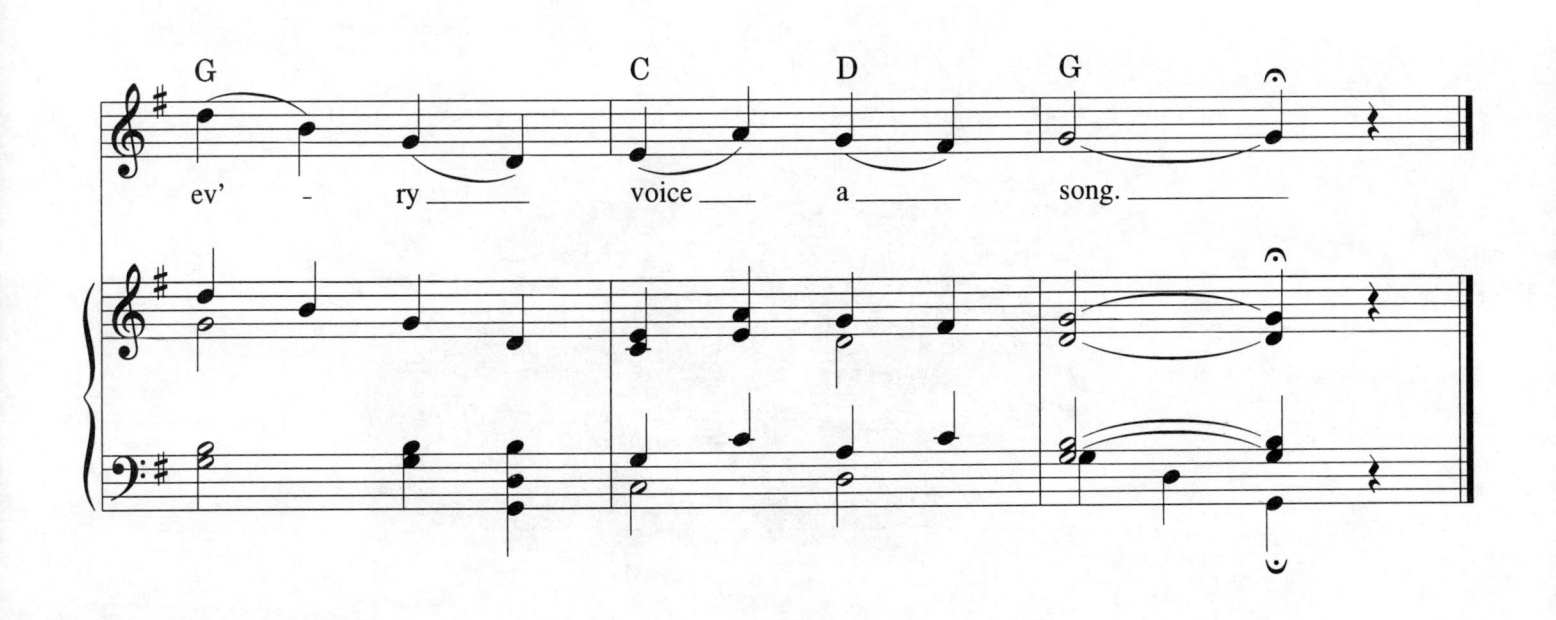

1) Hark! the glad sound! the Savior comes,
    The Savior promised long;
  Let ev'ry heart prepare him room,
    And ev'ry voice a song.

2) On Him the Spirit, largely poured,
    Exerts its sacred fire;
  Wisdom and might, and zeal, and love,
    His holy breast inspire.

3) He comes the prisoners to release,
    In Satan's bondage held;
  The gates of brass before Him burst,
    The iron fetters yield.

4) He comes from thickest film of vice,
    To clear the mental ray:
  And on the eyes oppressed with night,
    To pour celestial day.

5) He comes the broken heart to bind,
    The bleeding soul to cure;
  And with the treasures of his grace,
    T'enrich the humble poor.

6) His silver trumpets publish loud
    The jubilee of the Lord;
  Our debts are all remitted now,
    Our heritage restored!

7) Our glad hosannas, Prince of peace,
    Thy welcome shall proclaim;
  And heaven's eternal arches ring
    With Thy beloved name.

"Christmas Games."
From *Godey's Lady's Book and Magazine*, Dec., 1869.

GLAD TIDINGS

Mrs. R. N. Turner

Mrs. Julia H. Mosher

[♩. = 80]

Ring out the glad tid-ings of glo - - ry, For Je-sus our Sav-ior is King! Ring out, hap-py bells, the sto - ry, A-far o'er the earth let it ring. All glo-ry to

Chorus

1) Ring out the glad tidings of glory,
    For Jesus our Savior is King!
  Ring out, happy bells, the story,
    Afar o'er the earth let it ring.

Chorus: All glory to God in the highest,
       All glory and honor proclaim,
      The Savior has come to redeem us,
       All honor and praise to his name.

2) Ring far o'er the land and the ocean,
    The tidings of peace and goodwill,
  Let waves of sweet music arising,
    All hearts with the melody thrill.

3) Oh dearly we love the sweet story,
    The bells of the Christmas tide ring,
  And gladly we join in the chorus,
    Of honor and praise to the King.

GLORIOUS MORN

John Needham
R. F. Mann

A - wake, a - wake, a - rise, And hail the glo - rious morn!

Hark how the an - gels sing To you a Sav - ior

born; Now let our hearts in con - cert move,

And ev'-ry tongue be tuned to love.

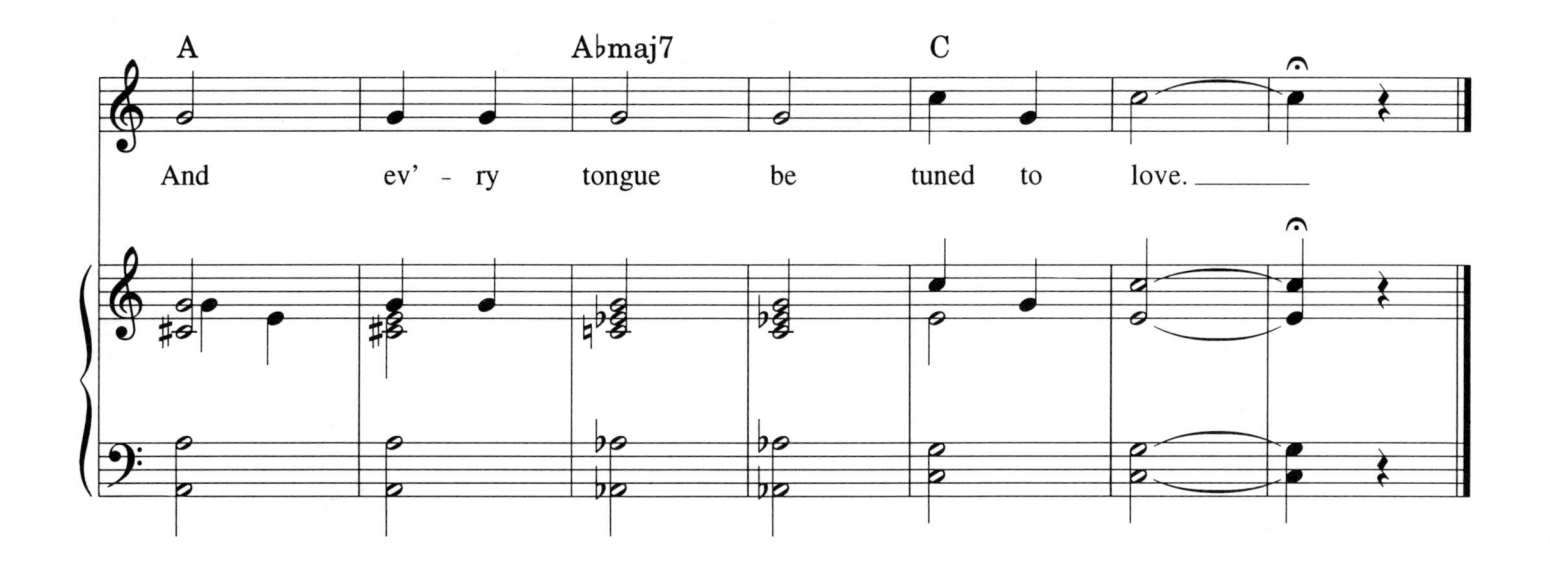

1) Awake, awake, arise,
   And hail the glorious morn!
   Hark how the angels sing
   To you a Savior born;
       Now let our hearts in concert move,
       And ev'ry tongue be tuned to love.

2) He mortals came to save
   From sin's tyrannic power;
   Come, with angels sing
   At this auspicious hour,
       Let every heart and tongue combine
       To praise the love, the grace divine.

3) The prophecies and types
   Are all this day fulfilled;
   With eastern sages join
   To praise this wondrous child:
       God's only Son is come to bless
       The earth with peace and righteousness.

4) Glory to God on high,
   For our Emmanuel's birth;
   To mortal men good will,
   And peace and joy on earth;
       With angels now we will repeat
       Their songs, still new and ever sweet.

GREAT CREATOR

Thomas Pestel Unknown

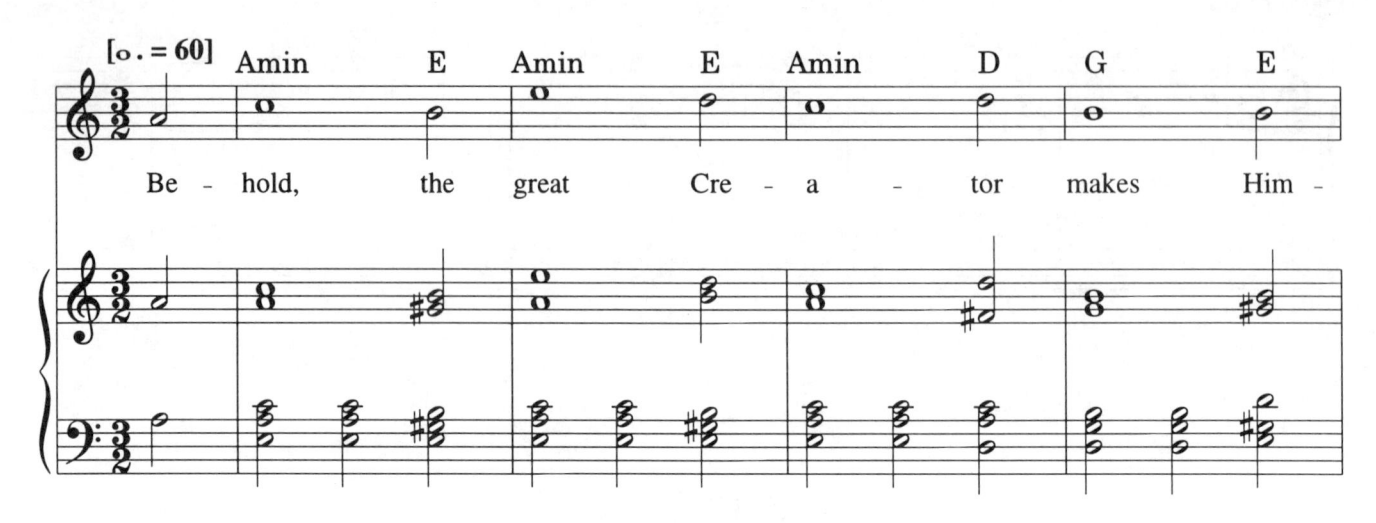

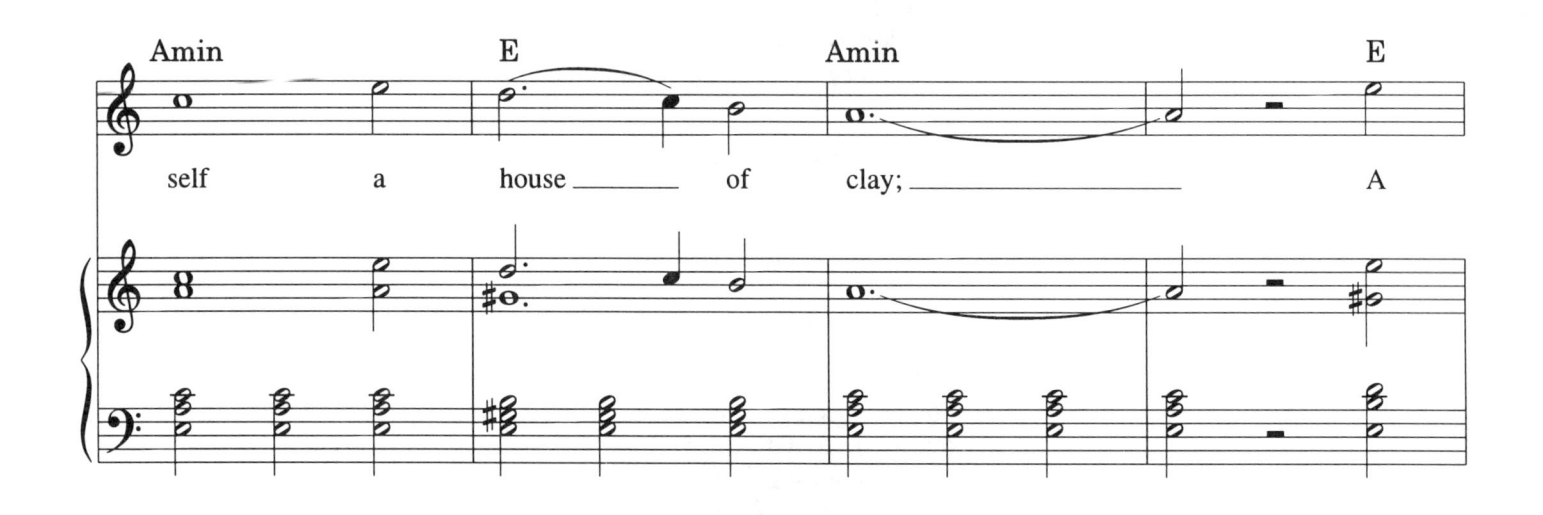

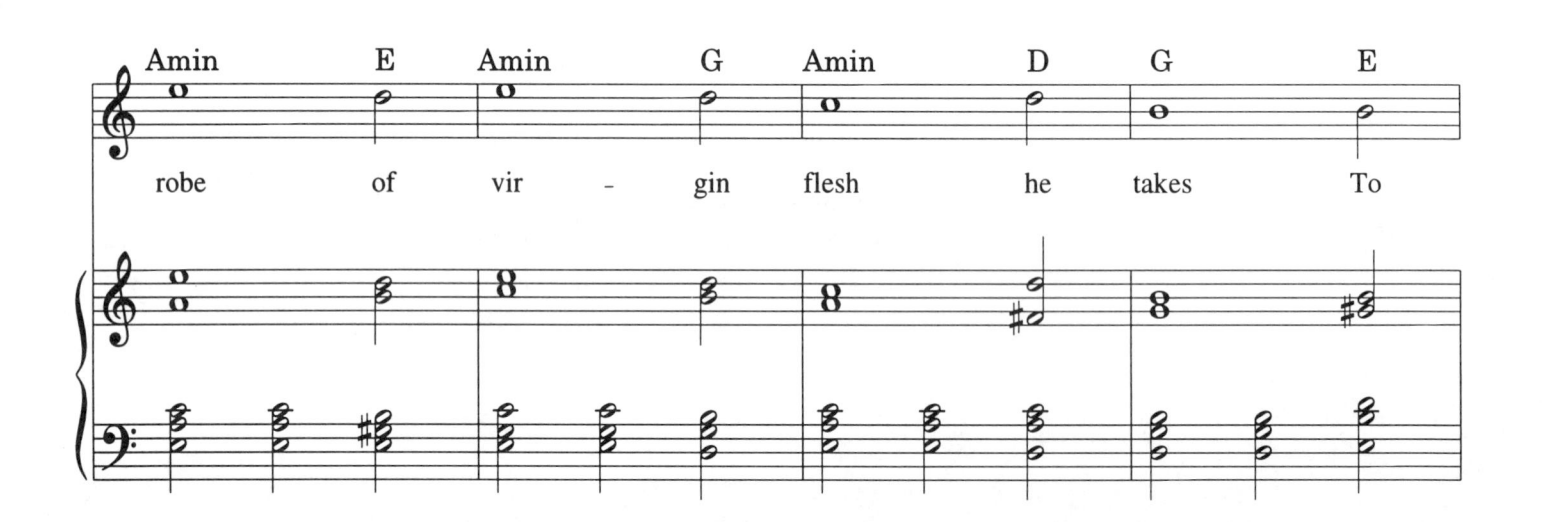

Behold, the great Cre-a-tor makes Himself a house of clay; A robe of virgin flesh he takes To

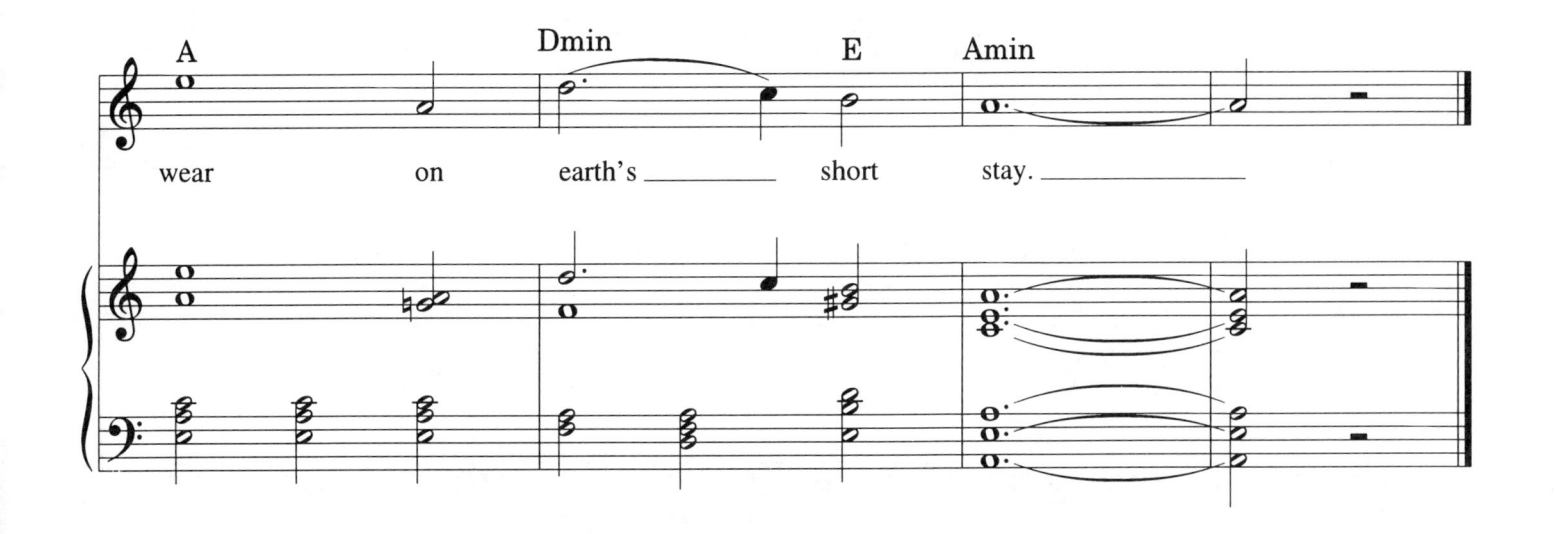

1) Behold, the great Creator makes
	Himself a house of clay;
   A robe of virgin flesh he takes
	To wear on earth's short stay.

2) Hark, hark! the wise eternal Word
	Like a weak infant cries;
   In form of servant is the Lord,
	And God in cradle lies.

3) This wonder struck the world amazed,
	It shook the starry frame;
   Squadrons of spirits stood and gazed,
	Then down in troops they came.

4) Glad shepherds ran to view this sight;
	A choir of angels sings,
   And eastern sages with delight
	Adore the King of Kings.

5) Join then, all hearts that are not stone,
	And all our voices prove,
   To celebrate this Holy One,
	The God of peace and love.

GREAT MILTON

George Richards
Unknown

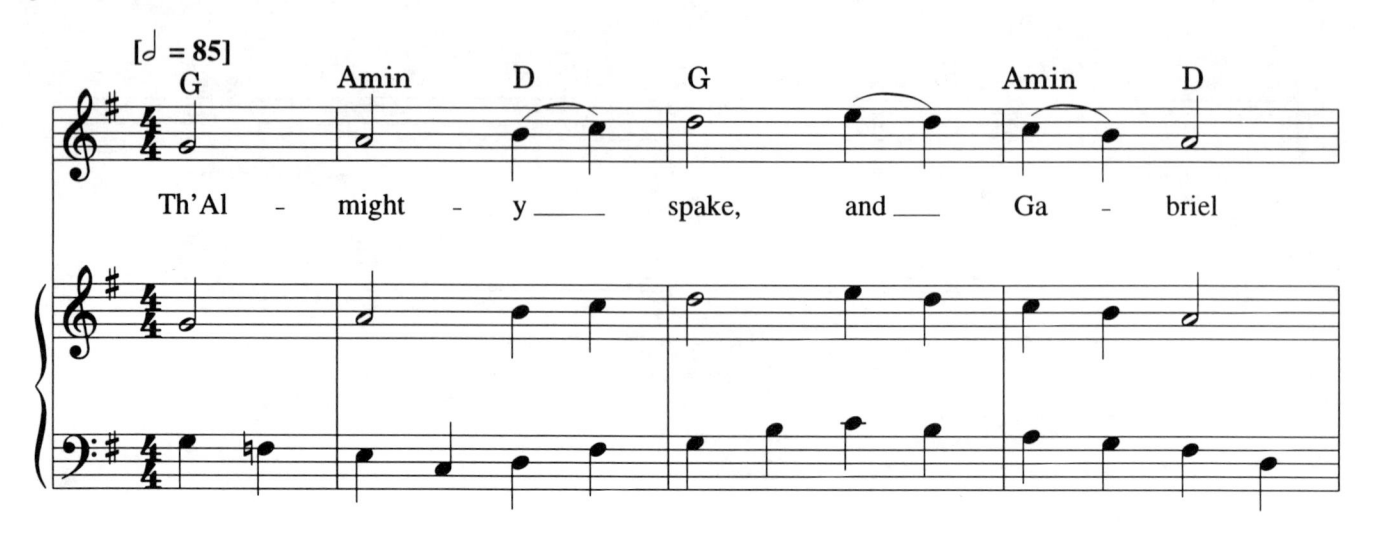

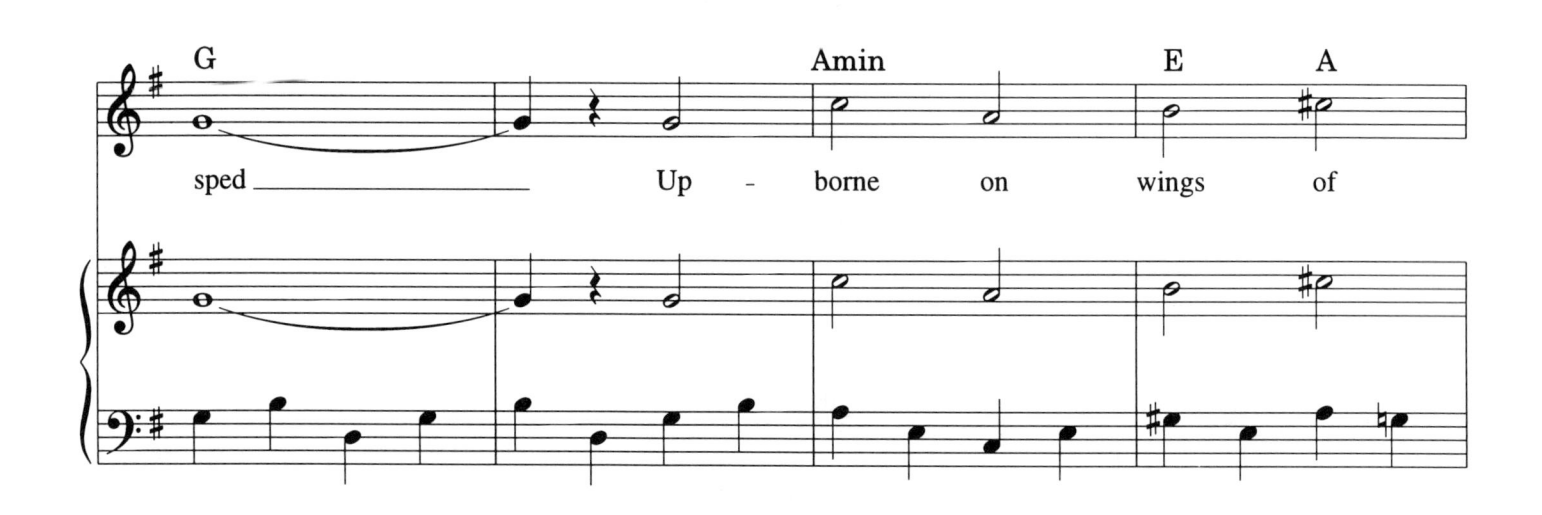

Th'Al - might - y ___ spake, and ___ Ga - briel sped ___ Up - borne on wings of light; ___ Je - ho - vah's ___ glo - ry round him spread, _____ And changed __ to ____ day __ the night. _____ Swift down to ____ earth th'arch - an - gel flew _____ From God's e - ter - nal __ throne; _____ His

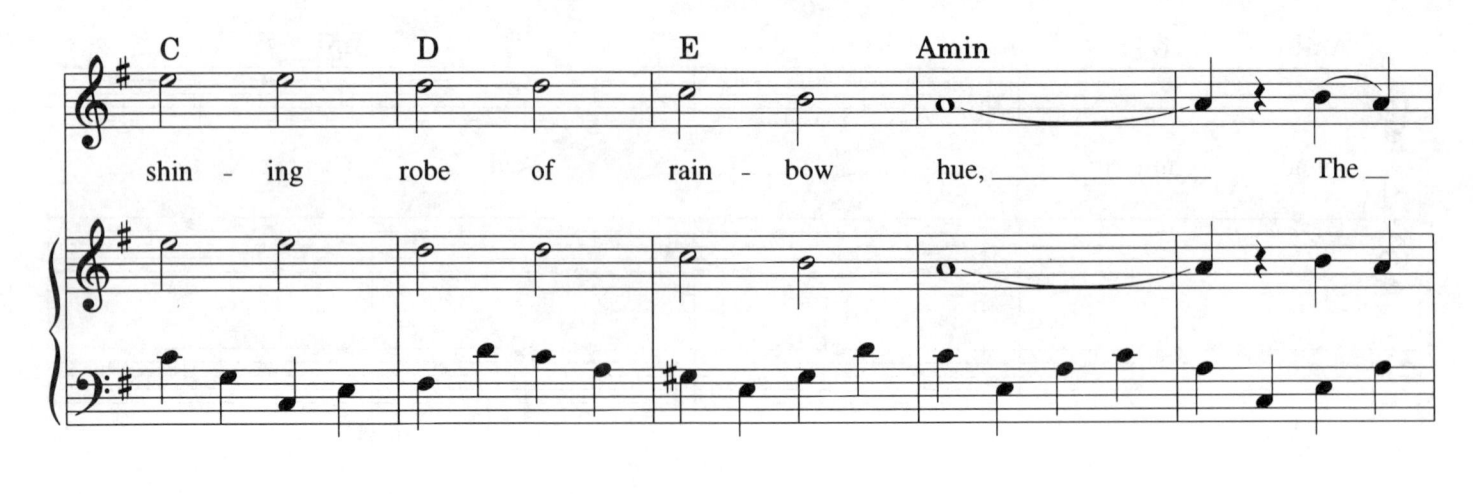

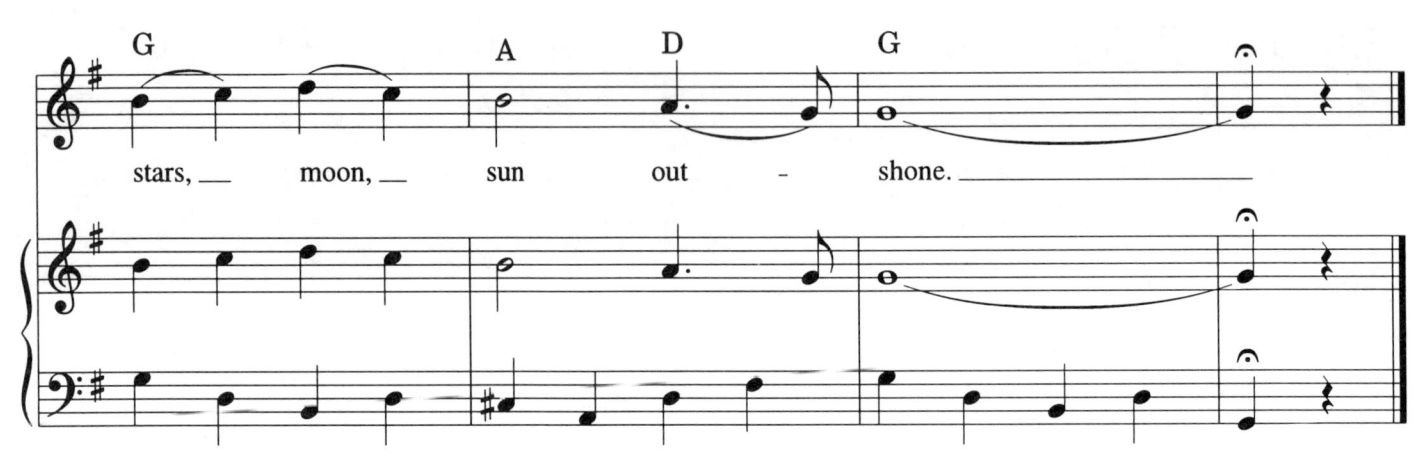

1) Th'Almighty spake, and Gabriel sped
    Upborne on wings of light;
   Jehovah's glory round him spread,
    And changed to day the night.

2) Swift down to earth th'archangel flew
    From God's eternal throne;
   His shining robe of rainbow hue,
    The stars, moon, sun outshone.

3) Ten thousand thousand left the sky
    To catch salvation's sound;
   One note of peace was heard on high,
    Glad tidings rolled around.

4) Shout, shout for joy; rejoice on earth;
    All hail this glorious morn;
   Rejoice, rejoice in Jesus' birth;
    Today are nations born.

5) From Zion's hills to worlds above,
    Reecho back the strain;
   And golden harps attuned to love,
    Thus sweep Ephratah's plain.

6) He comes, He comes, the Savior God;
    Goodwill, peace, joy for men;
   Glad tidings shout to all abroad;
    Amen, amen, amen.

"Christmas Post," by Thomas Nast. From *Harper's Weekly*, Jan. 4, 1879.

HARBOROUGH

Martin Madan
Charles Burney

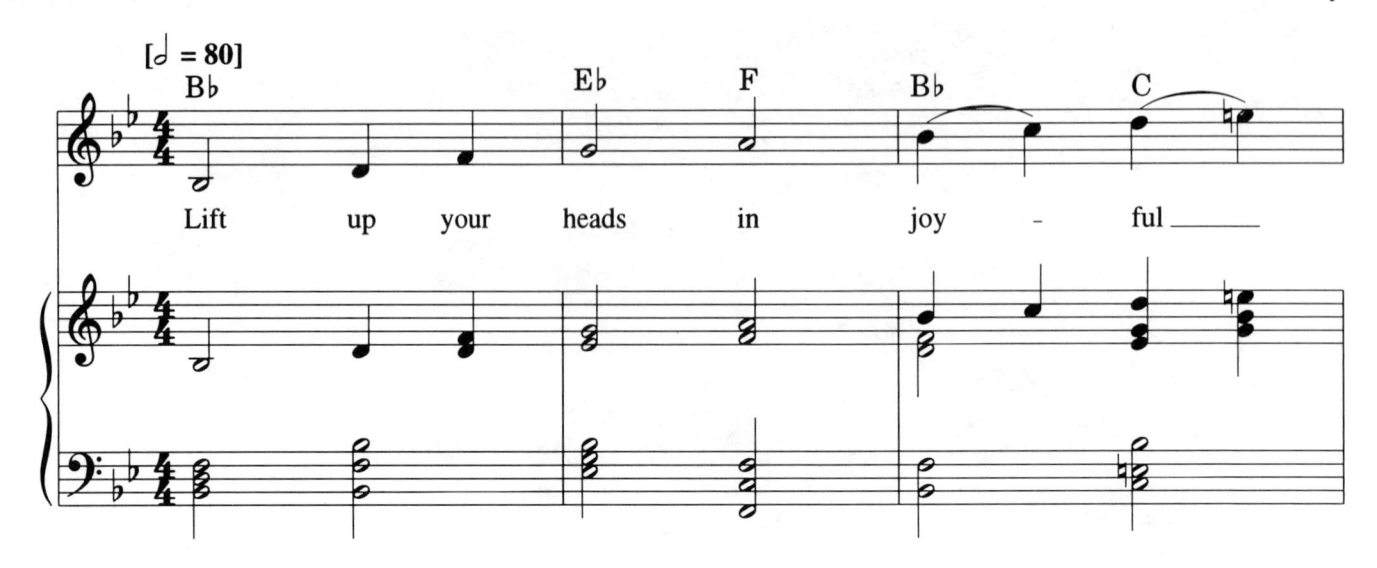

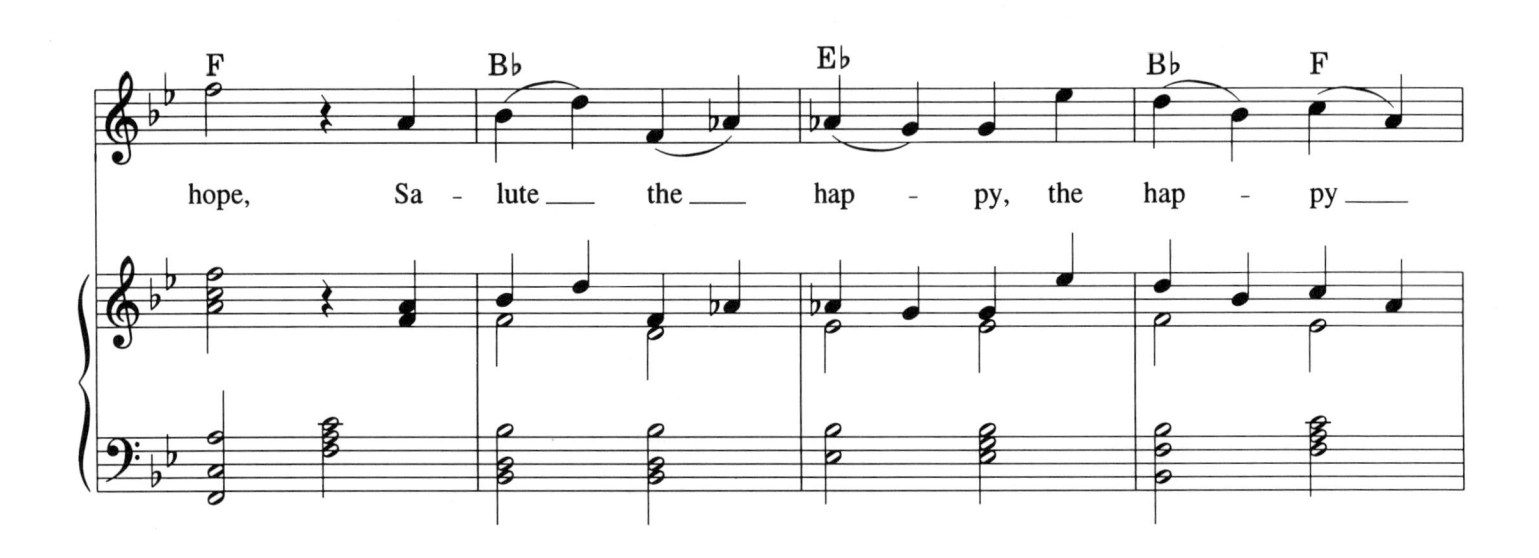

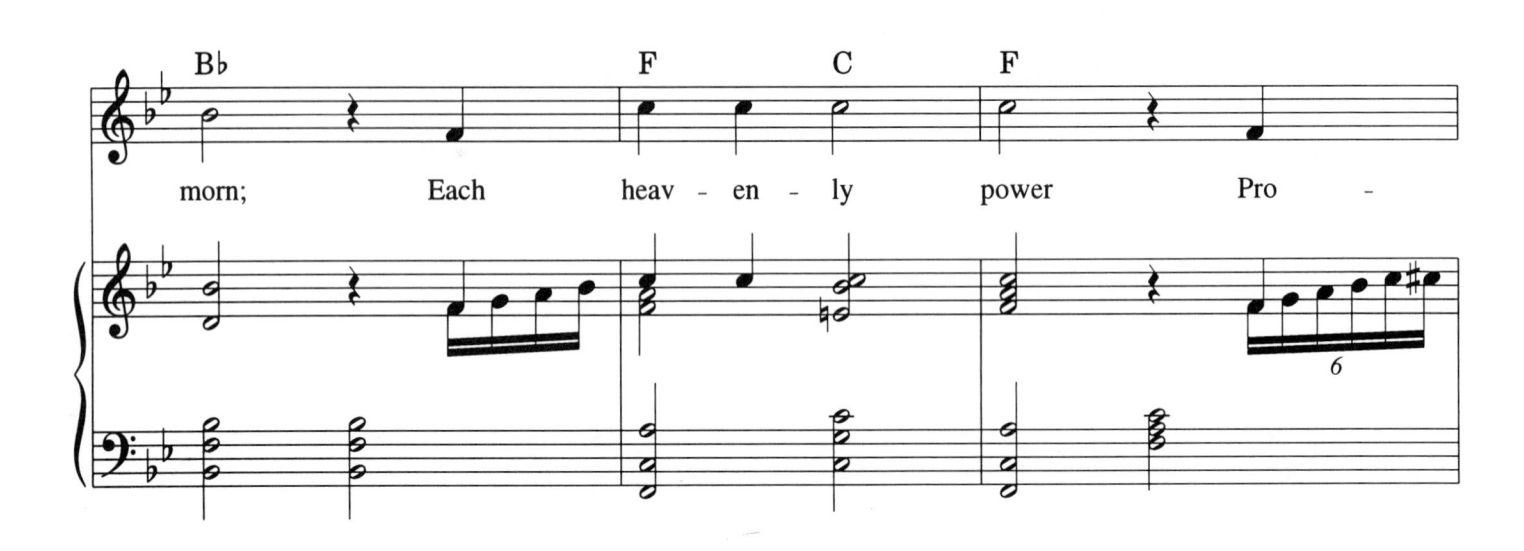

Lift up your heads in joyful hope, Salute the happy, the happy morn; Each heavenly power Pro-

B♭ D Gmin Cmin
claims the glad hour; Lo, Je - sus the
6
F B♭ E♭
rallentando
Sav - ior is born, Lo, Je - sus the
Cmin B♭ F B♭
Sav - ior is born!

1) Lift up your heads in joyful hope,
    Salute the happy morn;
        Each heavenly power
        Proclaims the glad hour;
    Lo, Jesus the Saviour is born!

2) All glory be to God on high,
    To Him all praise is due;
        The promise is sealed,
        The Saviour's revealed,
    And proves that the record is true.

3) Let joy around like rivers flow;
    Flow on, and still increase;
        Spread o'er the glad earth
        At Jesus' birth,
    For heaven and earth are at peace.

4) Now the good will of heaven is shown
    Toward Adam's helpless race;
        Messiah is come
        To ransom his own,
    To save them by infinite grace.

5) Then let us join the heavens above,
    Where hymning seraphs sing;
        Join all the glad powers,
        For their Lord is ours,
    Our Prophet, our Priest, and our King.

"Under the Mistletoe." From an engraving dated 1868.

HARVARD

Charles H. Gabriel
George J. Webb

[♩ = 120]

Come, let us sing a cheer-ful song, Let each one join his voice, Let ev'-ry heart to-day be glad, And ev'-ry soul re-joice; For 'tis the day that Christ was born, And brought good will to

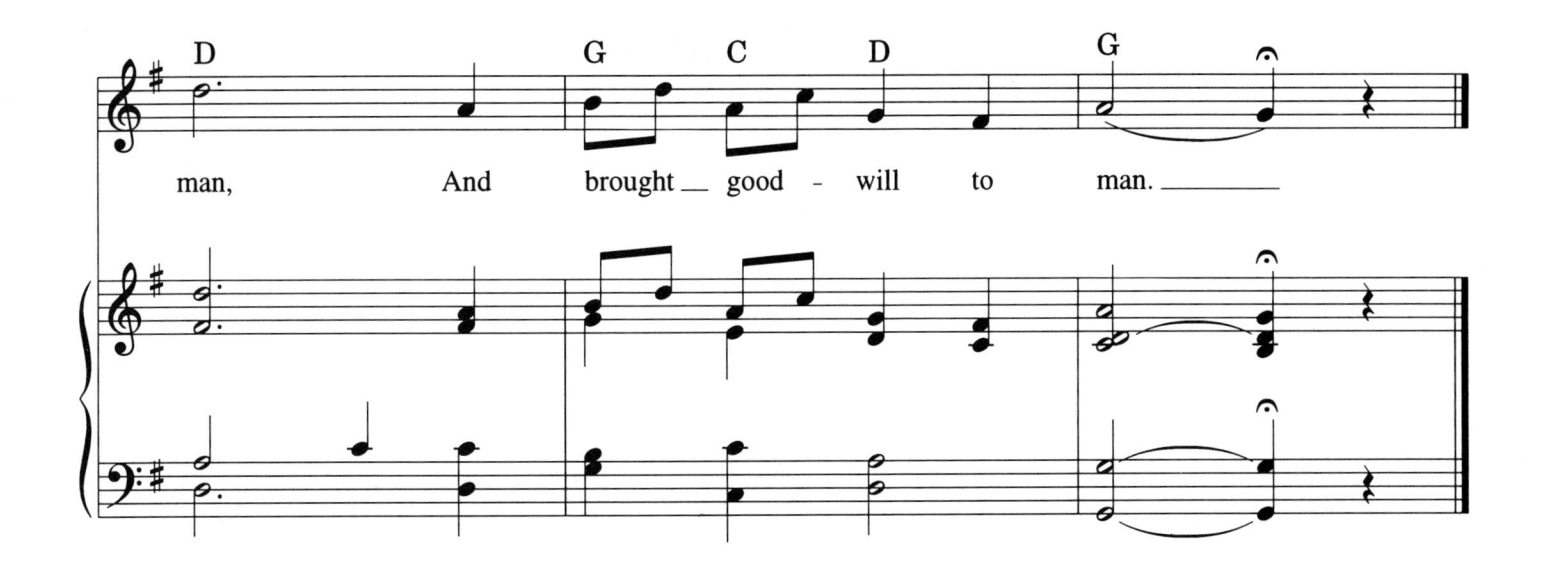

1) Come, let us sing a cheerful song,
   Let each one join his voice,
   Let ev'ry heart today be glad,
   And ev'ry soul rejoice;
   For 'tis the day that Christ was born,
   And brought good will to man.

2) The angels heard the joyful strains,
   Far out of Bethlehem;
   The angels sang the welcome news
   Upon that blessed morn,
   In songs rejoicingly they sang,
   "The Savior, Christ, is born."

3) Today in Bethlehem's stall is born
   A Savior, Christ the Lord;
   "Fear not, to thee I bring great joy:"
   From heaven, with sweet accord;
   To God the glory; peace on earth;
   Goodwill to all of man.

4) Reechoed through the lofty sky,
   'Twas God's eternal plan.
   He came to set the sinner free,
   Salvation to obtain.
   For all the souls that will but come
   And wash away their stain.

JAMAICA

William Billings   William Billings

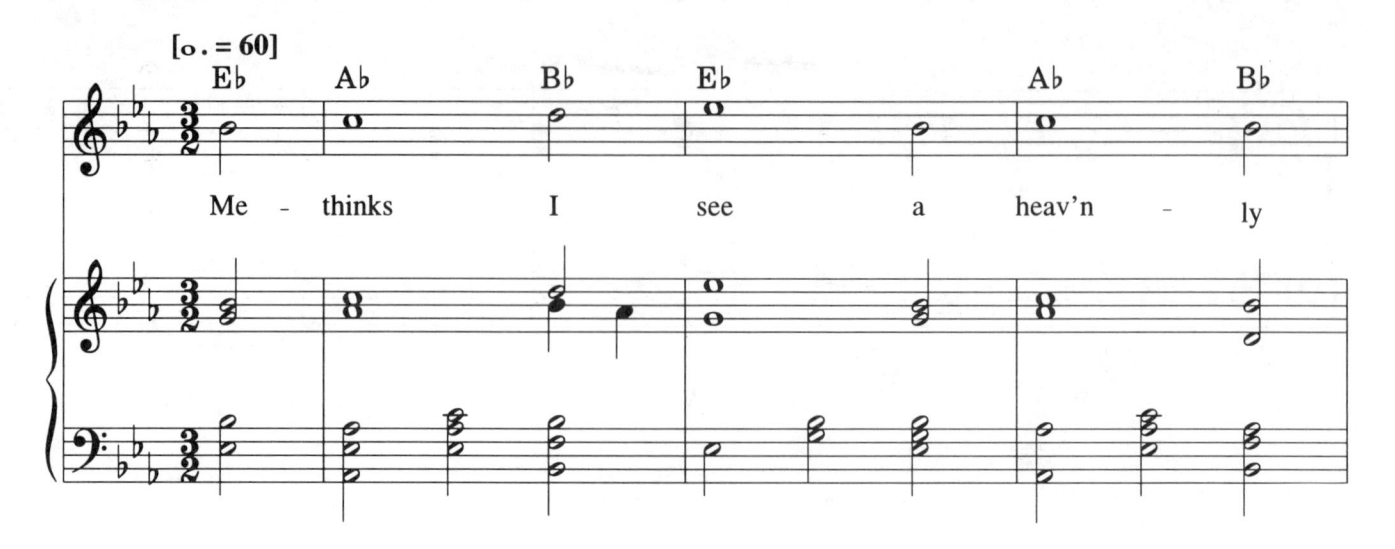

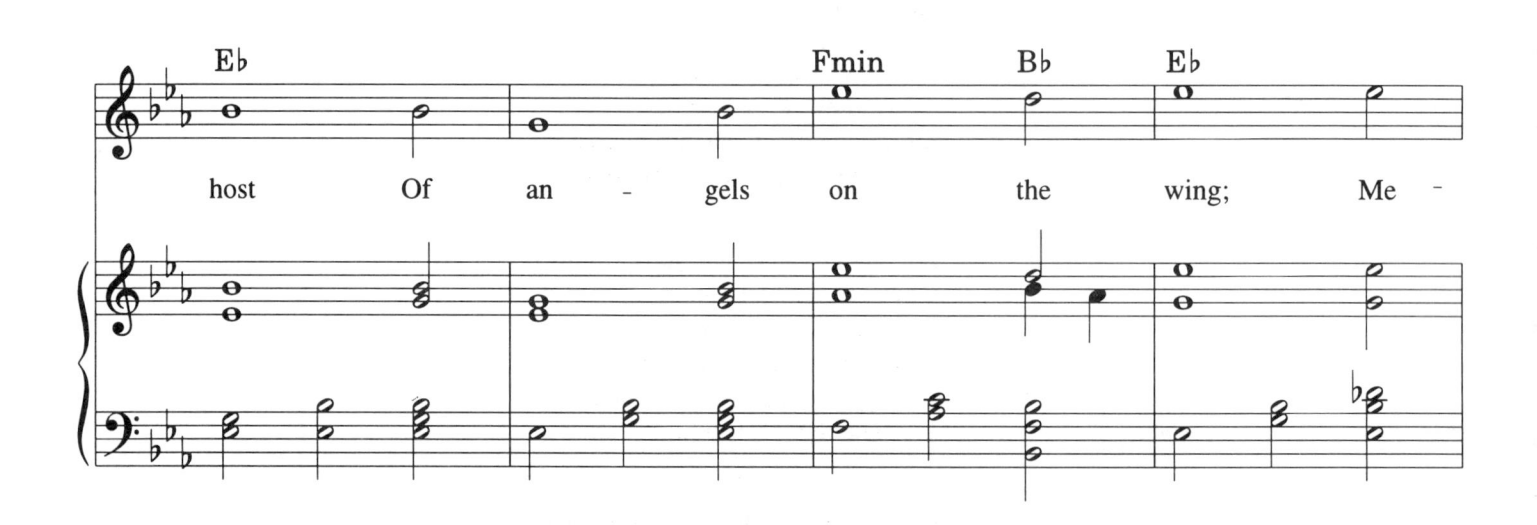

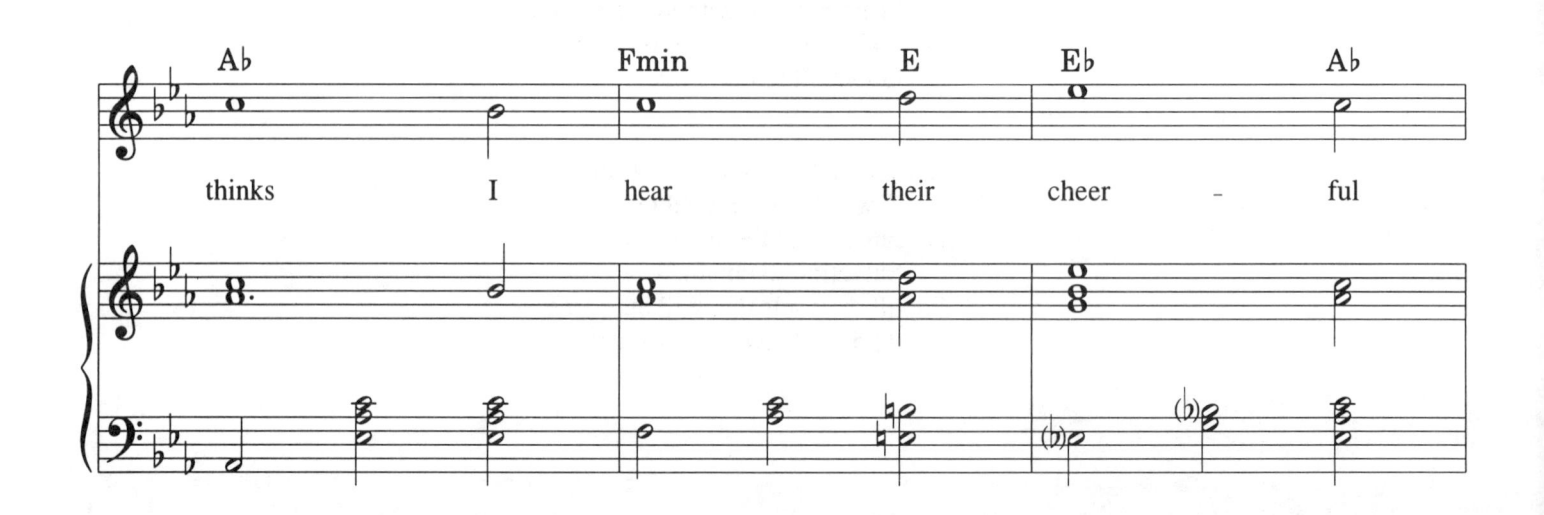

Me-thinks I see a heav'n-ly host Of an-gels on the wing; Me-thinks I hear their cheer-ful

notes, So mer - ri - ly they sing.

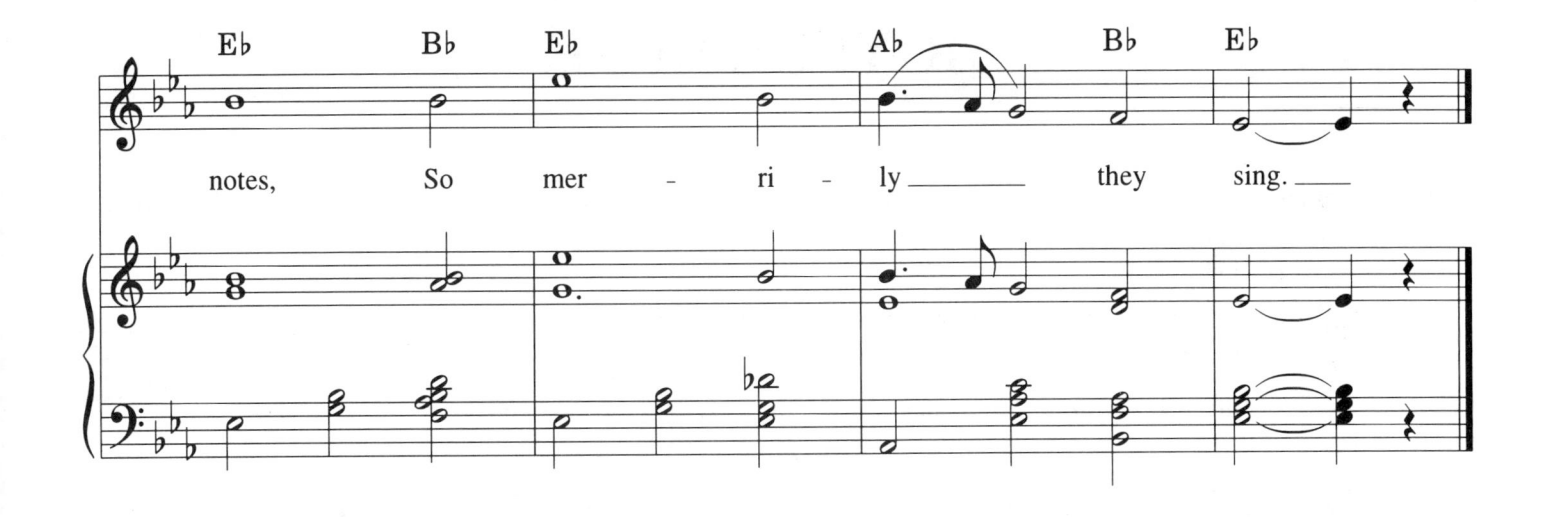

1) Methinks I see a heav'nly host
    Of angels on the wing;
   Methinks I hear their cheerful notes,
    So merrily they sing.

2) Let all your fears be banished hence,
    Glad tidings we proclaim;
   For there's a Savior born today,
    And Jesus is his name.

JOYFUL HOPE

Martin Madan Martin Madan

Lift up your heads in joy-ful hope, Sa-lute the hap-py__ morn; Sa-lute the hap-py__ morn; Each heav'n-ly power Pro-claims the glad hour; Lo, Je-sus the

1) Lift up your heads in joyful hope,
　　Salute the happy morn;
　　　Each heav'nly power
　　　Proclaims the glad hour;
　Lo, Jesus the Saviour is born!

2) All glory be to God on high,
　　To Him all praise is due;
　　　The promise is sealed,
　　　The Saviour's revealed,
　And proves that the record is true.

3) Let joy around like rivers flow;
　　Flow on, and still increase;
　　　Spread o'er the glad earth
　　　At Jesus' birth,
　For heaven and earth are at peace.

4) Now the good will of heaven is shown
　　Toward Adam's helpless race;
　　　Messiah is come
　　　To ransom his own,
　To save them by infinite grace.

5) Then let us join the heavens above,
　　Where hymning seraphs sing;
　　　Join all the glad powers,
　　　For their Lord is ours,
　Our Prophet, our Priest, and our King.

JOYFUL NEWS

Isaac Watts　　　　　　　　　　　　　　　　　　　　　　　　　　　William Tuckey

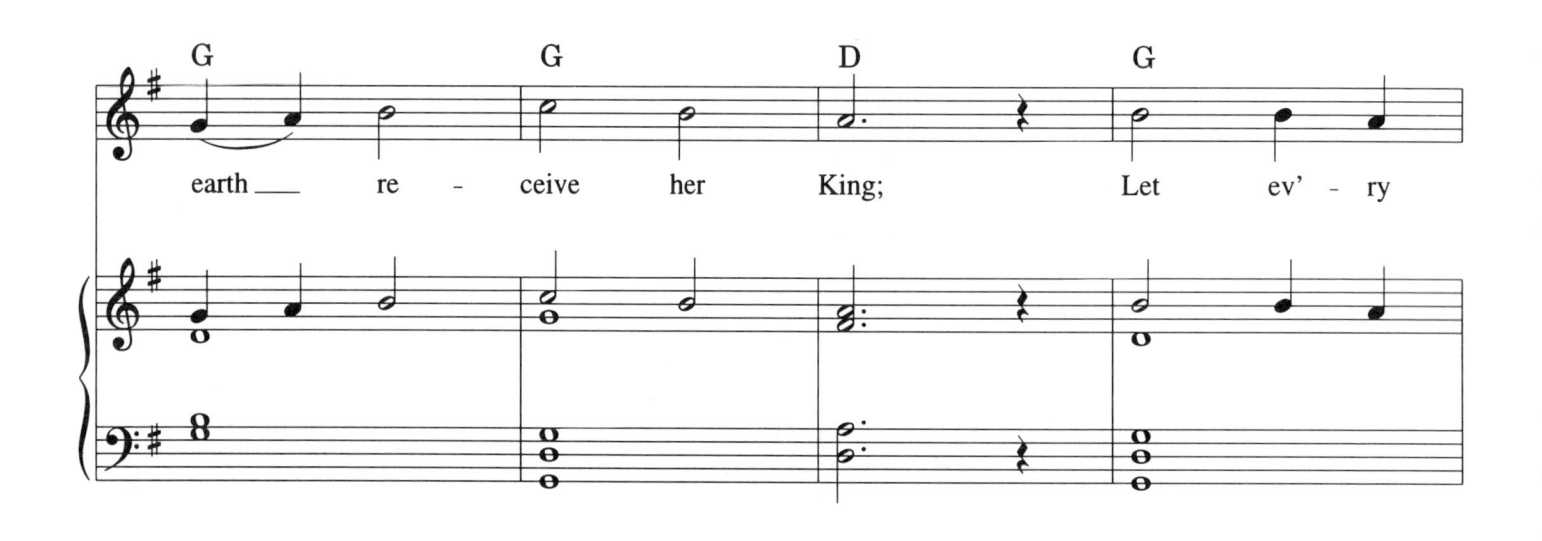

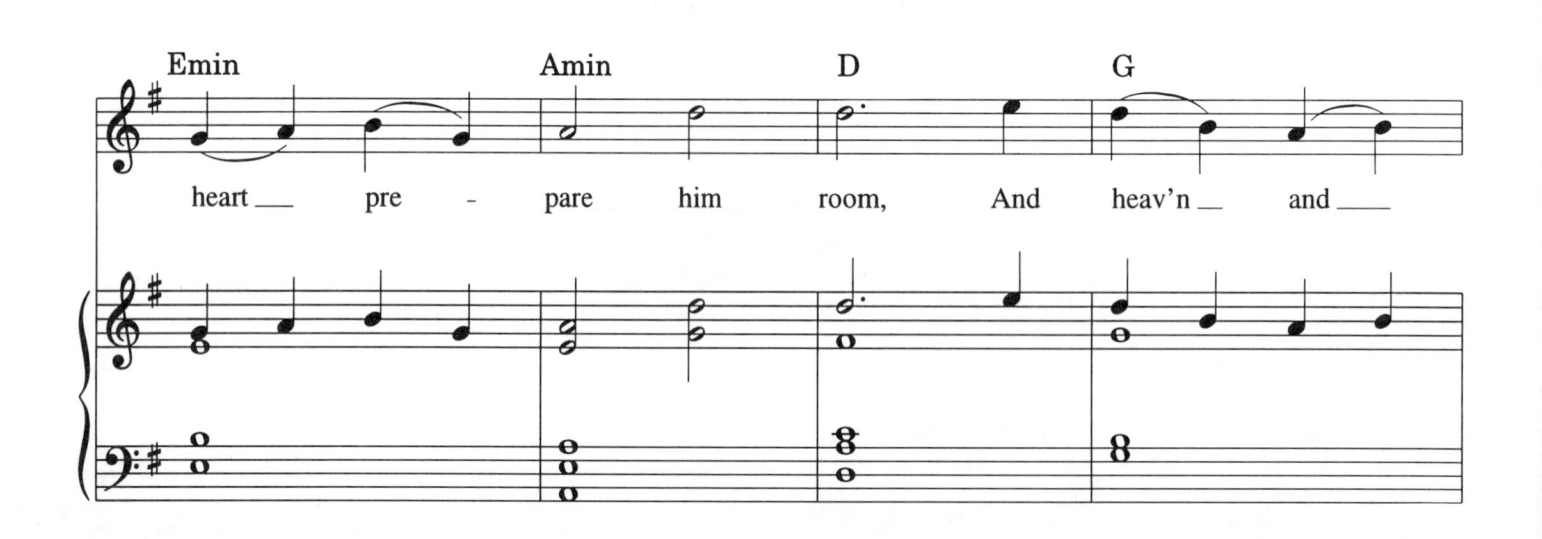

[♩ = 100]

Joy to the world;— the— Lord is come; Let earth— re-ceive her King; Let ev'-ry heart— pre-pare him room, And heav'n— and—

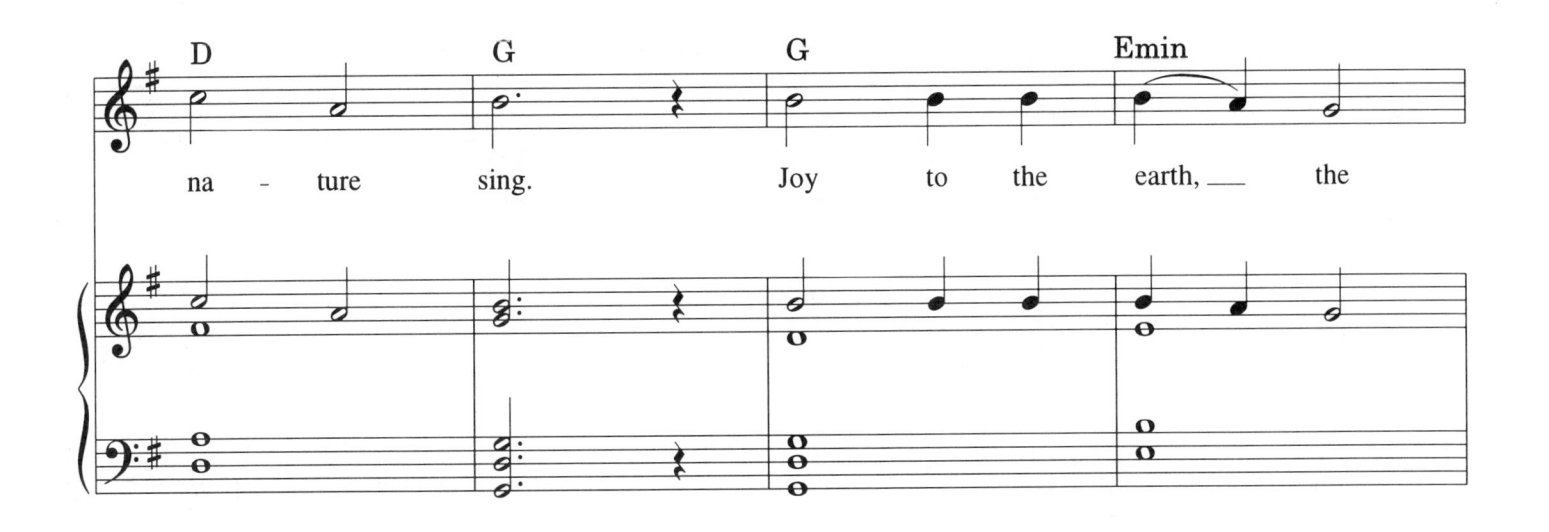

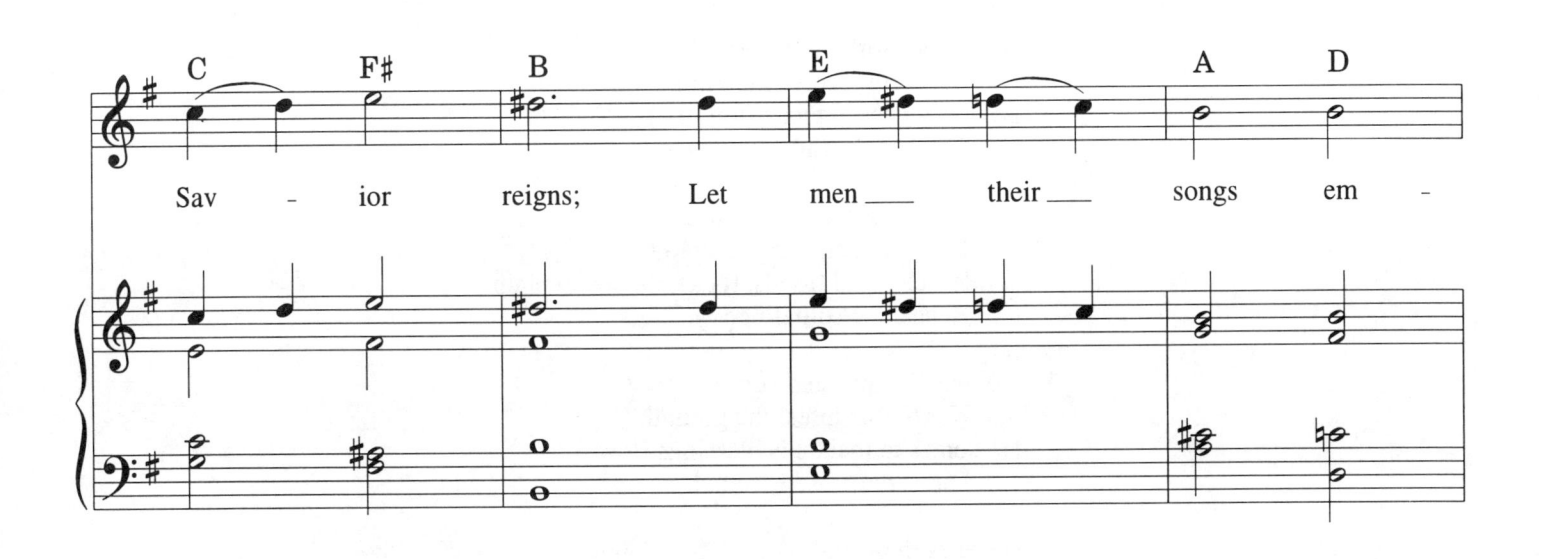

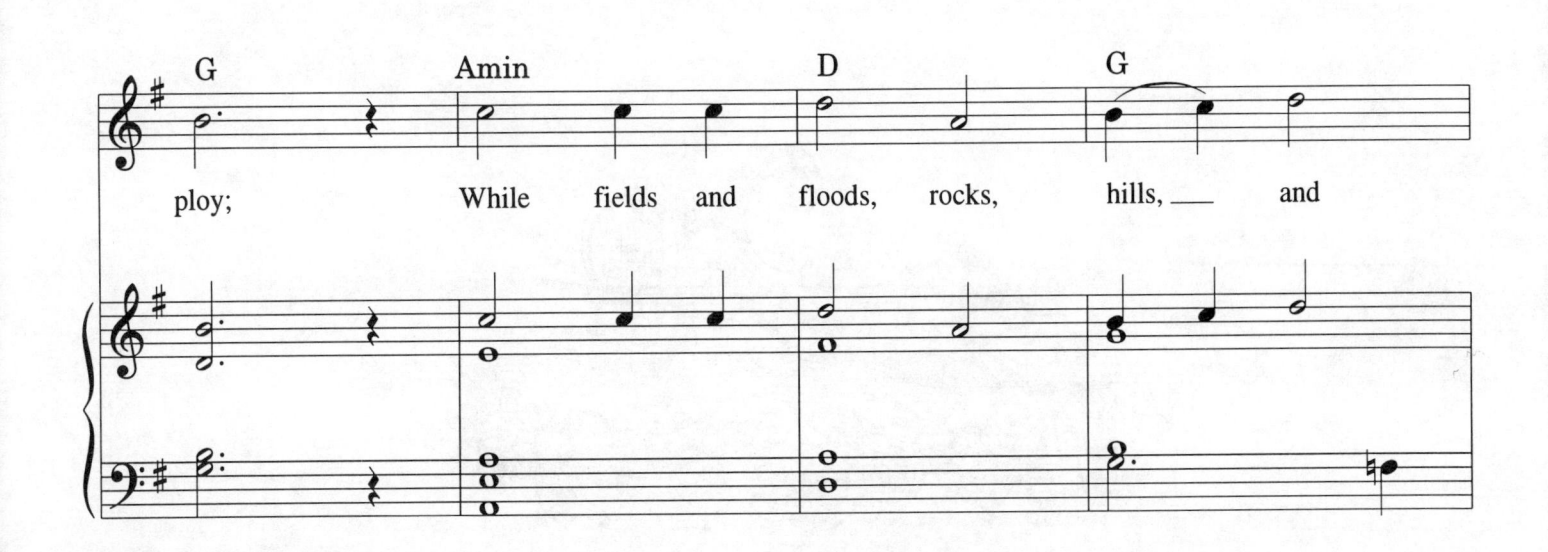

nature sing. Joy to the earth, the Savior reigns; Let men their songs employ; While fields and floods, rocks, hills, and

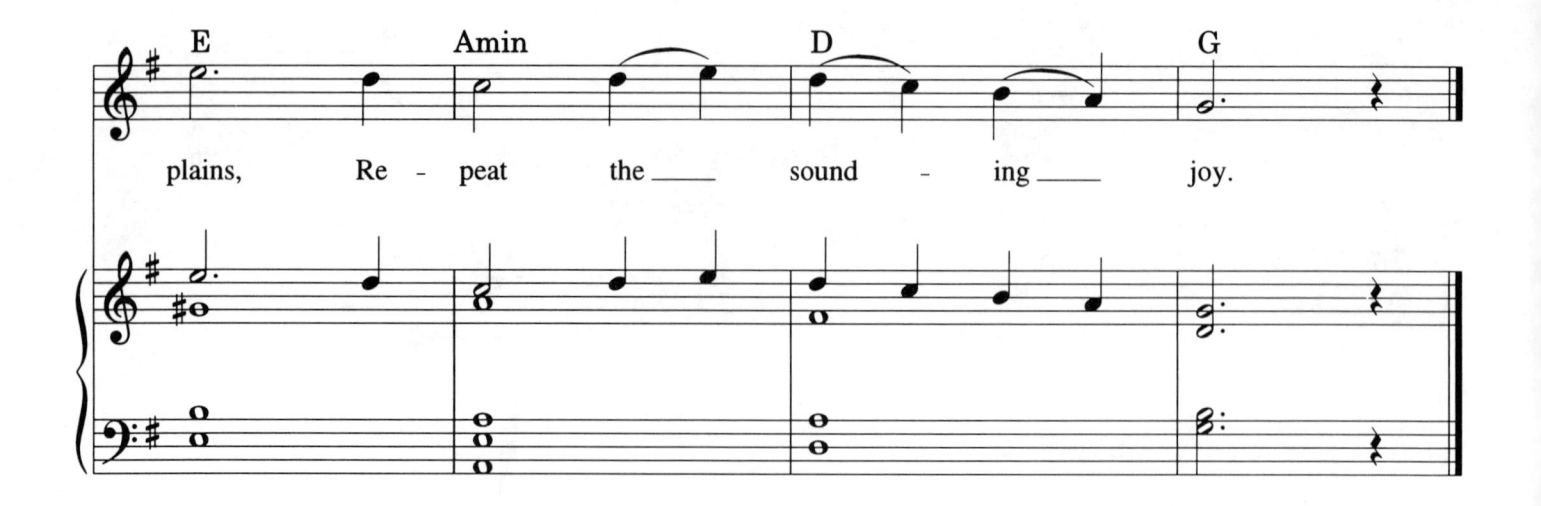

1) Joy to the world; the Lord is come;
   Let earth receive her King;
   Let ev'ry heart prepare him room,
   And heav'n and nature sing.

2) Joy to the earth, the Saviour reigns;
   Let men their songs employ;
   While fields and floods, rocks, hills, and plains,
   Repeat the sounding joy.

3) No more let sins and sorrows grow,
   Nor thorns infest the ground;
   He comes to make his blessings flow
   Far as the curse is found.

4) He rules the world with truth and grace,
   And makes the nations prove
   The glories of his righteousness,
   And wonders of his love.

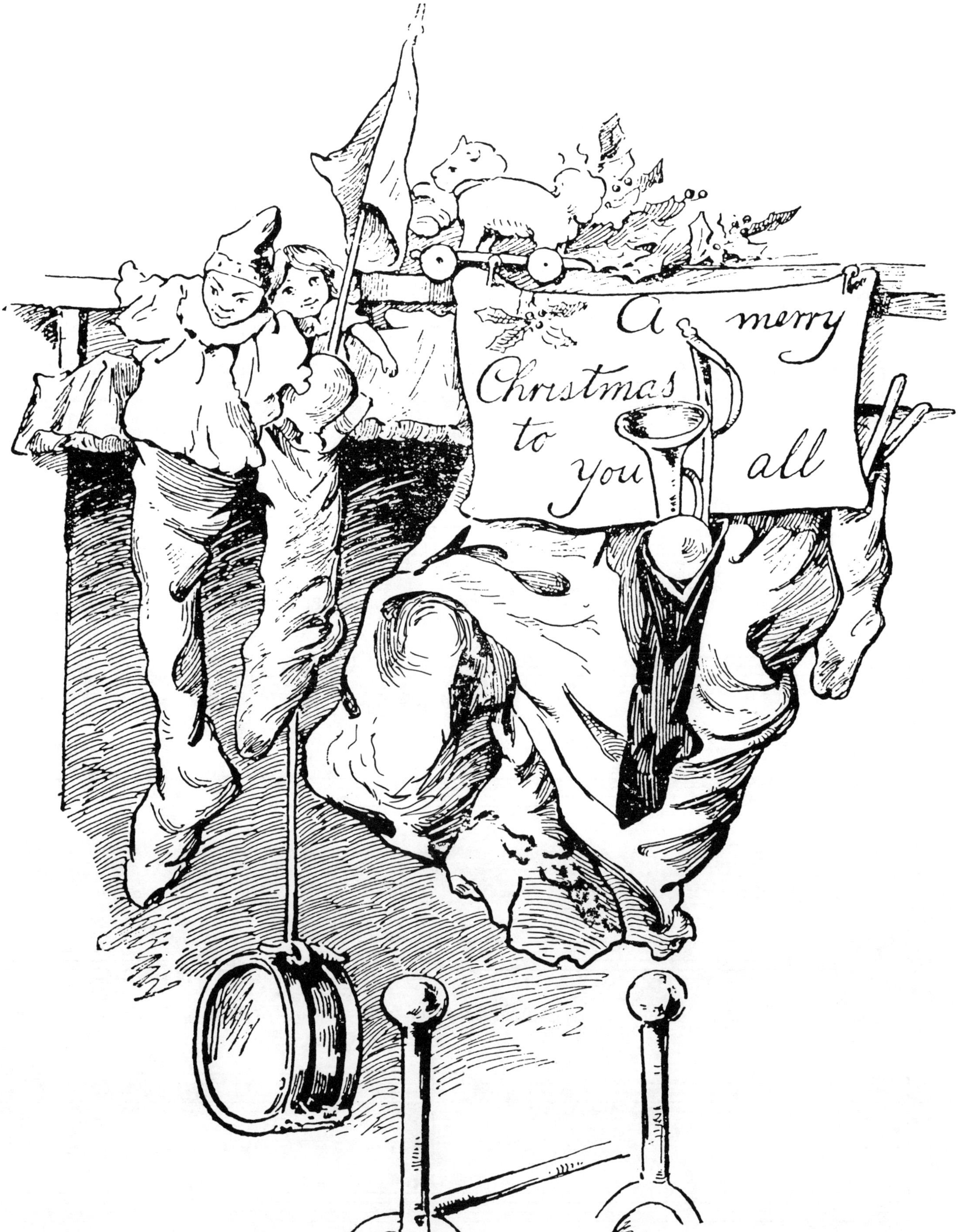
A merry
Christmas
to
you
all

JUBAL

Unknown   George J. Webb

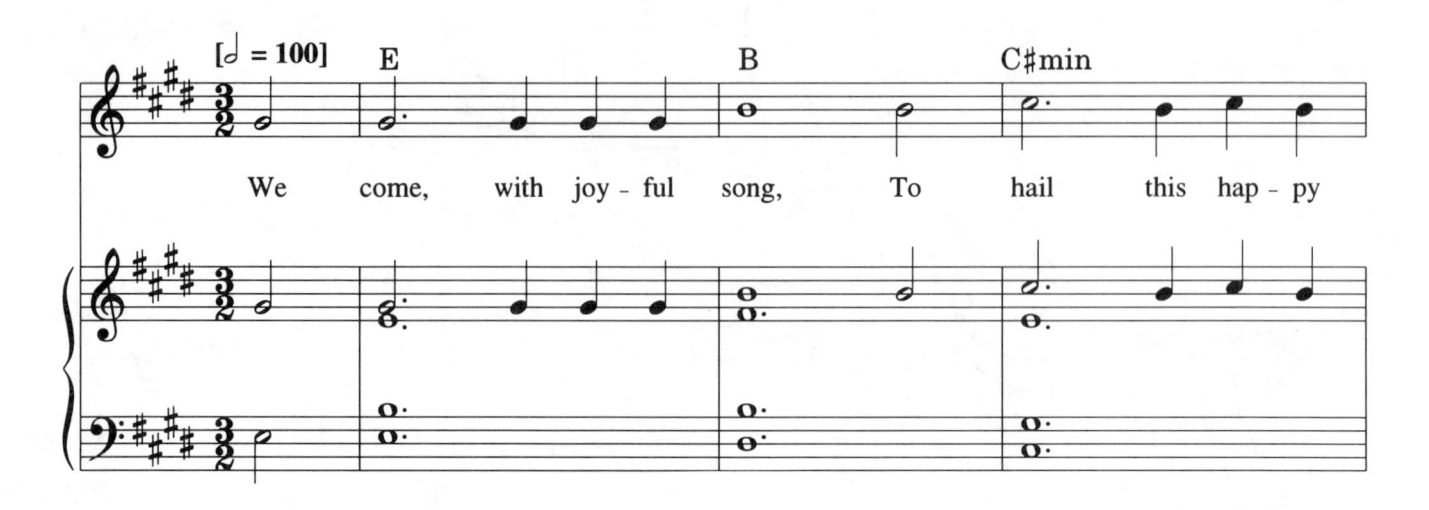

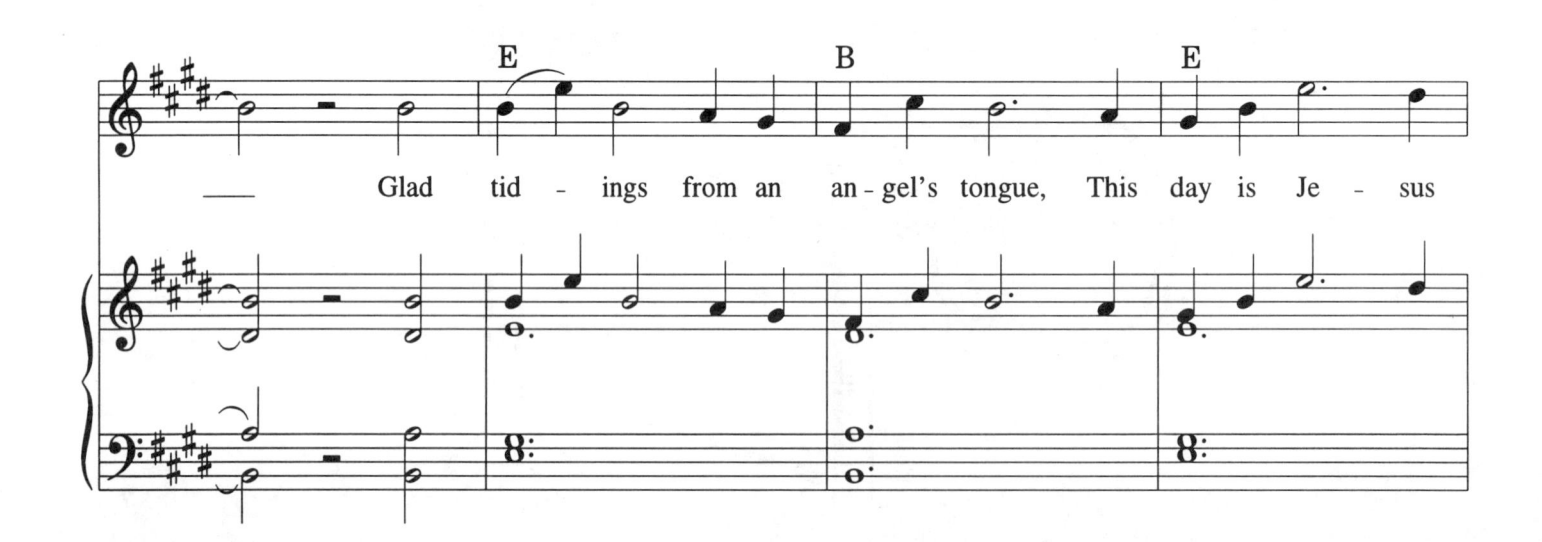

We come, with joy-ful song, To hail this hap-py morn; To hail this hap-py, hap-py morn; Glad tid-ings from an an-gel's tongue, This day is Je-sus

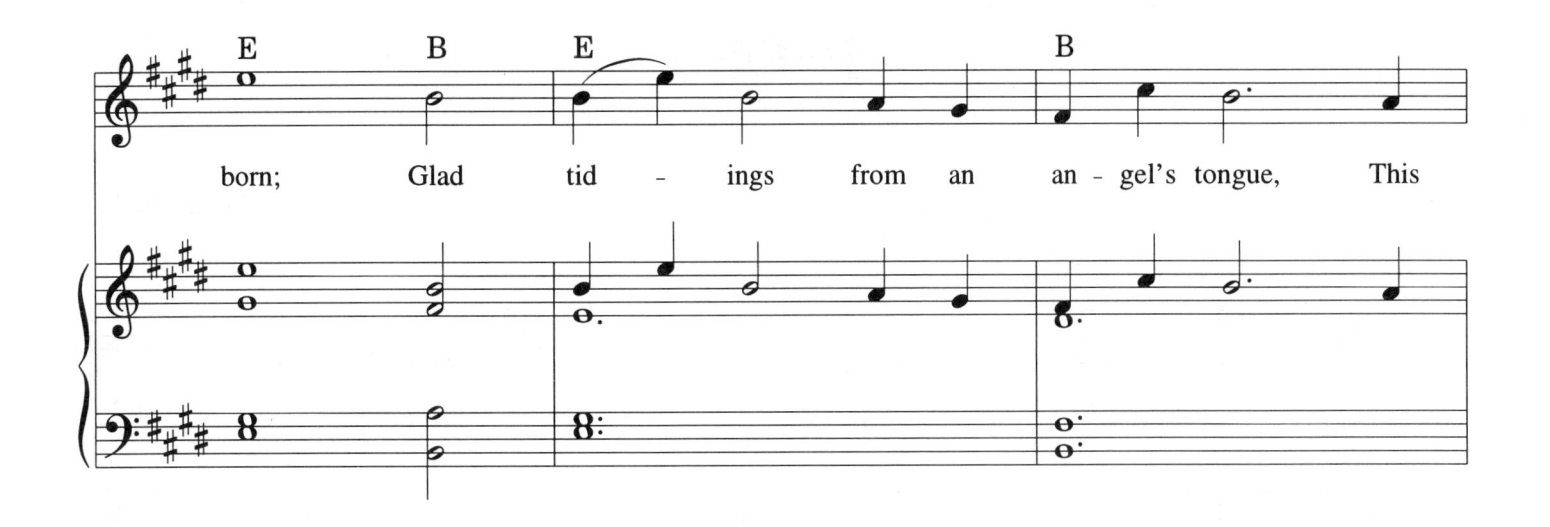

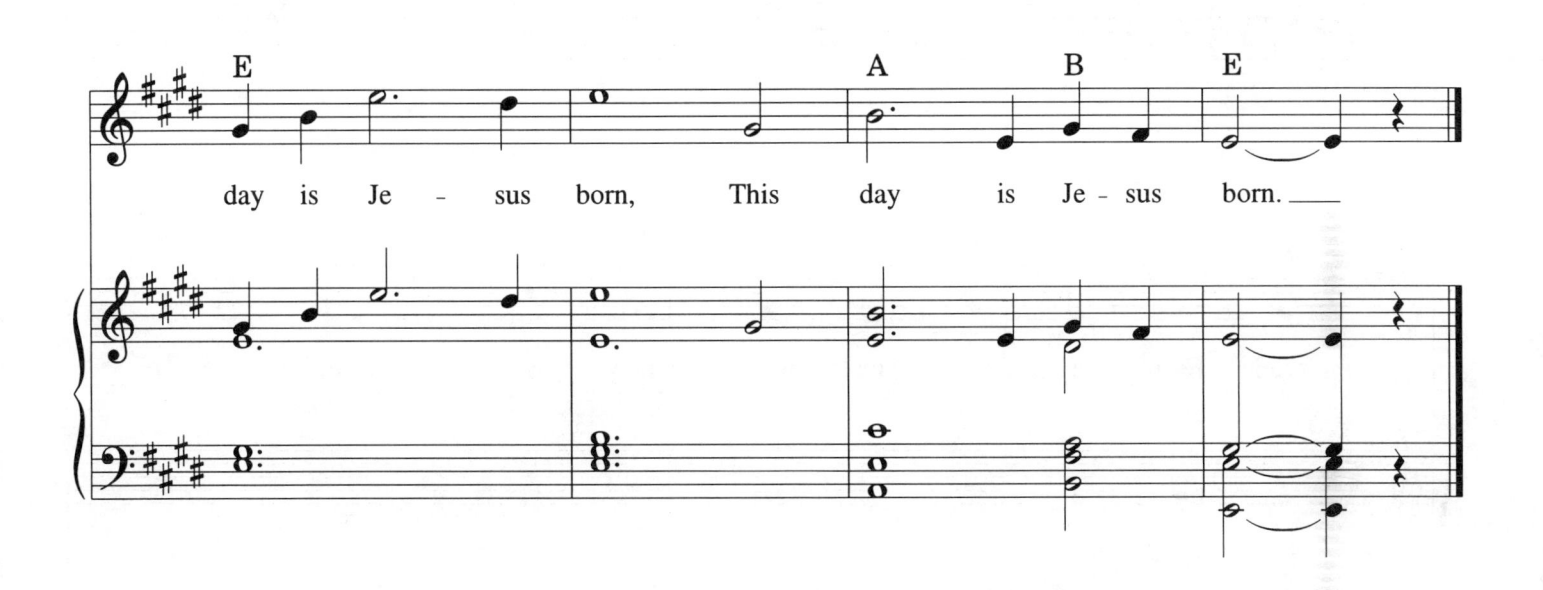

1) We come, with joyful song,
   To hail this happy morn;
   Glad tidings from an angel's tongue,
   This day is Jesus born.

2) Glory to God on high!
   All hail the happy morn;
   We join the anthems of the sky,
   And sing, the Saviour's born!

3) What transports doth his name
   To sinful men afford!
   His glorious titles we proclaim:
   A Saviour, Christ, the Lord.

JUDEA

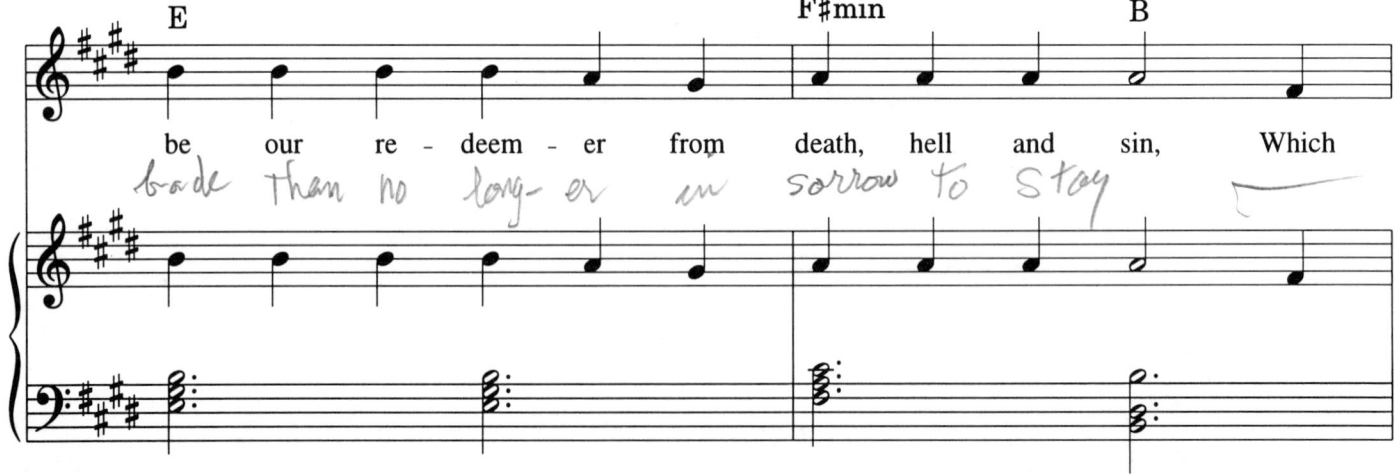

Traditional
William Billings

[♩. = 60]

A vir-gin un-spot-ted ye proph-et fore-told, Should bring forth a Sav-ior which now we be-hold; To be our re-deem-er from death, hell and sin, Which

Adam's trans-gres-sion in-volv-ed us in. Then_

Because that our saviour was born on this day (handwritten)

2nd time Nancy + D (handwritten)

Chorus
A little faster

let us be__ mer-ry, put sor-row a-way, Our Sav-ior Christ Je-sus was born on this day.___

1) A virgin unspotted ye prophet foretold,
    Should bring forth a Savior which now we behold;
   To be our redeemer from death, hell and sin,
    Which Adam's transgression involved us in.

Chorus: Then let us be merry, put sorrow away,
    Our Savior Christ Jesus was born on this day.

2) To Bethlehem, city of David, they came,
    Both Joseph and Mary, to answer by name
   The census of taxes which all had to pay,
    For Caesar commanded it done on that day.

3) But when they had entered the city so fair,
    A number of people so mighty was there
   That Joseph and Mary, whose substance was small,
    Could find in the inn there no lodging at all.

4) Then were they constrained in a stable to lie,
    Where horses and oxen they used for to tie;
   Their lodging so simple they took it no scorn,
    But ere the next morning our Savior was born.

5) The King of all kings to this world being brought,
    Small store of fine linen to wrap him was sought;
   But when she had swaddled her young son for sleep,
    'Twas naught but a manger she laid Him to keep.

6) Then God sent an angel from heaven so high,
    To certain poor shepherds in fields where they lie;
   And bade them no longer in sorrow to stay,
    Because that our Savior was born on this day.

7) Then presently after the shepherds did spy
    Vast numbers of angels to stand in the sky;
   They joyfully talked and sweetly did sing,
    To God be all glory, our heavenly King.

8) To teach us humility all this was done,
    And learn we from thence haughty pride for to shun;
   A manger his cradle who came from above,
    The great God of mercy, of peace, and of love.

LAMB OF GOD

Unknown   Aaron Williams

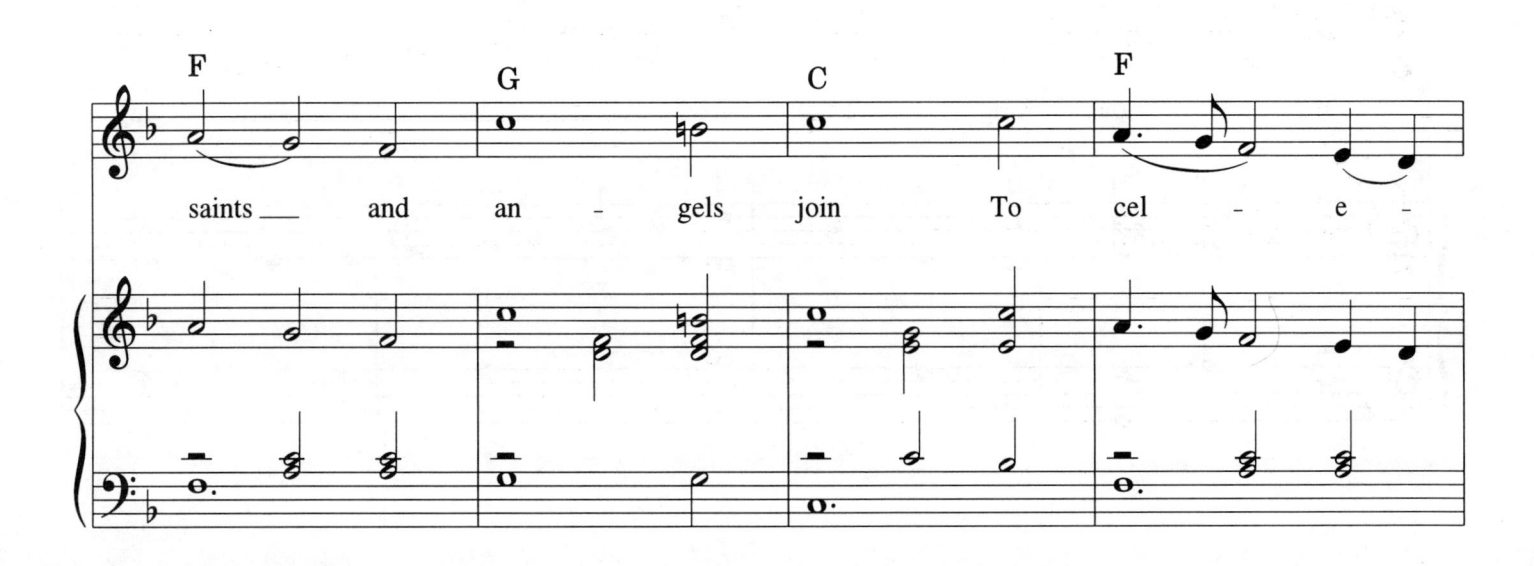

[♩ = 120]

Hail, hail, all glo-rious Lamb of God; Let saints and an - gels join To cel - e - brate thy praise a - broad, Whose name is

B C F F C F C
all ___ di - vine. Hail ev - er blessed ___ and
F G C F B♭ C Edim
glo - rious King, Thou great ___ in -
F D G C G C F
car - nate God; Who didst ___ to us ___ sal -

Gmin C F C F B♭
va - tion bring Through thine own
F C F
pre - cious blood.
Chorus
F
Hal - le - lu - jah,
F C F
hal - le - lu - jah
F G C A♭ A♭min C F
hal - le - lu - jah, hal - le - lu - jah, hal - le - lu - jah,
Gmin C F D Gmin C F
hal - le - lu - jah, hal - le - lu - jah, hal - le - lu - jah!

1) Hail, hail, all glorious Lamb of God;
    Let saints and angels join
  To celebrate thy praise abroad,
    Whose name is all divine.

  Hail ever blessed and glorious King,
    Thou great incarnate God;
  Who didst to us salvation bring
    Through thine own precious blood.

  Hallelujah!

2) Jesus, the lamb, who dwells on high,
    Fulfill'd th'eternal plan,
  As was foretold by prophecy,
    To save that rebel man.

  Behold! the long-expected sight
    Has now appear'd on earth;
  Behold! the darkness turn'd to light,
    At dear Emmanuel's birth!

  Hallelujah!

3) Thus did the holy angels sing,
    As shepherds they drew near;
  "Glad-tidings of great joy we bring,
    Therefore you need not fear!"

  "For unto you this day is born
    A Saviour, Christ the Lord!"
  Man to restore, unto his throne,
    And to fulfil his word.

  Hallelujah!

4) "All glory be to God on High!"
    The song let mortals aid;
  To Christ, that dwells above the sky,
    Be endless blessings paid.

  Thus we'd commemorate the day
    Of our dear Saviour's birth:
  O praise the Lord, give thanks and pray,
    For "peace to men on earth."

  Hallelujah!

Illustration by Randolph Caldecott.
From *Old Christmas, from the Sketch Book of Washington Irving*, 1875.

LANCASTER

Traditional   Traditional

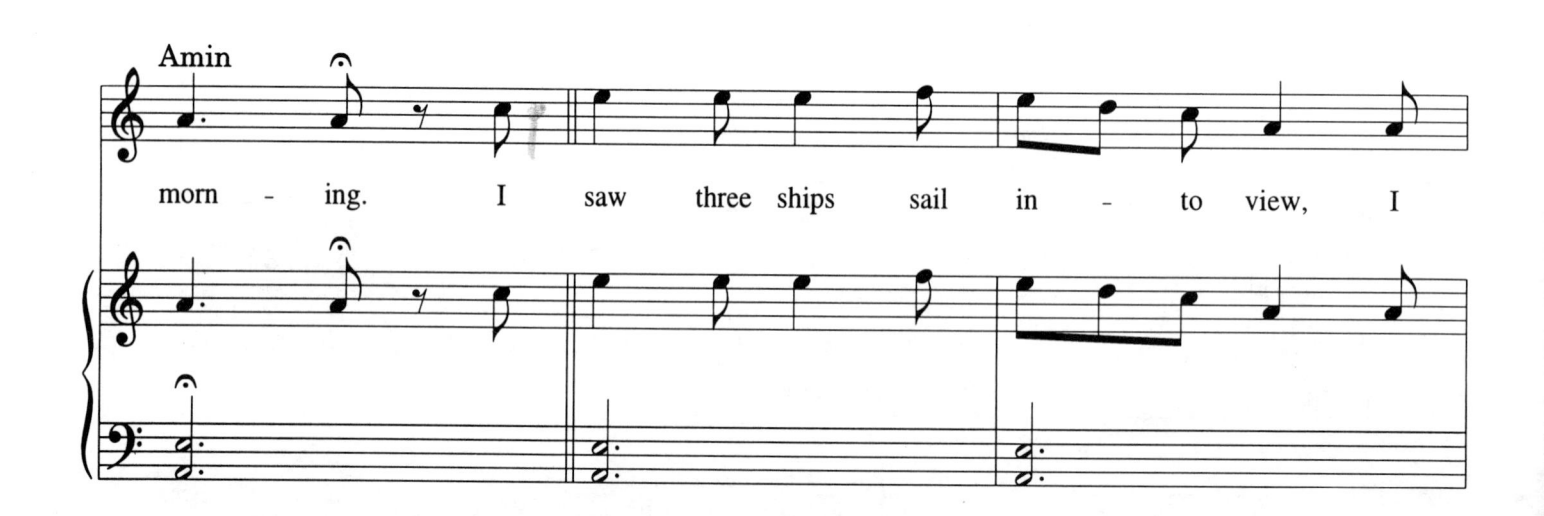

[♩. = 100]

As I sat on a sunny bank, As I sat on a sunny bank, As I sat on a sunny bank, On Christmas day in the morning. I saw three ships sail into view, I

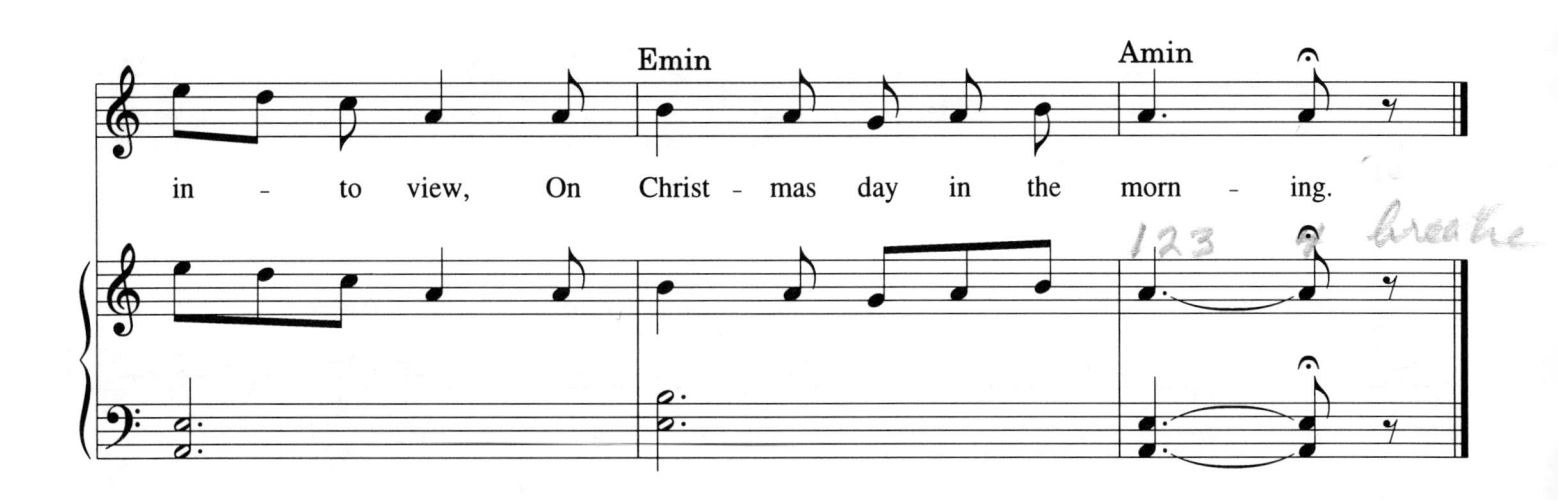

1. As I sat on a sunny bank,
On Christmas Day in the morning.

Ref. I saw three ships sail into view
On Christmas Day in the morning.

2. And who do you think I saw in those ships
'Twas Joseph and his fair lady.

Ref.

Then he did whistle and she did sing
On Christmas Day in the morning.

Ref.

3. And all the bells on earth did ring
On Christmas Day in the morning.

Ref.

For the joy of the new born King
On Christms Day in the morning.

LONDON

Isaac Watts
Dr. Samuel Arnold

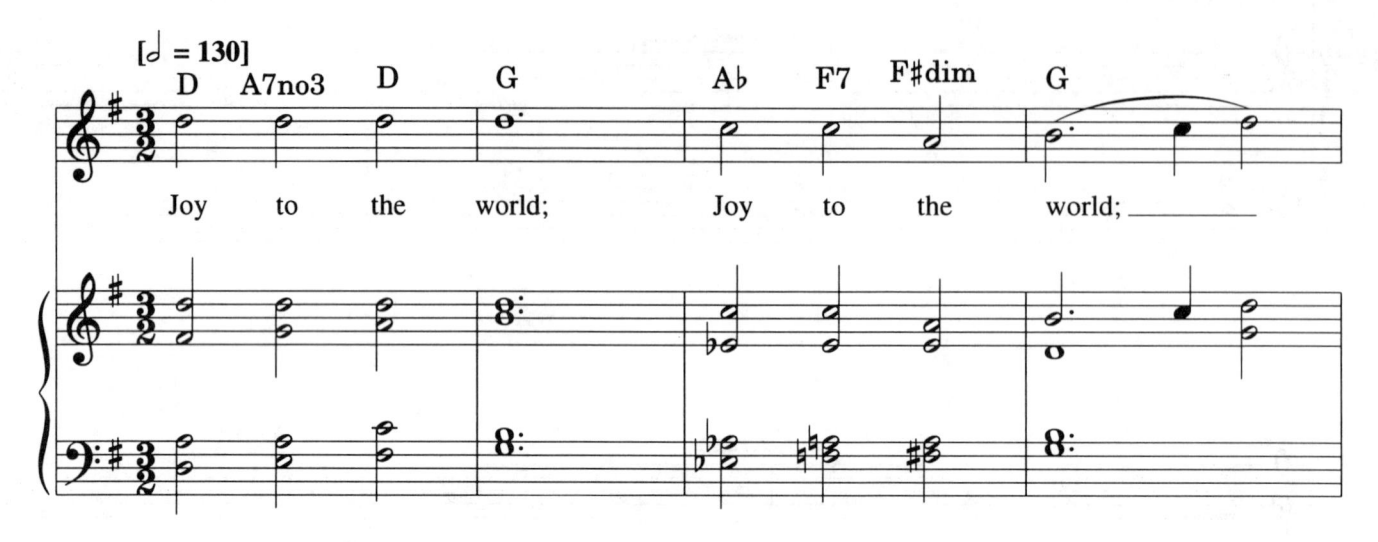

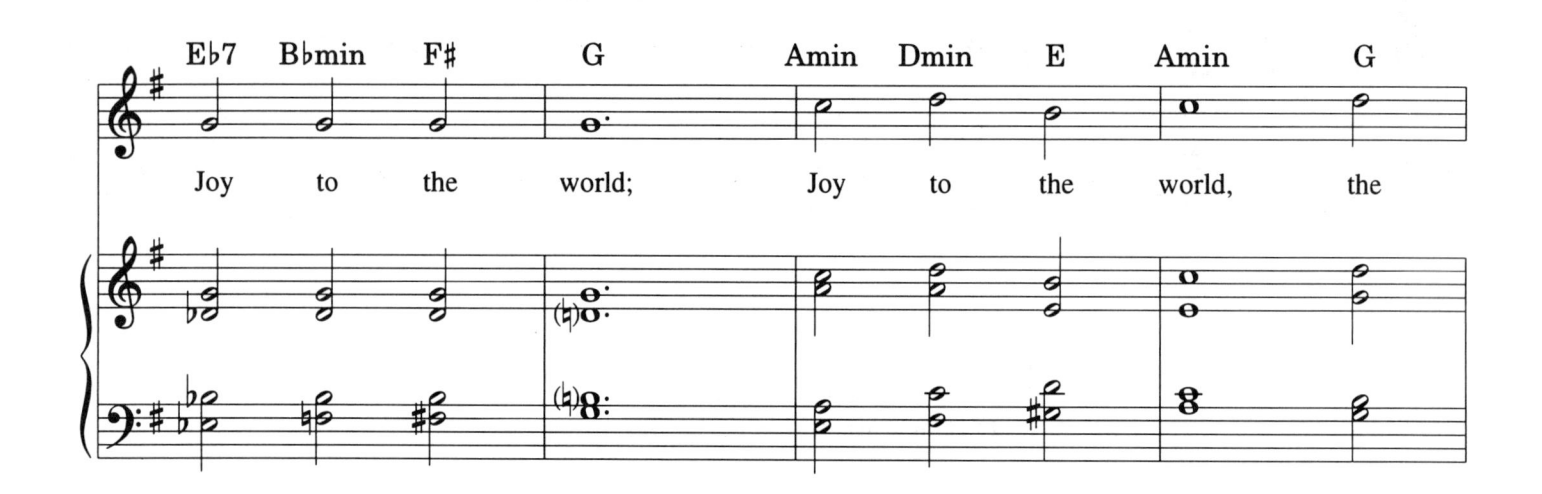

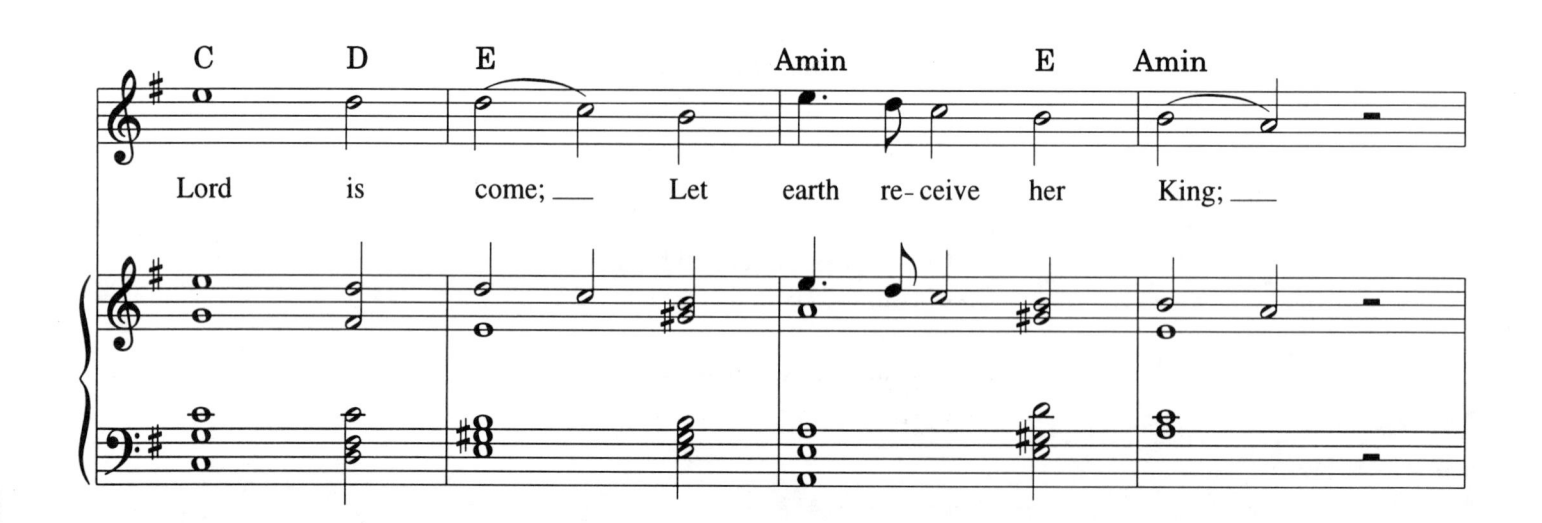

Joy to the world; Joy to the world; Joy to the world; Joy to the world, the Lord is come; Let earth re-ceive her King;

D G E♭ D G
Let ev' - ry __ heart pre - pare __ him __ room, And heav'n __ and
E A D A B7no3 A D
na - - ture sing. Joy to the earth,
G C E Amin E
the Sav - ior reigns; Let men ____ their songs ____ em -

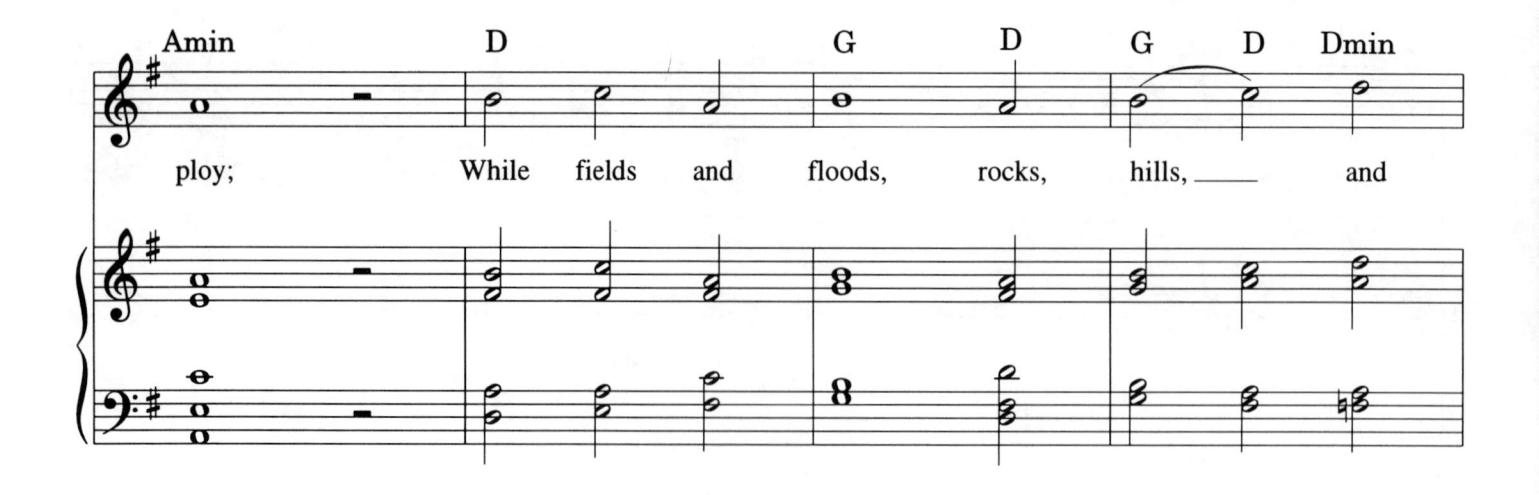

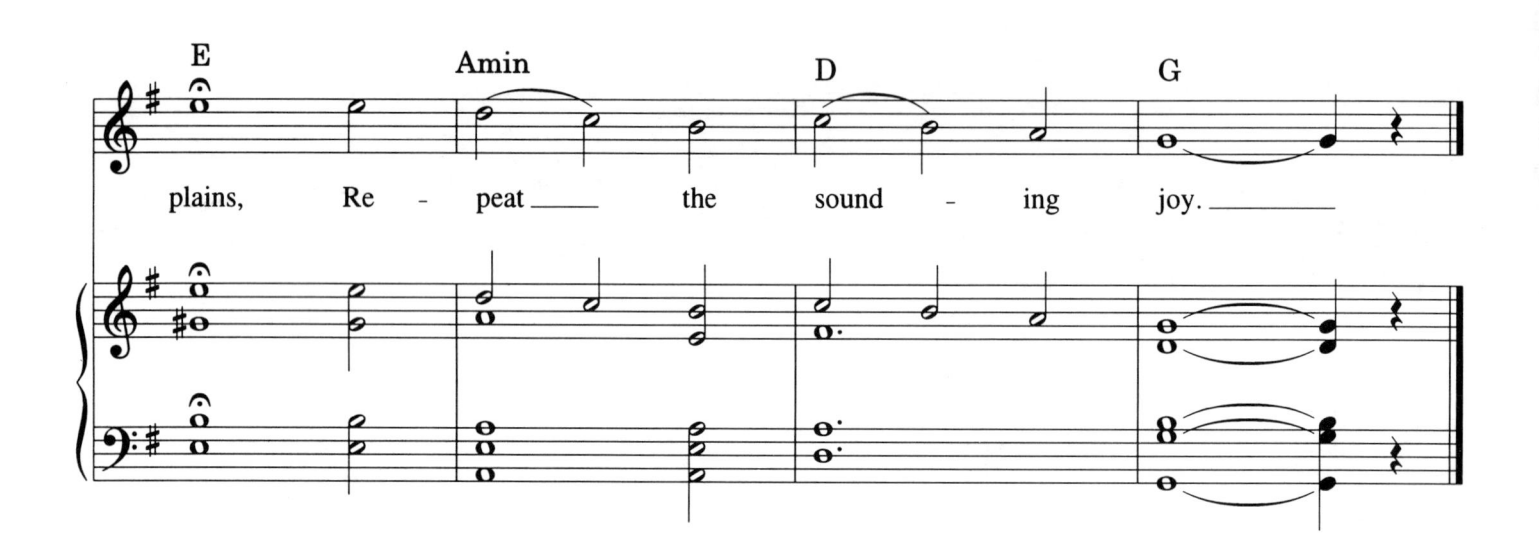

Joy to the world; the Lord is come;
   Let earth receive her King;
Let ev'ry heart prepare him room,
   And heav'n and nature sing.

Joy to the earth, the Saviour reigns;
   Let men their songs employ;
While fields and floods, rocks, hills, and plains,
   Repeat the sounding joy.

No more let sins and sorrows grow,
   Nor thorns infest the ground;
He comes to make his blessings flow
   Far as the curse is found.

He rules the world with truth and grace,
   And makes the nations prove
The glories of his righteousness,
   And wonders of his love.

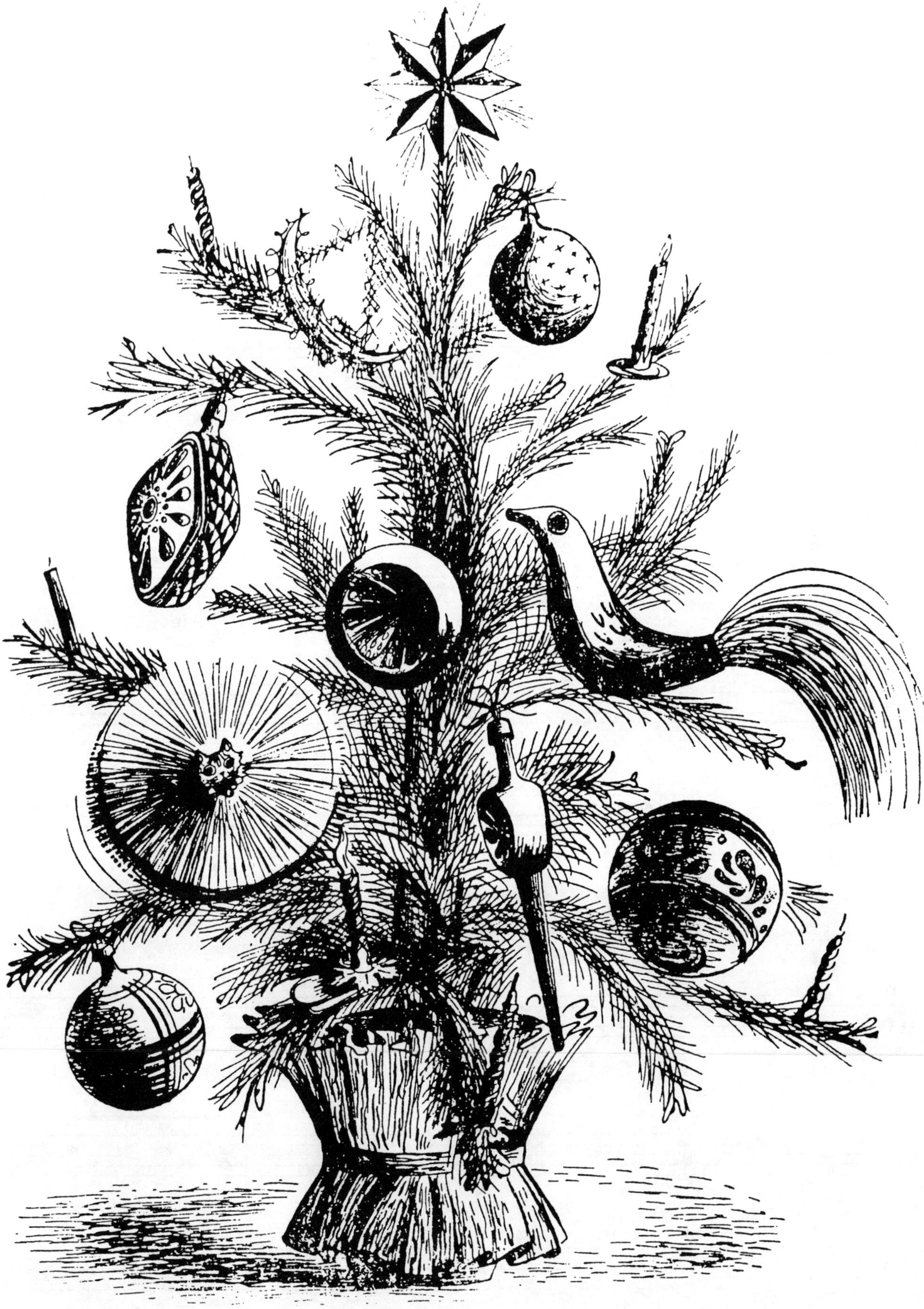

MESSENGER

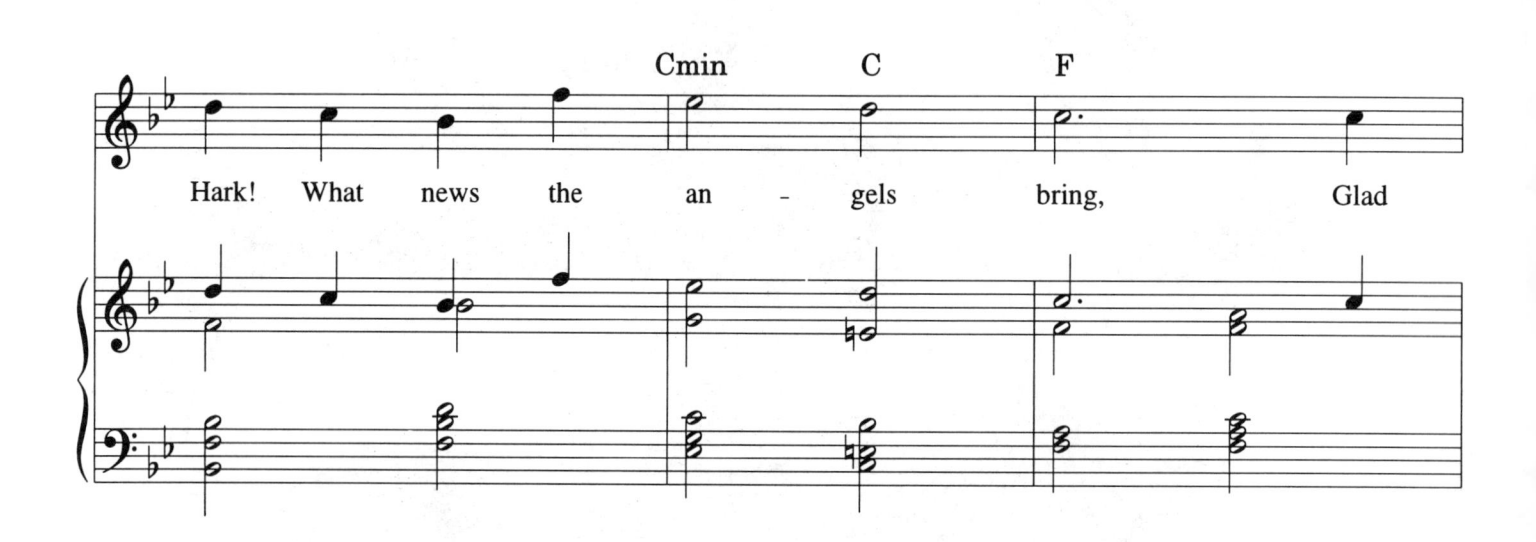

Unknown Unknown

Hark! Hark! Hark! Hark! Hark!

Hark! What news the angels bring, Glad tidings, Glad tidings of a new-born

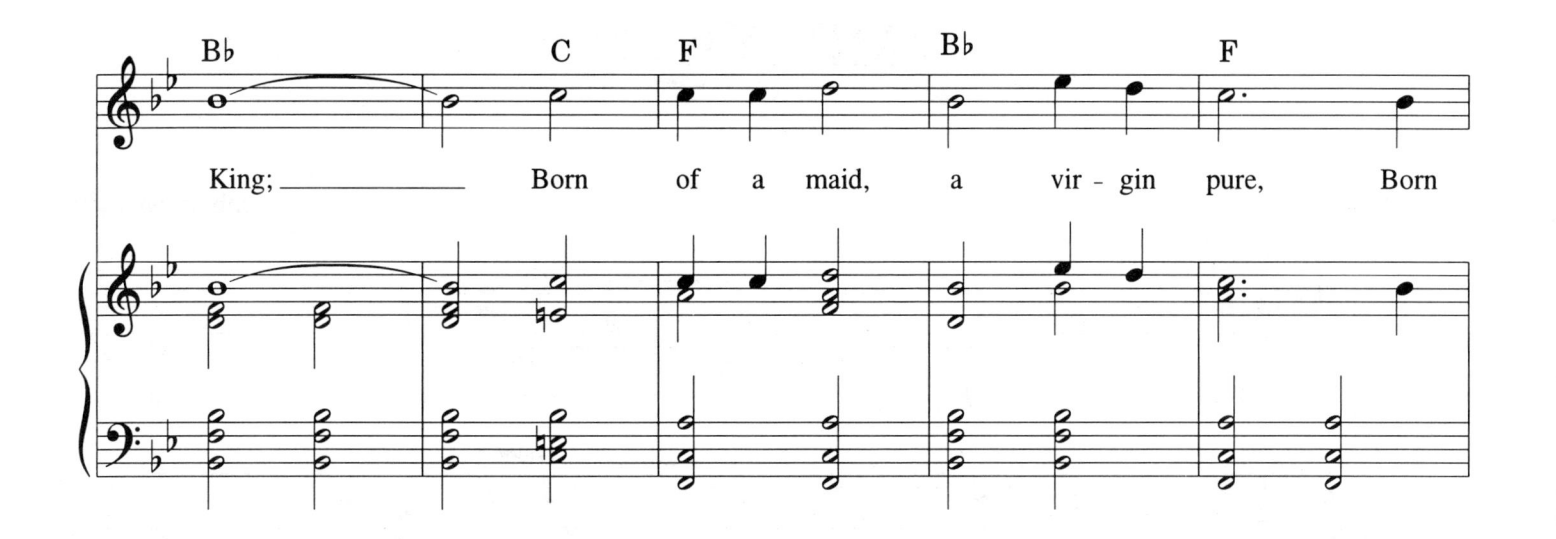

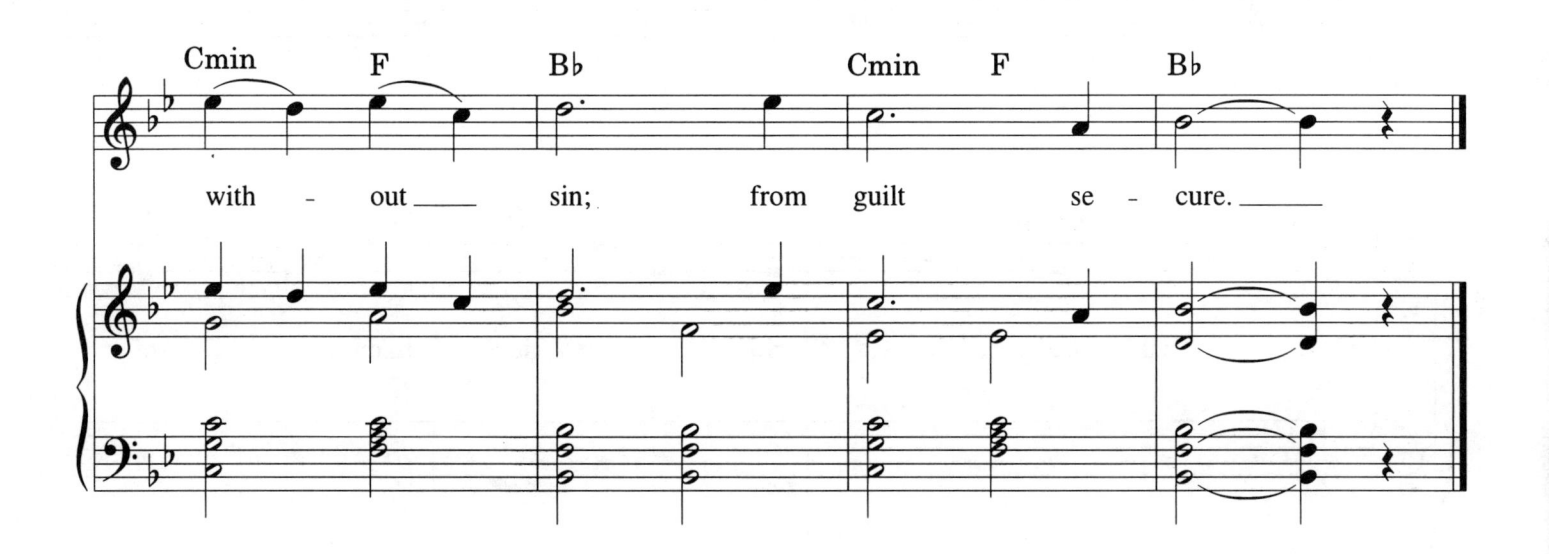

Hark! Hark! What news the angels bring,
    Glad tidings of a new born King;
Born of a maid, a virgin pure,
    Born without sin; from guilt secure.

MILFORD

Unknown
Joseph Stephenson

Hail, hail, all glo - rious Lamb of God; Hail, hail, all glo - rious Lamb of God; Let saints and an - gels join, To

G C E
cel - e - brate thy praise a - broad, Whose name is
Amin D G
all di - vine. To cel - e - brate thy
Emin Cmin D G
praise Whose name is all di - vine.

1) Hail, hail, all glorious Lamb of God;
       Let saints and angels join,
   To celebrate thy praise abroad,
       Whose name is all divine.

2) Hail ever blessed and glorious King,
       Thou great incarnate God;
   Who didst to us salvation bring
       Through thine own precious blood.

3) Jesus, the lamb, who dwells on high,
       Fulfill'd th'eternal plan,
   As was foretold by prophecy,
       To save that rebel man.

4) Behold! the long-expected sight
       Has now appear'd on earth;
   Behold! the darkness turn'd to light,
       At dear Emmanuel's birth!

5) Thus did the holy angels sing,
       As shepherds they drew nigh;
   "Glad-tidings of great joy we bring,
       Therefore you need not fear!"

6) "For unto you this day is born
       A Saviour, Christ the Lord!"
   Man to restore, unto his throne,
       And to fulfil his word.

7) "All glory be to God on High!"
       The song let mortals aid;
   To Christ, that dwells above the sky,
       Be endless blessings paid.

8) Thus we'd commemorate the day
       Of our dear Saviour's birth;
   O praise the Lord, give thanks and pray,
       For "peace to men on earth."

"The Snow Battle." From *Harper's Weekly*, c. 1872.

MILTON

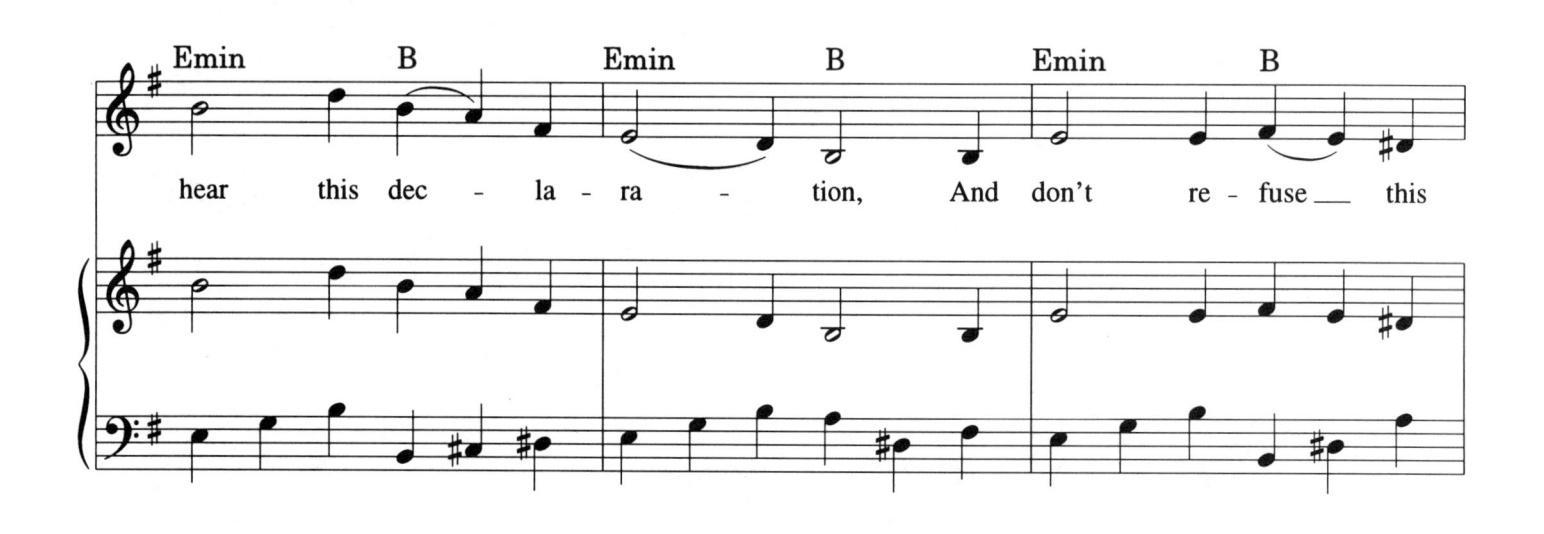

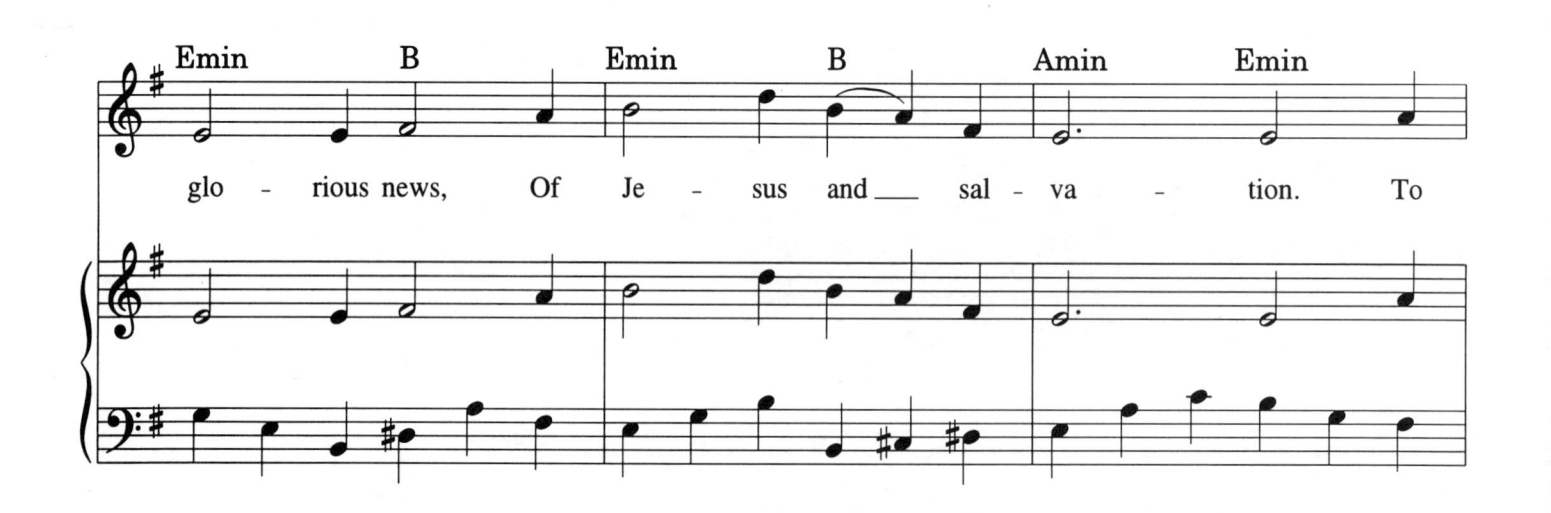

Traditional
William Walker

[♩. = 80]

Ye nations all, on you I call, Come hear this declaration, And don't refuse this glorious news, Of Jesus and salvation. To roy - al Jews came first the news Of Christ the great Mes-si - ah, As was fore-told by proph-ets old: I-sa - iah, Jer - i - mi - ah.

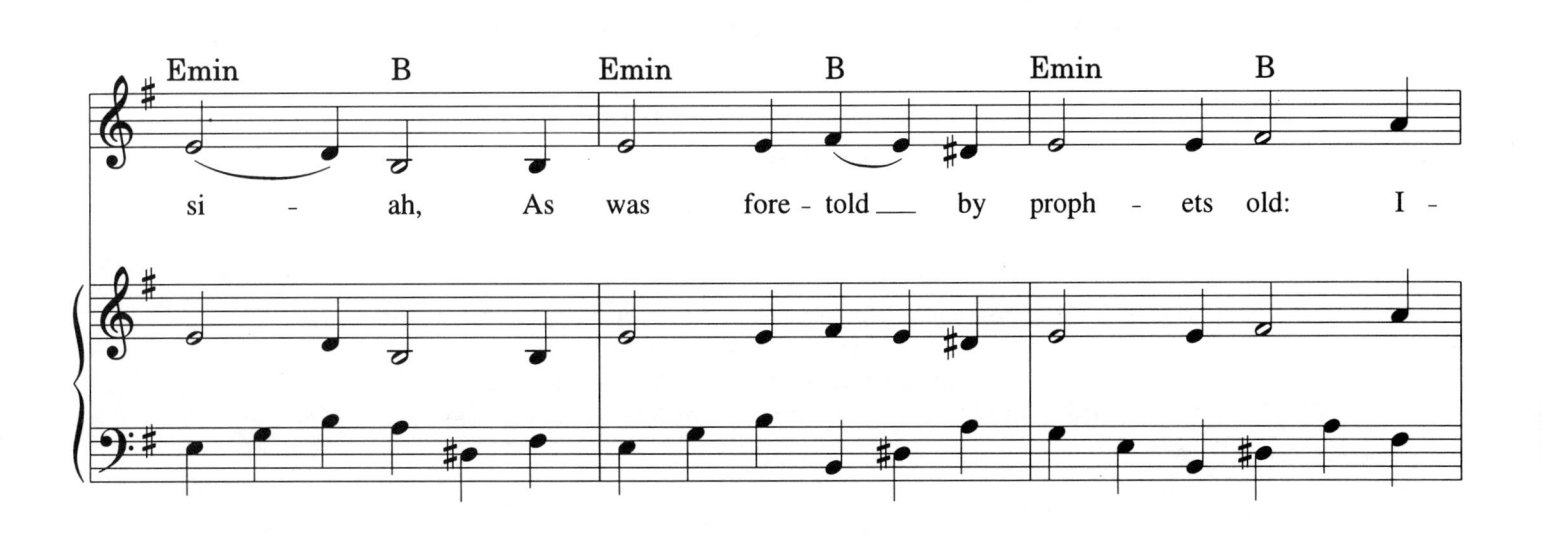

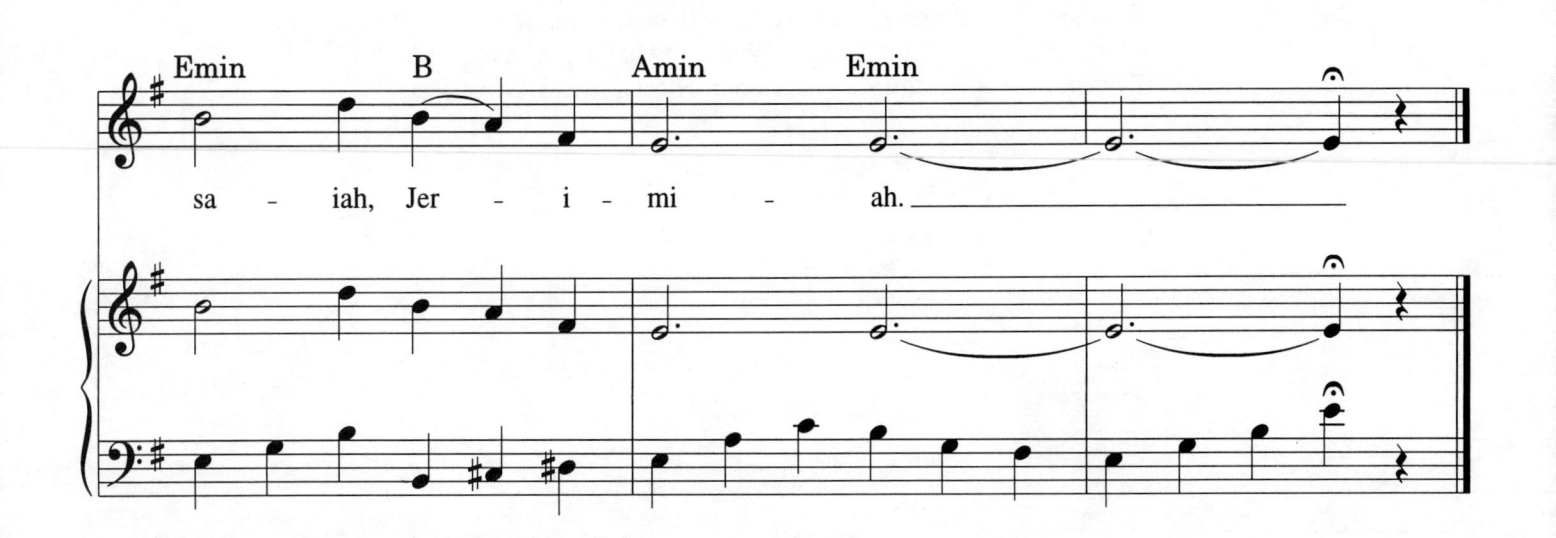

1) Ye nations all, on you I call, Come, hear this declaration,
   And don't refuse this glorious news, Of Jesus and salvation.
   To royal Jews came first the news Of Christ the great Messiah,
   As was foretold by prophets old: Isaiah, Jeremiah.

2) To Abraham the promise came, And to his seed for ever,
   A light to shine in Isaac's line, By scripture we discover;
   Hail promised morn, the Saviour's born, The glorious Mediator;
   God's blessed word made flesh and blood, Assumed the human nature.

3) His parents poor in earthly store, To entertain the stranger,
   They found no bed to lay his head, But in the ox's manger;
   No royal things, as used by kings, Were seen by those that found him,
   But in the hay the stranger lay, With swaddling bands around Him.

4) On the same night a glorious light To shepherds there appeared,
   Bright angels came in shining flame, They saw and greatly feared;
   The angels said, Be not afraid, Although we much alarm you,
   We do appear good news to bear, As now we will inform you.

5) The city's name is Bethlehem, In which God hath appointed,
   This glorious morn a Saviour's born, For Him God hath anointed;
   By this you'll know, if you will go, To see this little stranger,
   His lovely charms in Mary's arms, Both lying in a manger.

6) When this was said, straightway was made, A glorious sound from heaven,
   Each flaming tongue an anthem sung, To men a Saviour's given;
   In Jesus' name, the glorious theme, We elevate our voices,
   At Jesus' birth be peace on earth, Meanwhile all heaven rejoices.

7) Then with delight they took their flight, and winged their way to glory,
   The shepherds gazed and were amazed, To hear the pleasing story;
   To Bethlehem they quickly came, The glorious news to carry,
   And in the stall they found them all, Joseph, the Babe, and Mary.

8) The shepherds then returned again To their own habitation,
   With joy of heart they did depart, Now they have found salvation;
   Glory, they cry, to God on high, Who sent His Son to save us,
   This glorious morn the Saviour's born, His name it is Christ Jesus.

"Oatman's Fifth Avenue Skating Rink—First Lesson in Skating."
From *Harper's Weekly,* Jan. 12, 1867.

MT. EPHRAIM

Isaac Watts
Benjamin Milgrove

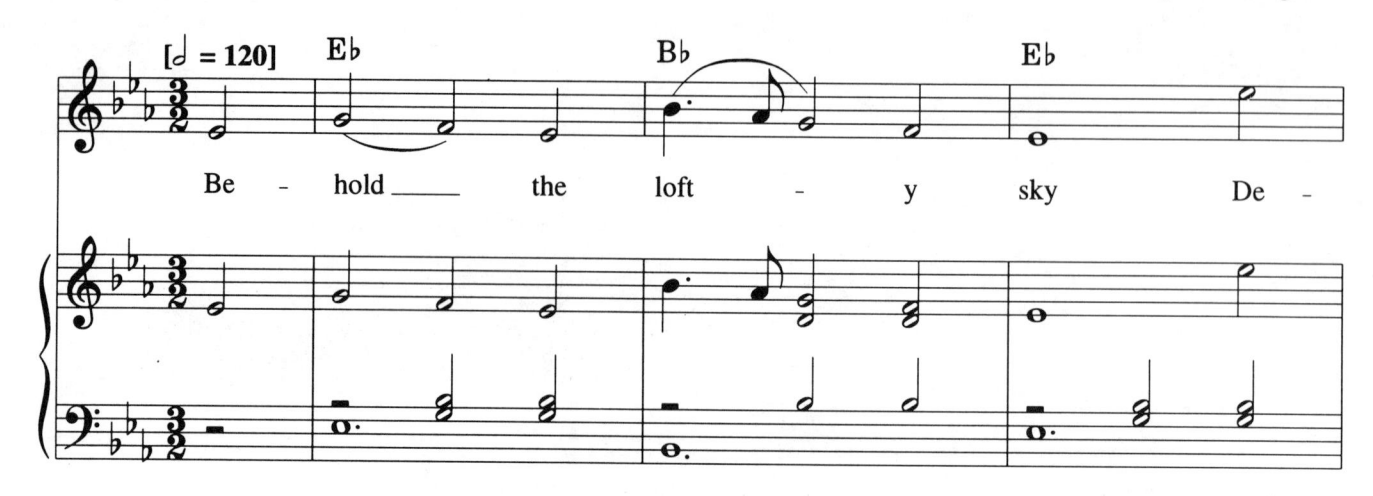

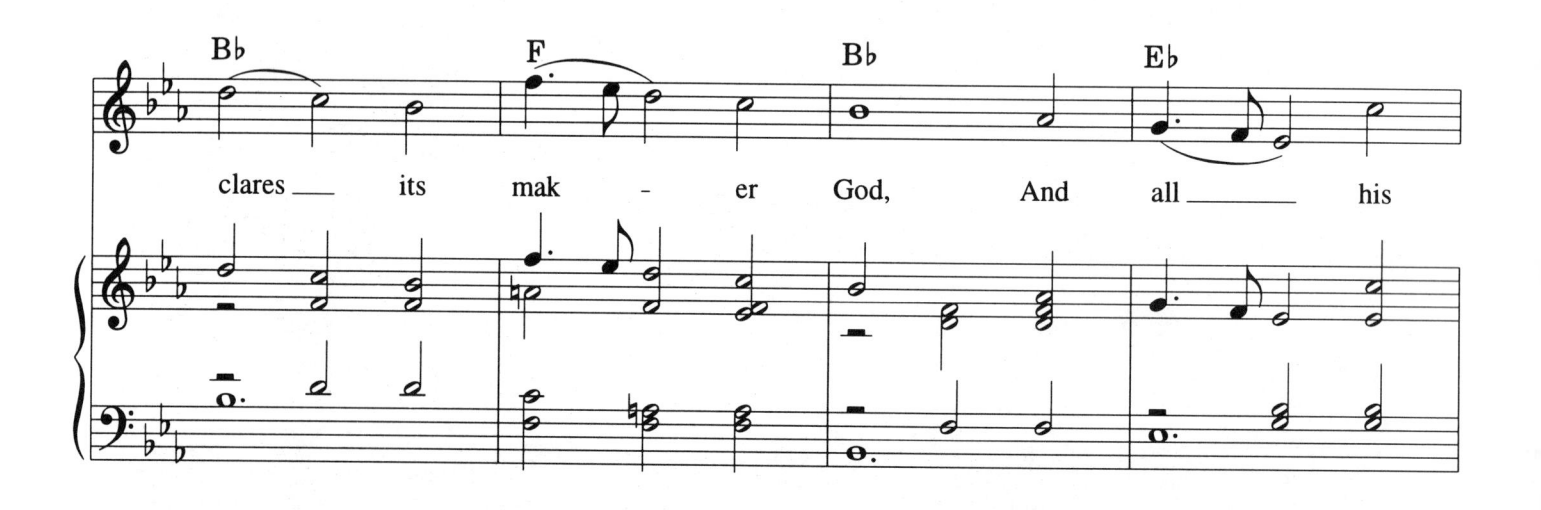

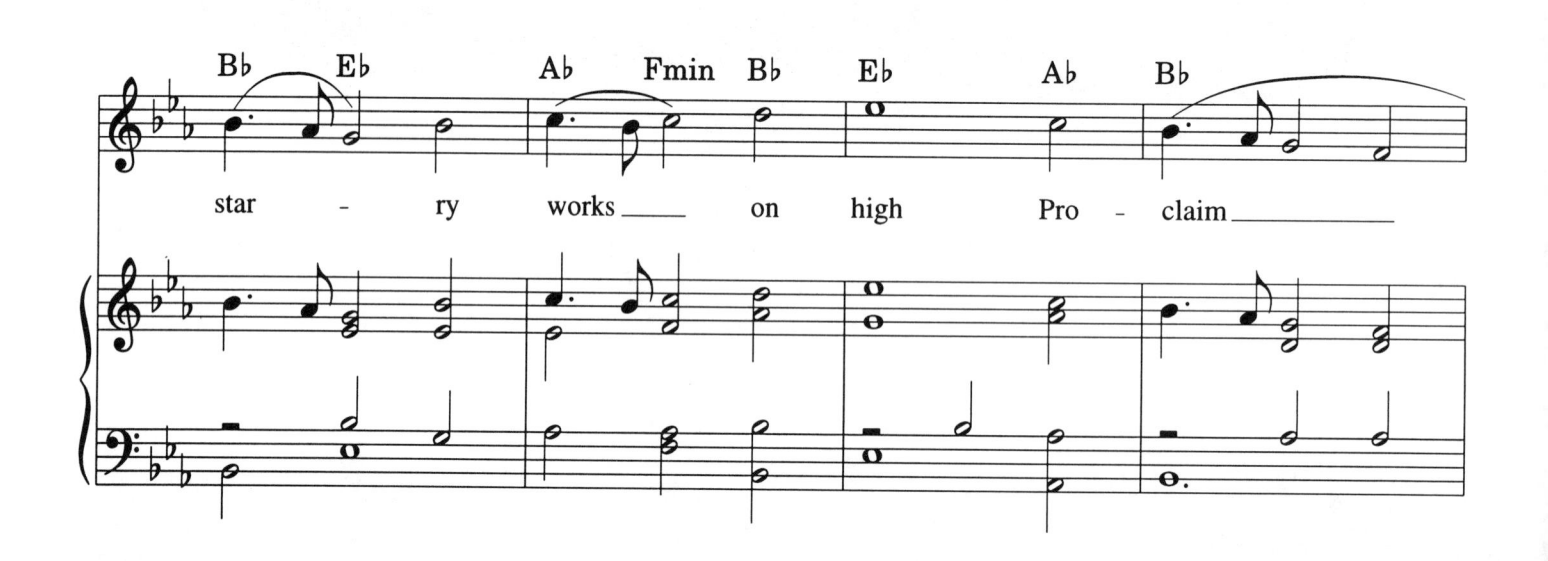

[♩ = 120]

Be-hold ____ the loft - y sky De-clares ____ its mak - er God, And all ____ his star - ry works ____ on high Pro-claim ____

136

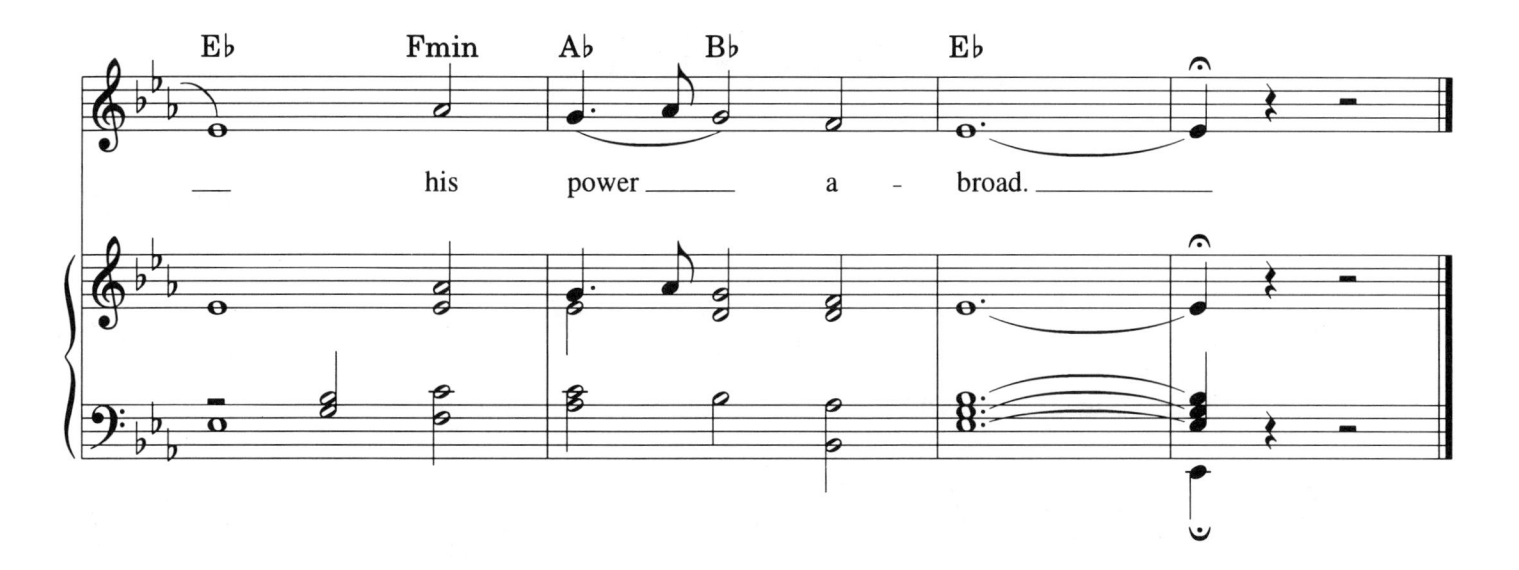

1) Behold the lofty sky
   Declares its maker God,
     And all his starry works on high
   Proclaim his power abroad.

2) The darkness and the light
   Still keep their course the same;
     While night to day and day to night
   Divinely teach his name.

3) In every different land
   Their general voice is known;
     They show the wonders of his hand,
   And orders of his throne.

4) Ye Christian lands rejoice,
   Here he reveals his word,
     We are not left to nature's voice
   To bid us know the lord.

5) His statutes and commands
   Are set before our eyes,
     He puts his gospel in our hands,
   Where our salvation lies.

6) His laws are just and pure,
   His truth without deceit,
     His promises forever sure,
   And his rewards are great.

7) Not honey to the taste
   Affords so much delight,
     Nor gold that has the furnace past
   So much allures the slight.

8) While of thy works I sing,
   Thy glory to proclaim,
     Accept the praise, my God, my King,
   In my Redeemer's name.

NATIVITY

Isaiah 9:6   George J. Webb

Un-to us a child is born, Un-to us a son is given; And the gov-ern-ment shall be up-on his shoul-der; And his name shall be call-ed Won-der-ful,

Coun - sel - lor, the Might - y God, The ev - er-last - ing Fa - ther, the Prince of Peace. Prince of Peace, Prince of Peace. Un - to

G D G Emin A
us a child is born, Un - to us a son is
D C G
given; And the gov - ern-ment shall be up - on his
D G C D
shoul - der; And his name shall be call - ed
G E♭ D
Won - der - ful, Coun - sel - lor, the Might - y

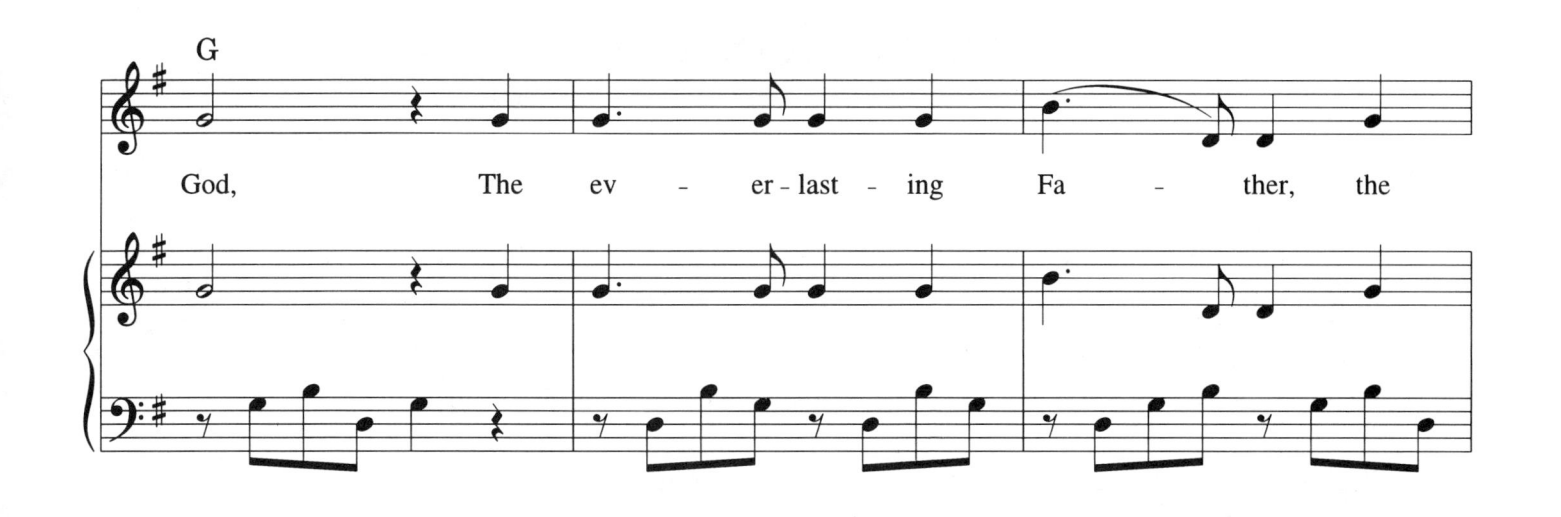

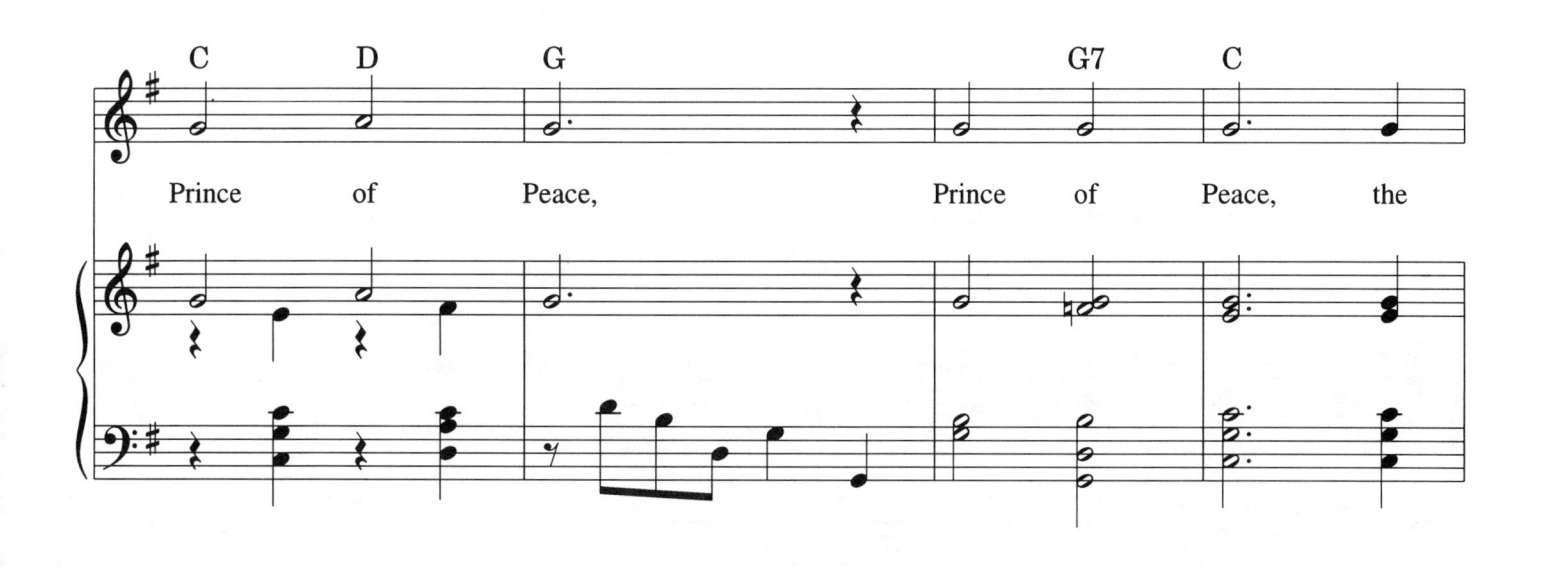

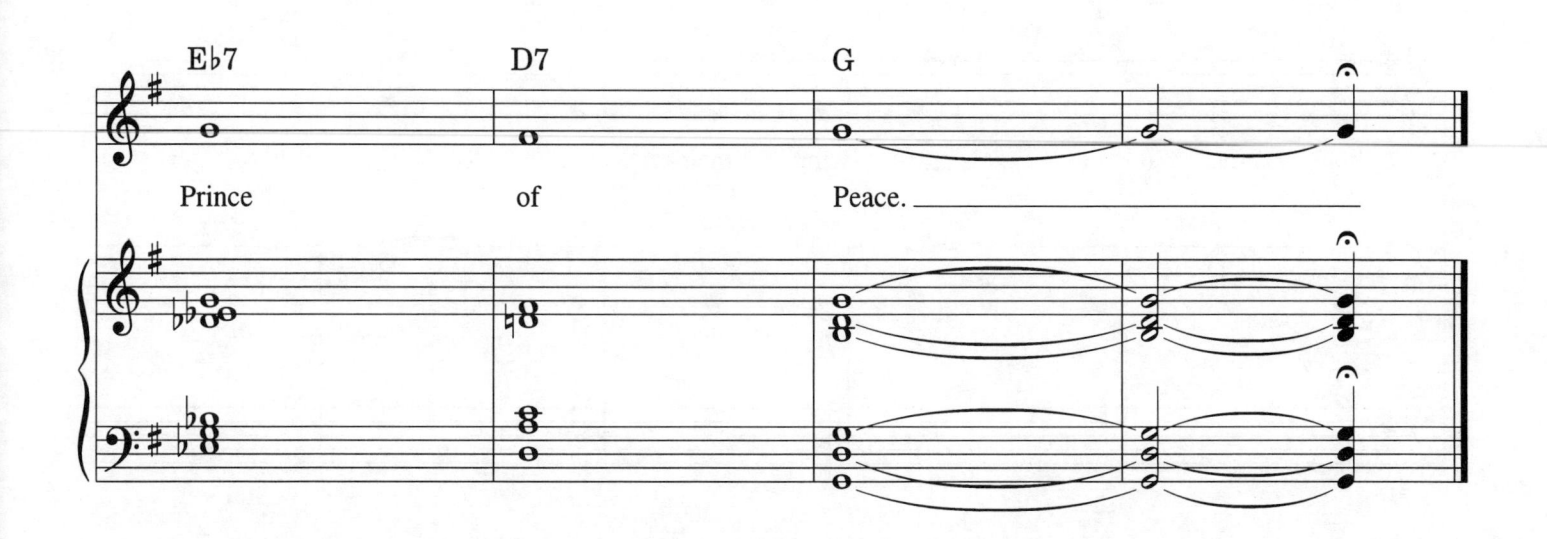

God, The ev-er-last-ing Fa-ther, the Prince of Peace, Prince of Peace, the Prince of Peace.

NEW HOSANNA

Unknown
H. S. Rees

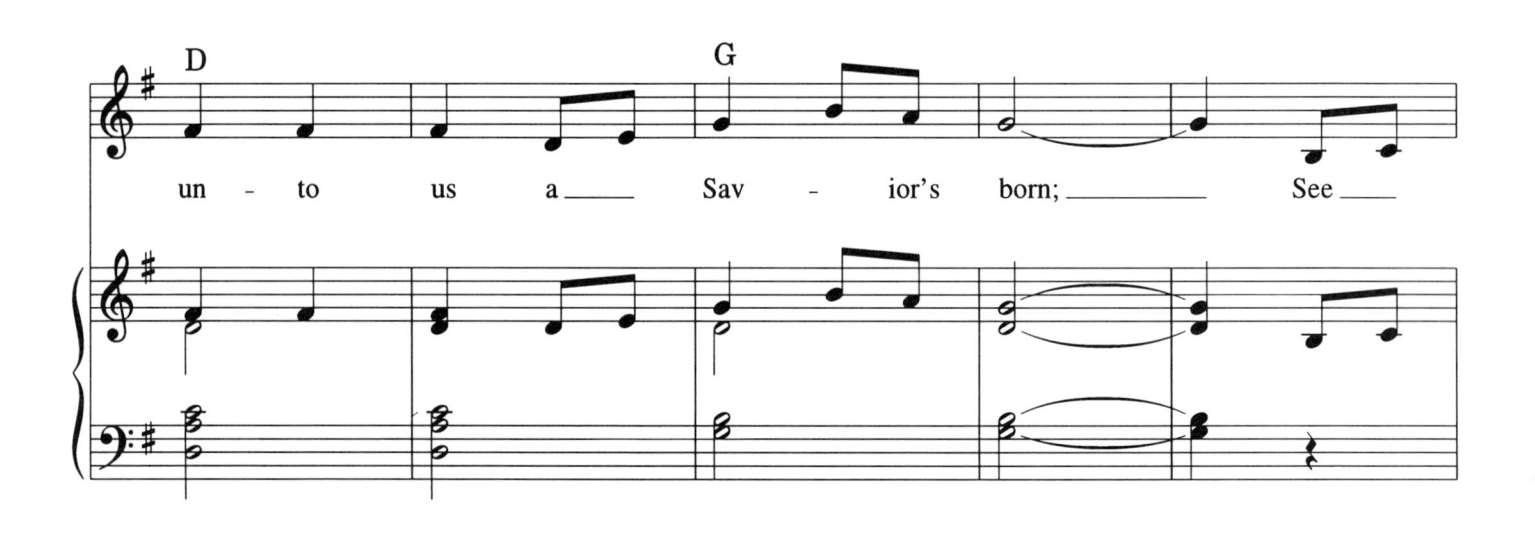

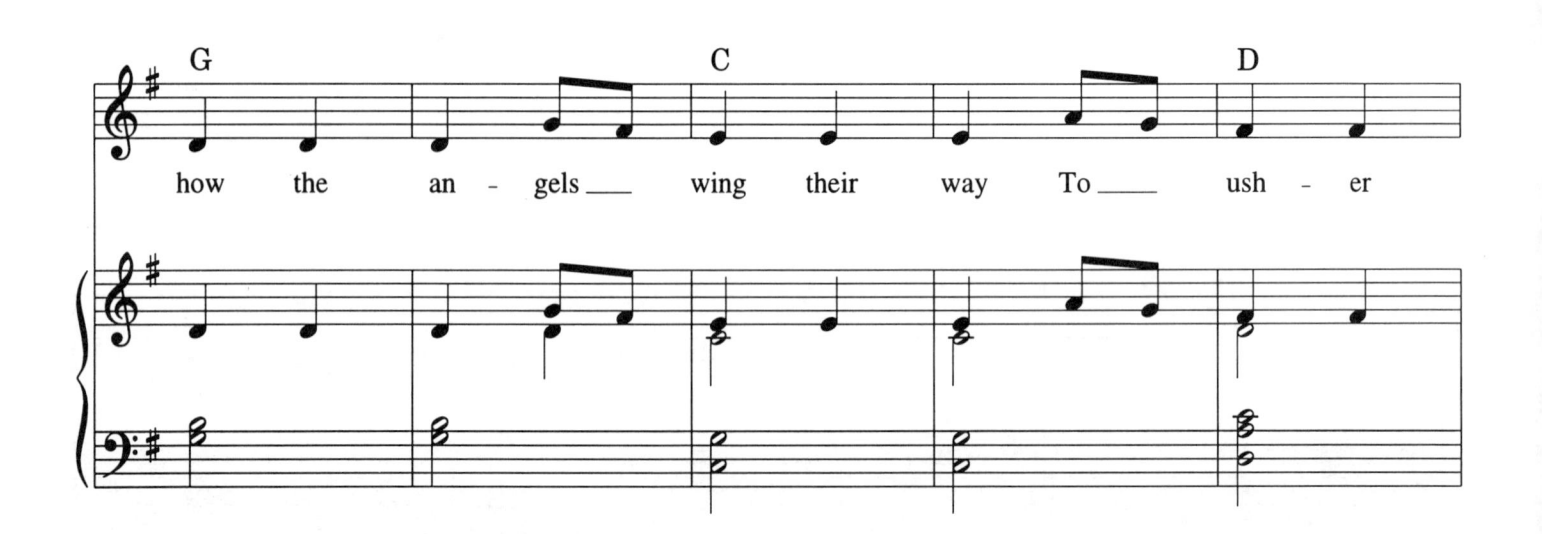

Wake, O my soul, and hail the morn, For unto us a Savior's born; See how the angels wing their way To usher

Chorus
D G D
in the glo - rious day. Glo - ry,
G D
glo - ry, let us sing, While heav'n and
G G
earth his prais - es ring, Ho - san -

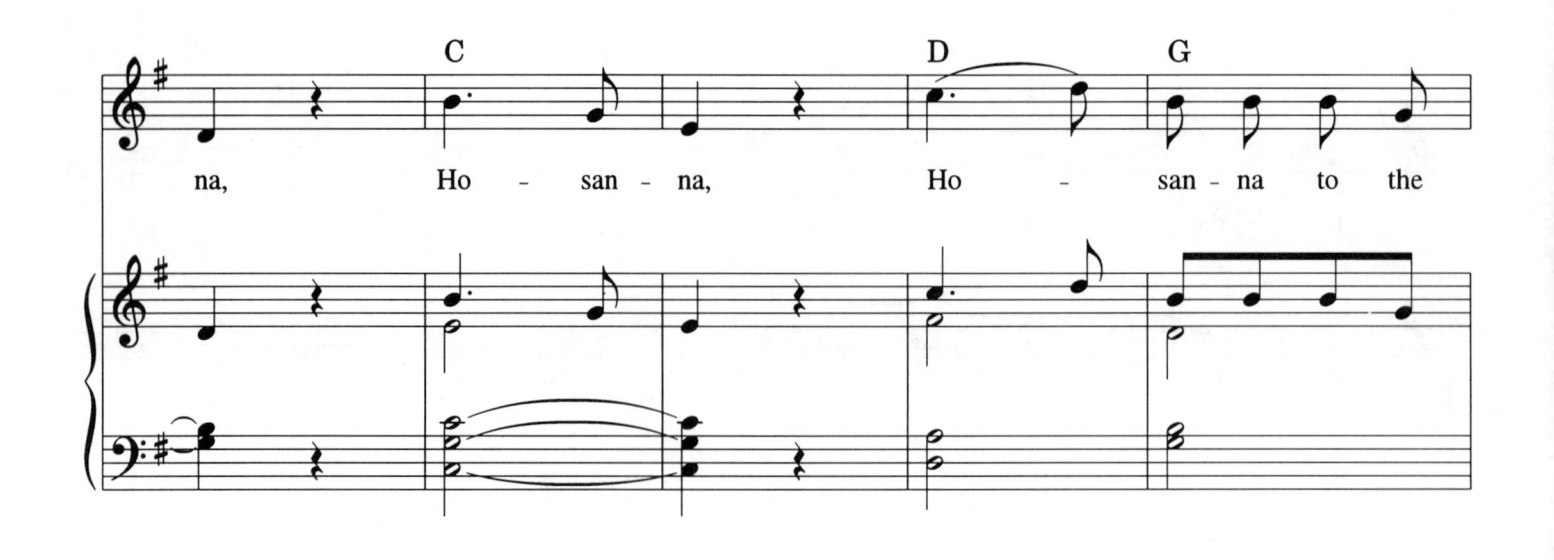

na, Ho - san - na, Ho - san - na to the Lamb of God. Glo - ry, glo - ry let us sing, While heav'n and earth his prais - es

1) Wake, O my soul, and hail the morn,
   For unto us a Savior's born;
   See how the angels wing their way
   To usher in the glorious day.

Chorus Glory, glory, let us sing,
   While heav'n and earth his praises ring,
   Hosanna to the Lamb of God.

2) Hark, what sweet music, what a song,
   Sounds from the bright celestial throng;
   Sweet song, whose melting sounds impart
   Joy to each raptured listening heart.

3) Come, join the angels in the sky,
   Glory to God who reigns on high;
   Let peace and love on earth abound,
   While time revolves and years roll round.

OXFORD

Anne Steele
John Massengale

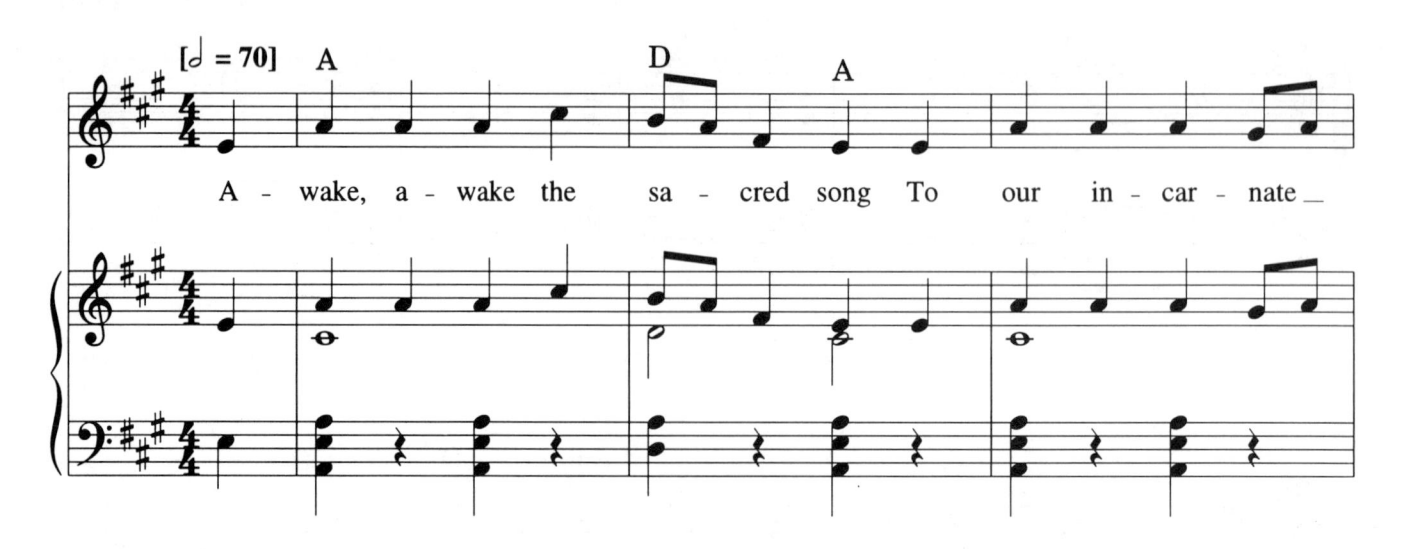

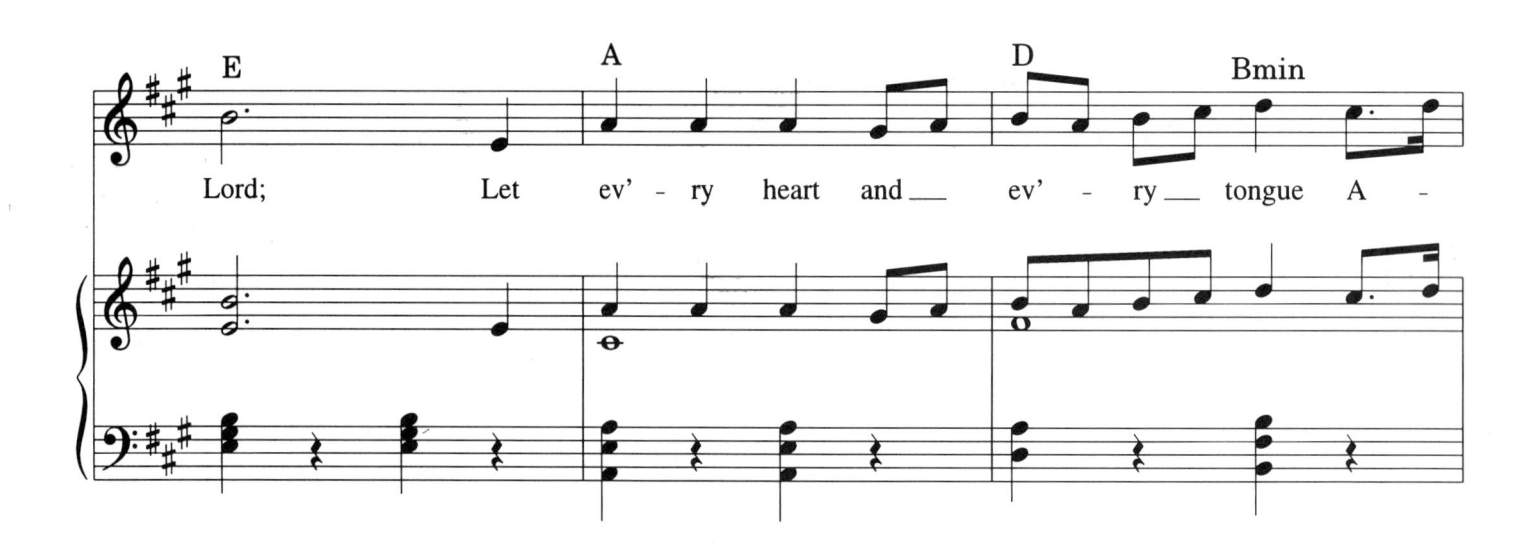

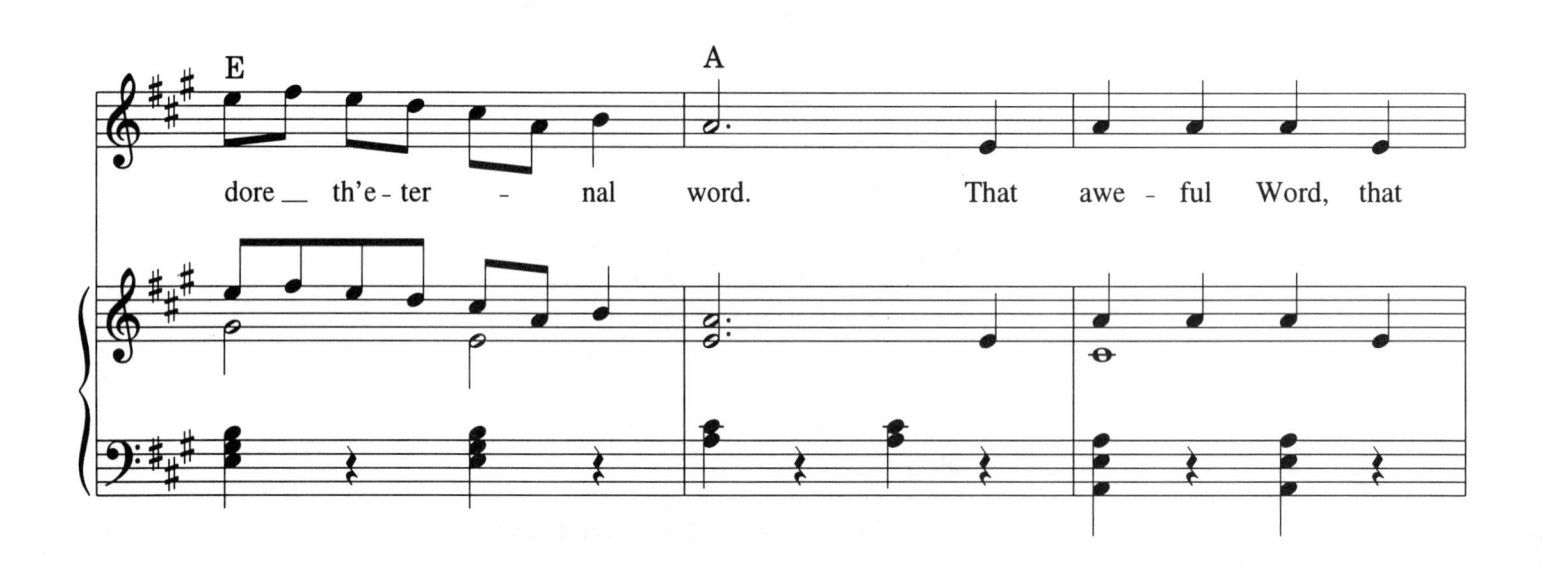

A-wake, a-wake the sa-cred song To our in-car-nate Lord; Let ev'-ry heart and ev'-ry tongue A-dore th'e-ter-nal word. That awe-ful Word, that

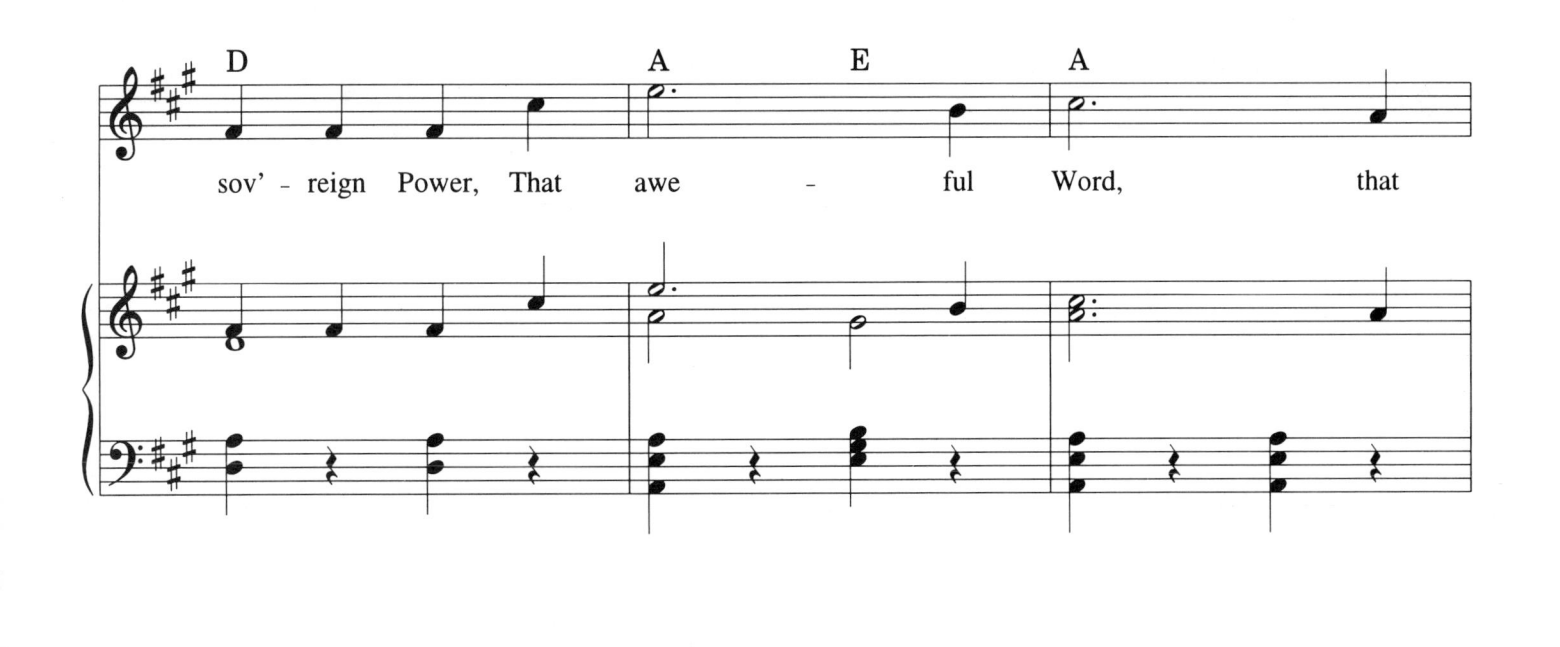

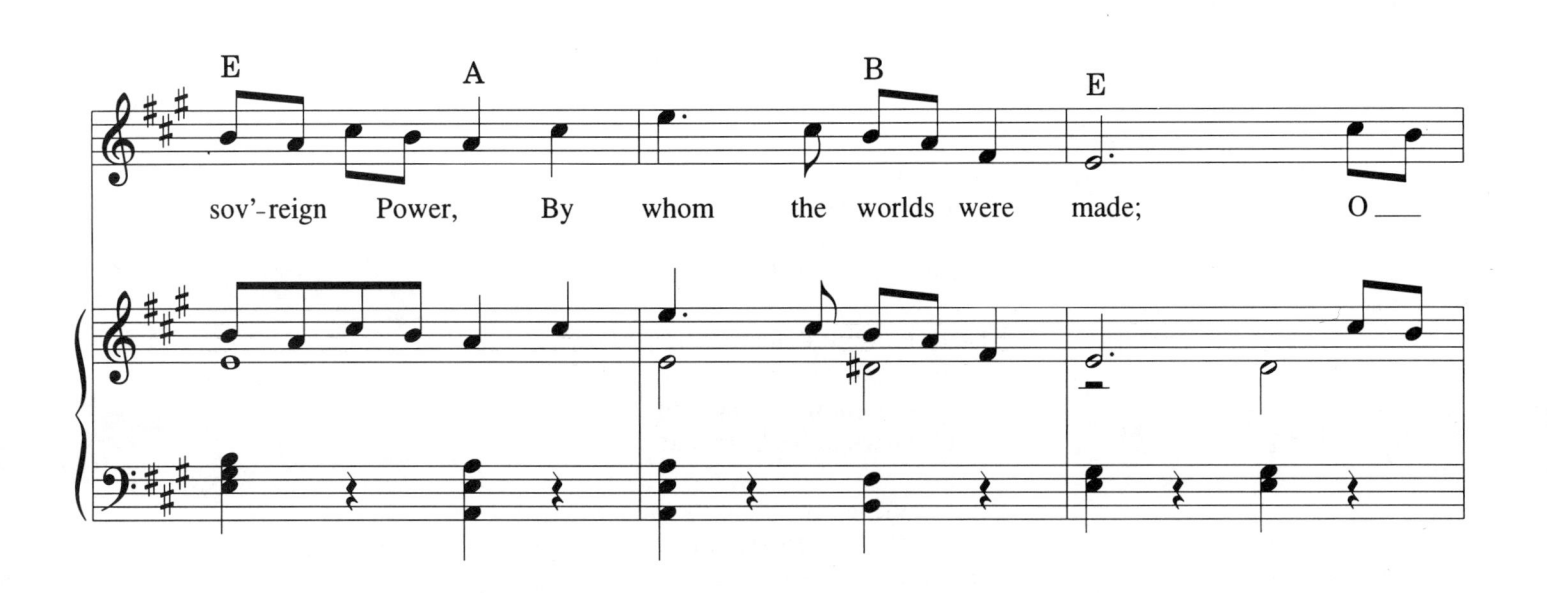

sov'-reign Power, That awe - ful Word, that sov'-reign Power, By whom the worlds were made; O hap-py morn! il-lus-trious hour! Was once _____ in flesh __ ar - rayed. _____

Awake, awake the sacred song
    To our incarnate Lord;
Let ev'ry heart and ev'ry tongue
    Adore th'eternal word.

That aweful Word, that sov'reign Power,
    By whom the worlds were made;
O happy morn! illustrious hour!
    Was once in flesh arrayed.

Then shone almighty power and love,
    In all their glorious forms;
When Jesus left his throne above
    To dwell with sinful worms.

To dwell with misery below,
    The Saviour left the skies;
And sank, to wretchedness and woe,
    That worthless man might rise.

Adoring angels tun'd their songs
    To hail the joyful day;
With rapture then, let mortal tongues
    Their grateful worship pay.

What glory, Lord, to thee is due!
    With wonder we adore;
But could we sing as angels do,
    We'd love and praise thee more.

"A Christmas Welcome," by Edward Hughes.
From *Illustrated London News* (Christmas Supplement), Dec. 16, 1871.

PAXTON

E. H. Sears
Unknown

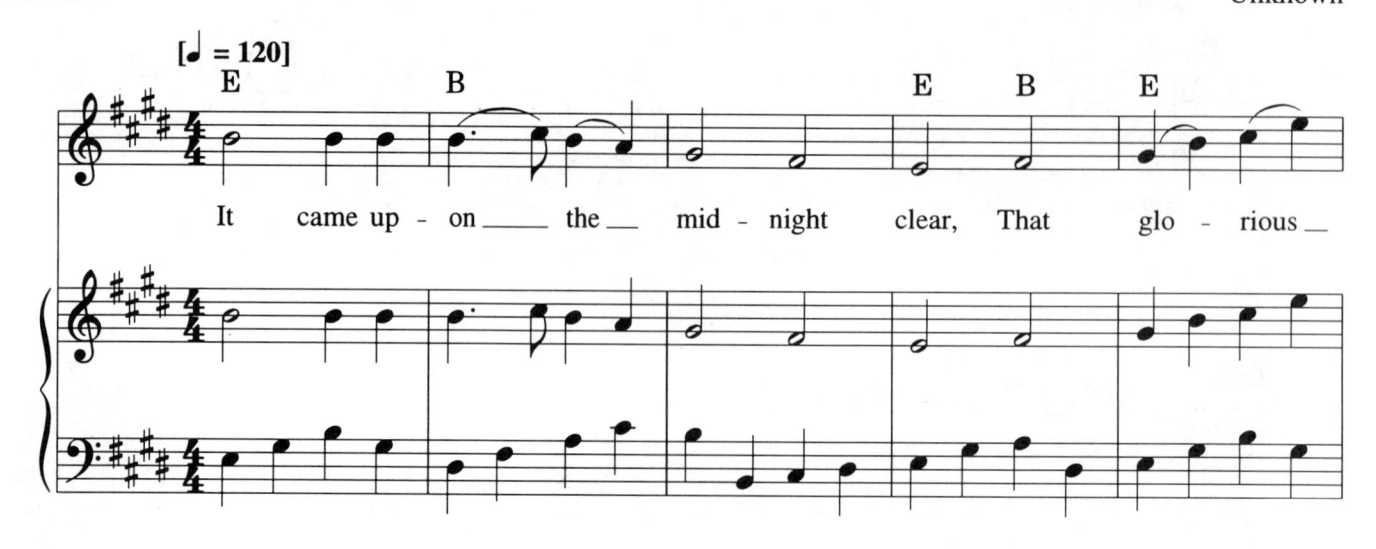

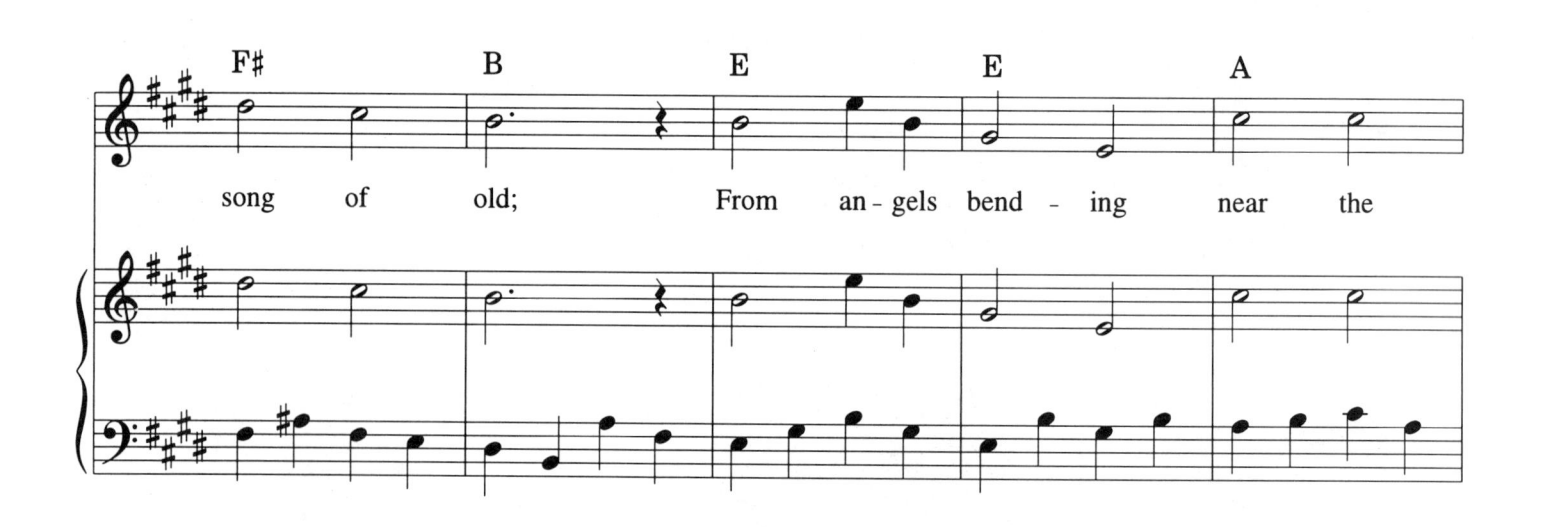

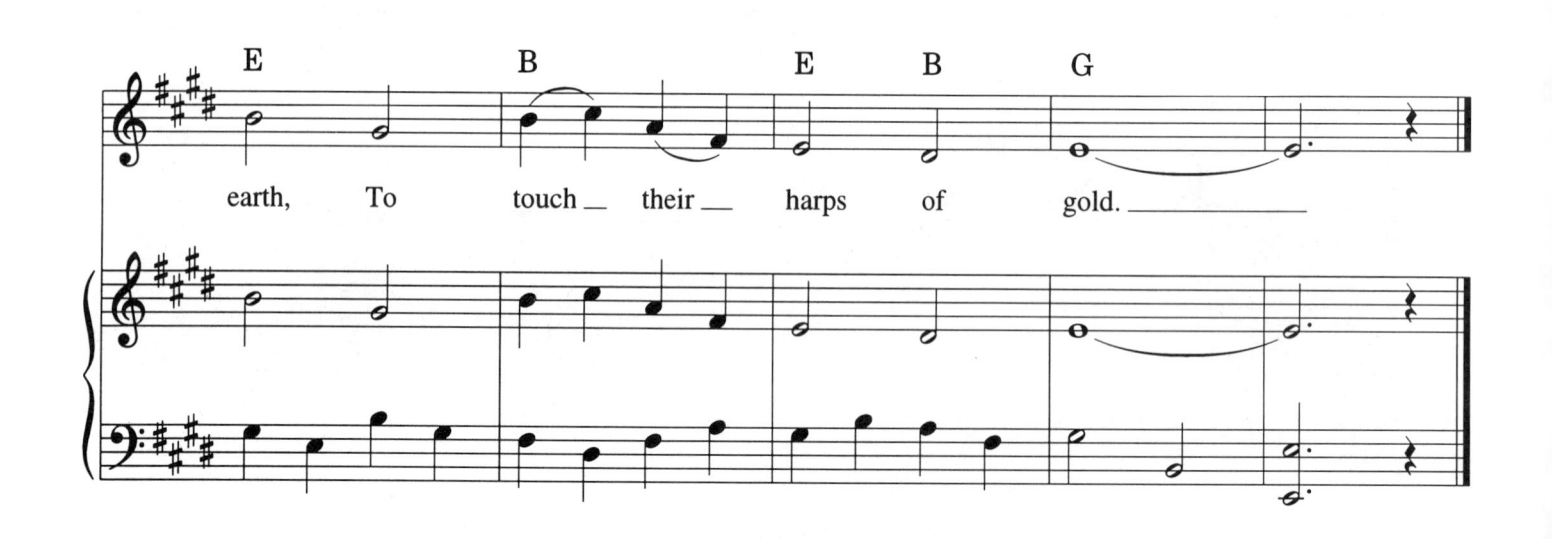

It came upon the midnight clear, That glorious song of old; From angels bending near the earth, To touch their harps of gold.

It came upon the midnight clear,
    That glorious song of old;
From angels bending near the earth,
    To touch their harps of gold.

Peace on the earth, good will to men,
    From heaven's all-gracious King!
The world in solemn stillness lay
    To hear the angels sing.

Still through the cloven skies they come
    With peaceful wings unfurled
And still their heavenly music floats
    O'er all the weary world.

Above its sad and lowly plains
    They bend on hovering wing;
And ever o'er its Babel-sounds
    The blessed angels sing.

Yet with the woes of sin and strife
    The world has suffered long;
Beneath the angel-strain have rolled
    Great praises in man's song.

And man, at war with man, hears not
    The love-song which they bring;
O hush the noise, ye men of strife,
    And hear the angels sing.

And ye, beneath life's crushing load,
    Whose forms are bending low,
Who toil along the climbing way
    With painful steps and slow,

Look, now! for glad and golden hours
    Come swiftly on the wing;
O rest besides the weary road
    And hear the angels sing.

For lo, the days are hastening on,
    By prophet-bards foretold,
When, with the ever-circling years,
    Comes round the age of gold.

When peace shall over all the earth
    Its ancient splendours sling,
And the whole world give back the song
    Which now the angels sing.

RANDOLPH

Isaac Watts   Nahum Mitchell

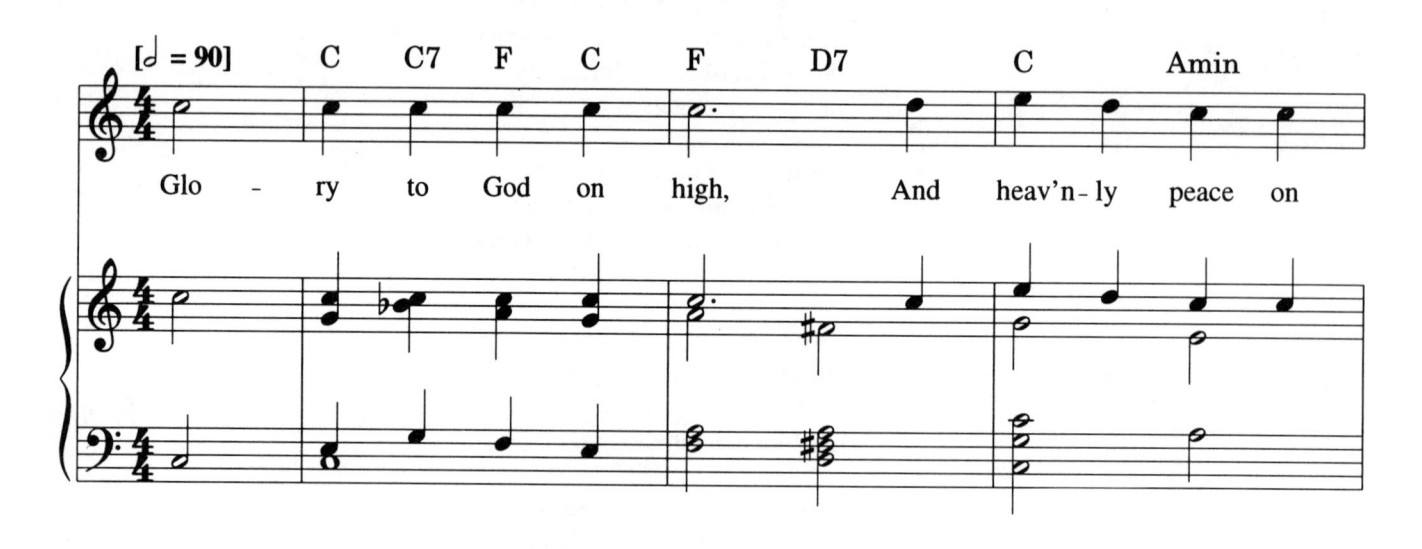

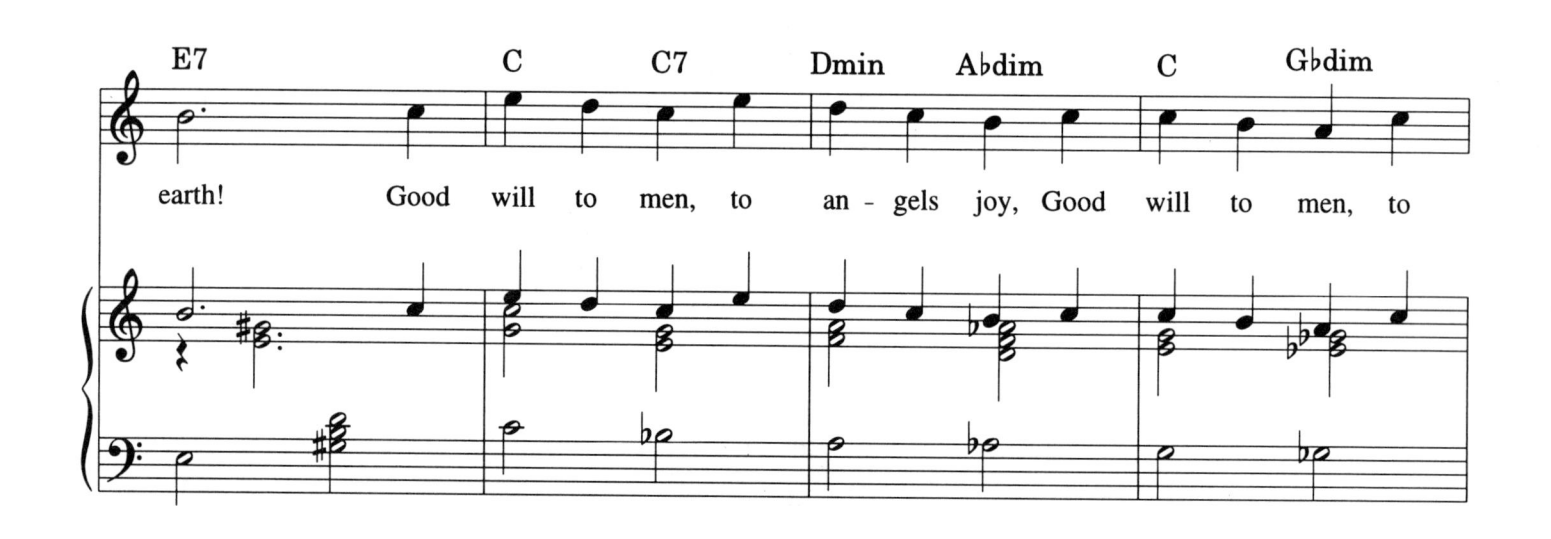

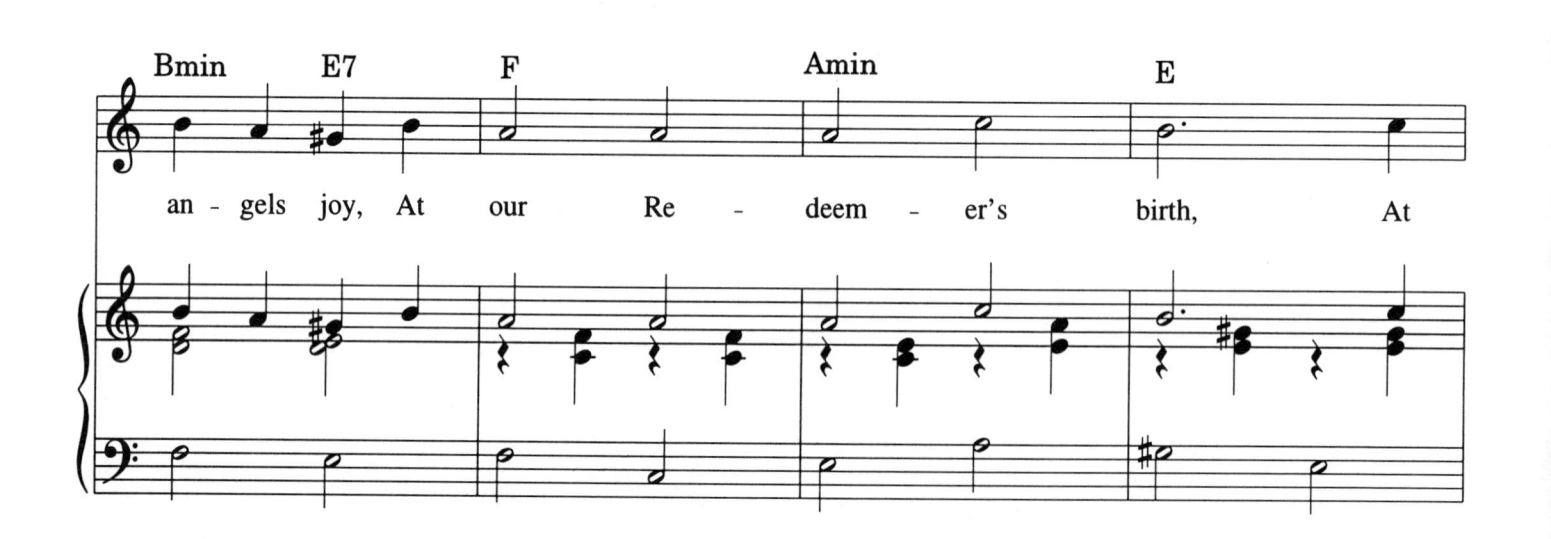

Glo-ry to God on high, And heav'n-ly peace on earth! Good will to men, to an-gels joy, Good will to men, to an-gels joy, At our Re-deem-er's birth, At

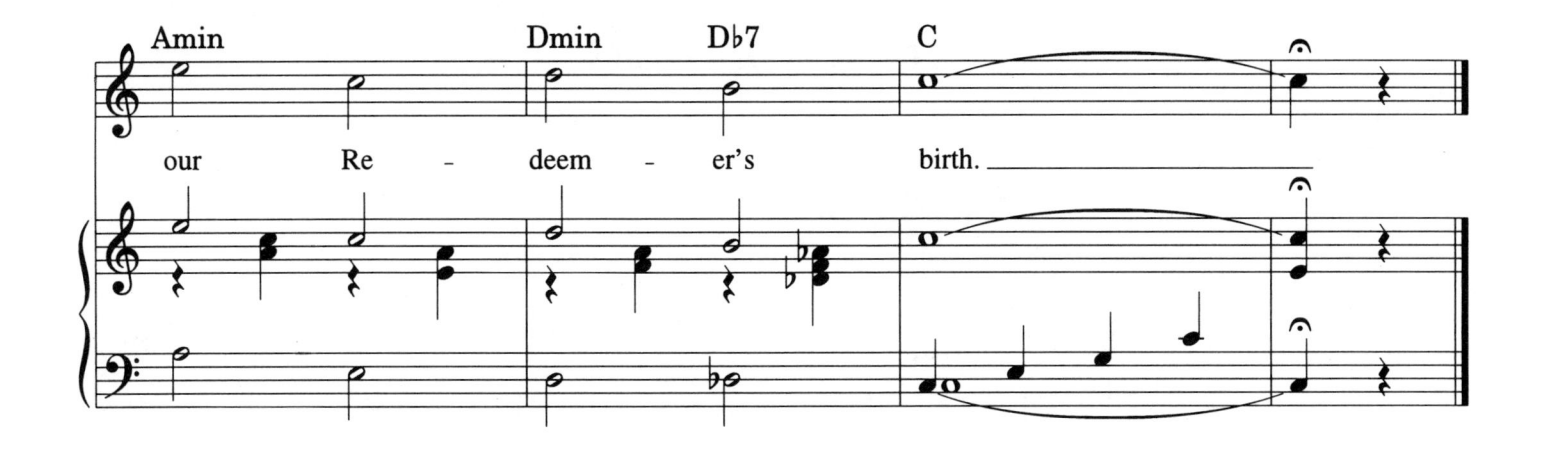

1) Glory to God on high,
   And heav'nly peace on earth!
       Good will to men, to angels joy,
   At our Redeemer's birth.

2) In worship so divine
   Let saints employ their tongues;
       With the celestial hosts we join,
   And loud repeat their songs.

3) Behold, the grace appears,
   The promise is fulfilled;
       Mary, the righteous virgin, bears
   And Jesus is the child.

4) The Lord, the highest God,
   Calls him his only Son;
       He bids him rule the lands abroad,
   And gives him David's throne.

5) O'er Jacob shall he reign
   With a peculiar sway;
       The nations shall his grace obtain,
   His kingdom ne'er decay.

6) To bring the glorious news,
   A heav'nly form appears;
       He tells the shepherds of their joys,
   And banishes their fears.

7) "Go, humble swains," said he,
   "To David's city fly;
       The promised infant, born to-day,
   Doth in a manger lie."

8) "With looks and hearts serene
   Go visit Christ your king;"
       And straight a flaming troop was seen;
   The shepherds heard them sing.

9) Glory to God on high,
   And heavenly peace on earth,
       Good-will to men, to angels joy,
   At our Redeemer's birth!

REDEEMER

Traditional   Traditional

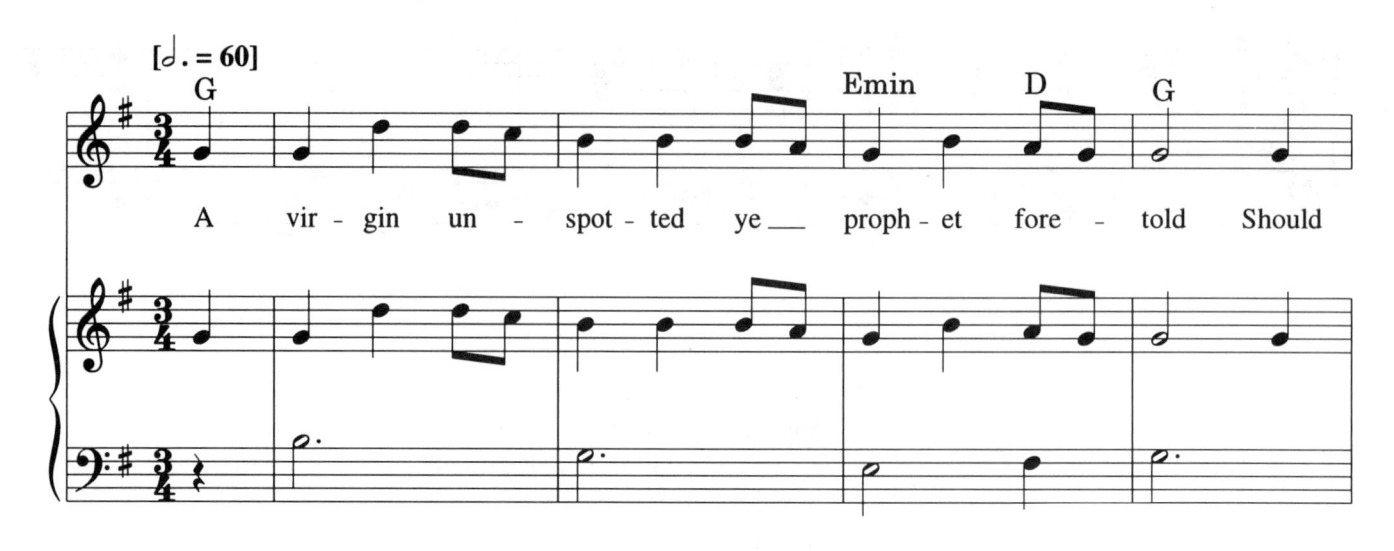

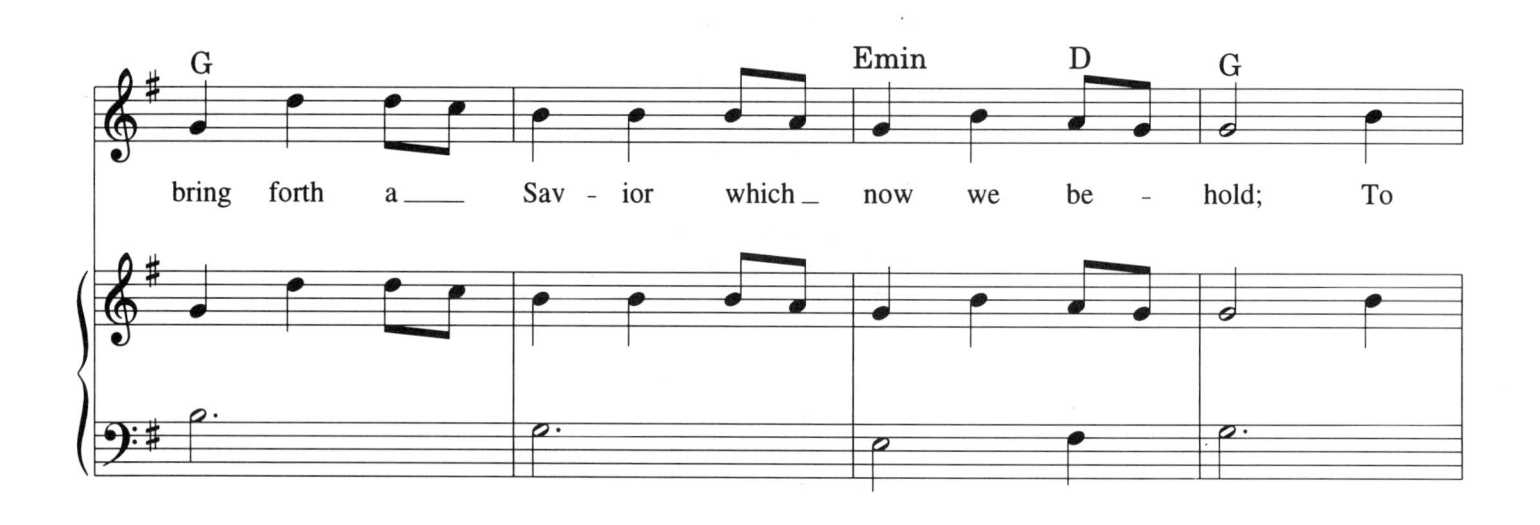

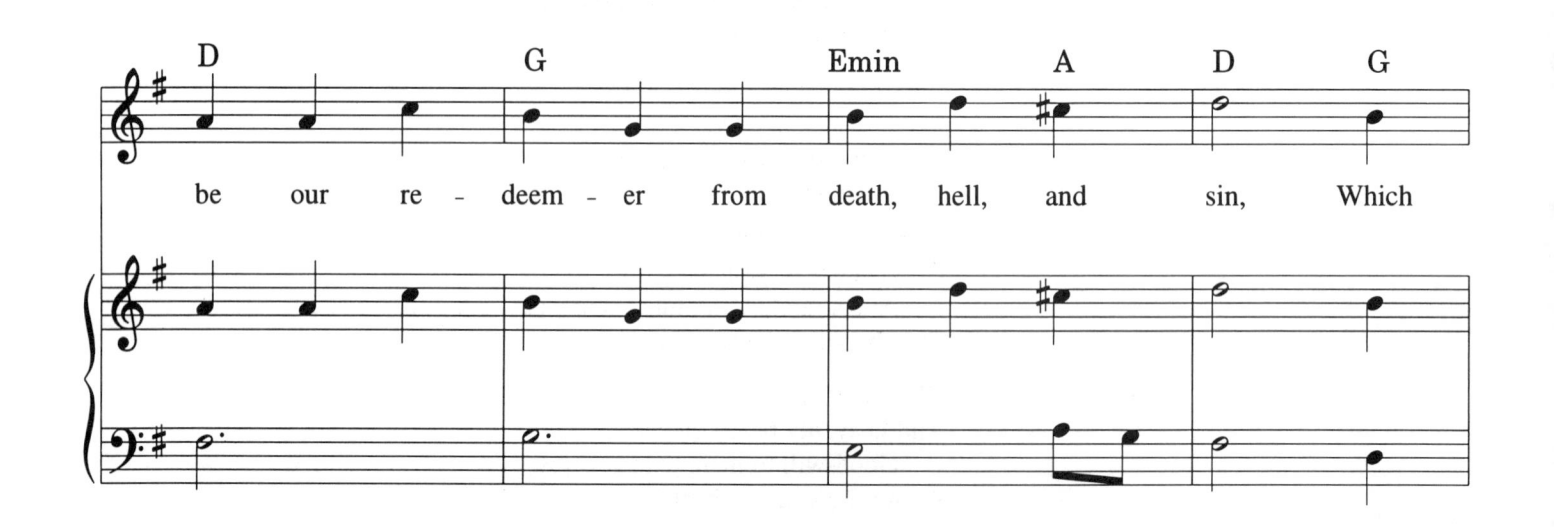

[♩. = 60]

A virgin un-spotted ye__ proph-et fore-told Should

bring forth a__ Sav-ior which__ now we be-hold; To

be our re-deem-er from death, hell, and sin, Which

154

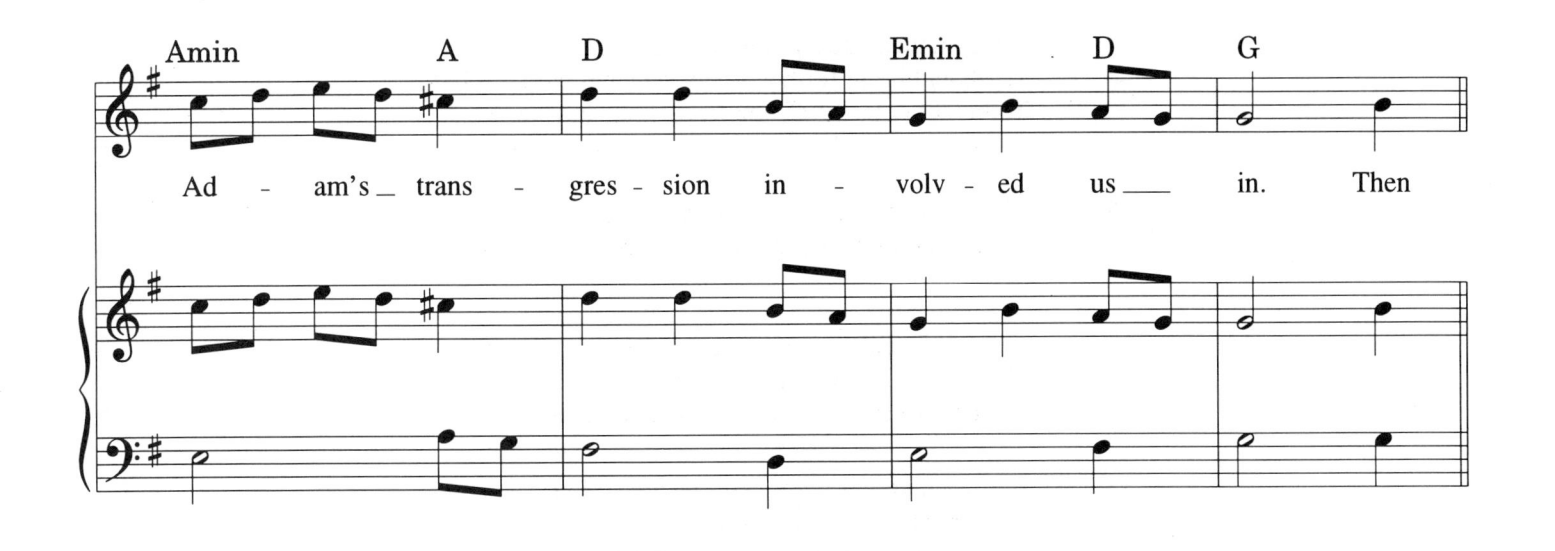

Adam's transgression involved us in. Then

Chorus

let us be merry, put sorrow away, Our Savior Christ Jesus was born on this day.

1) A virgin unspotted ye prophet foretold
    Should bring forth a Savior which now we behold;
   To be our redeemer from death, hell, and sin,
    Which Adam's transgression involved us in.

Chorus: Then let us be merry, put sorrow away,
    Our Savior Christ Jesus was born on this day.

2) To Bethlehem, city of David, they came,
    Both Joseph and Mary, to answer by name
   The census of taxes which all had to pay,
    For Caesar commanded it done on that day.

3) But when they had entered the city so fair,
    A number of people so mighty was there
   That Joseph and Mary, whose substance was small,
    Could find in the inn there no lodging at all.

4) Then were they constrained in a stable to lie,
    Where horses and oxen they used for to tie;
   Their lodging so simple they took it no scorn,
    But ere the next morning our Savior was born.

5) The King of all kings to this world being brought,
    Small store of fine linen to wrap him was sought;
   But when she had swaddled her young son for sleep,
    'Twas naught but a manger she laid Him to keep.

6) Then God sent an angel from heaven so high,
    To certain poor shepherds in fields where they lie;
   And bade them no longer in sorrow to stay,
    Because that our Savior was born on this day.

7) Then presently after the shepherds did spy
    Vast numbers of angels to stand in the sky;
   They joyfully talked and sweetly did sing,
    To God be all glory, our heavenly King.

8) To teach us humility all this was done,
    And learn we from thence haughty pride for to shun;
   A manger his cradle who came from above,
    The great God of mercy, of peace, and of love.

REDEMPTION

Unknown Asahel Benham, Sr.

[♩ = 100]

Hark! hark! glad tidings charm our ears, Angelic music fills the spheres; Earth spreads the sound with decent mirth, A God, a God is born _____ on earth. _____ A God is _____ born! The val-leys cry; A God is _____ born! the hills re-ply; The ev'-ning re-peats to won-der-ing morn, A God, a God on

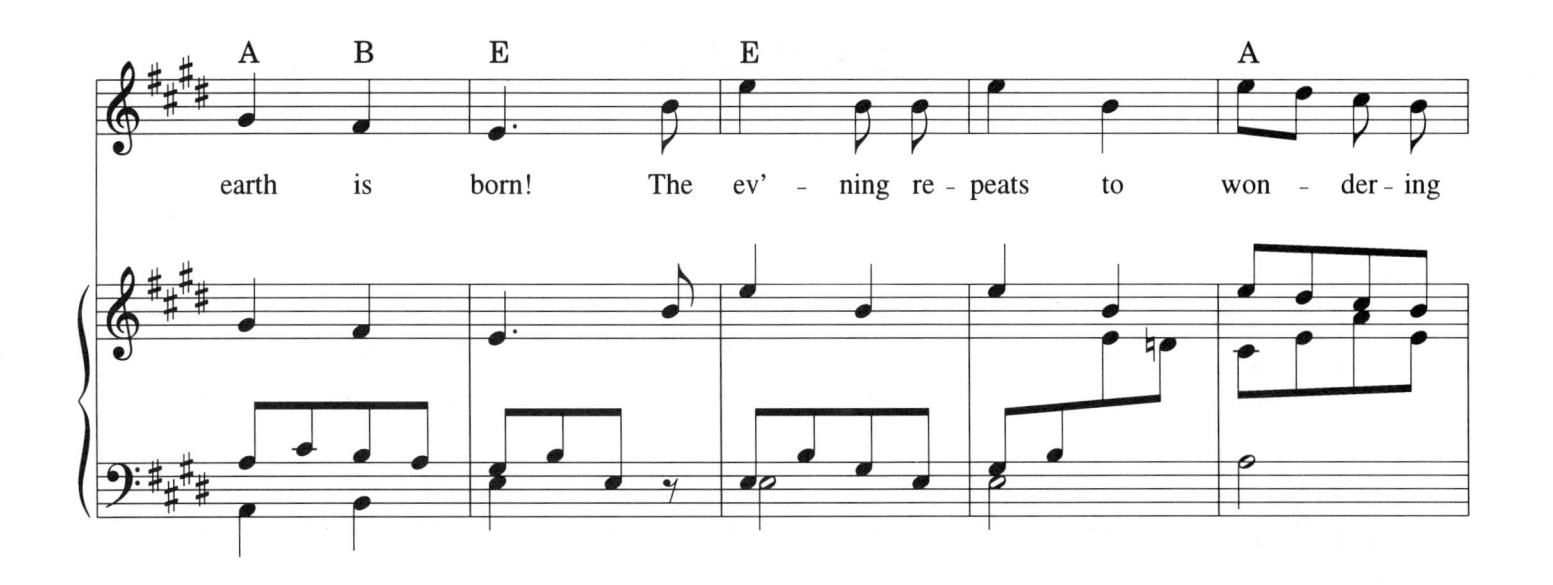

Hark! hark! glad tidings charm our ears,
Angelic music fills the spheres;
Earth spreads the sound with decent mirth,
A God, a God is born on earth!

A God is born! the valleys cry;
A God is born! the hills reply;
The ev'ning repeats to wondering morn,
A God, a God on earth is born!

REJOICE

Isaac Watts

Leonard P. Breedlove

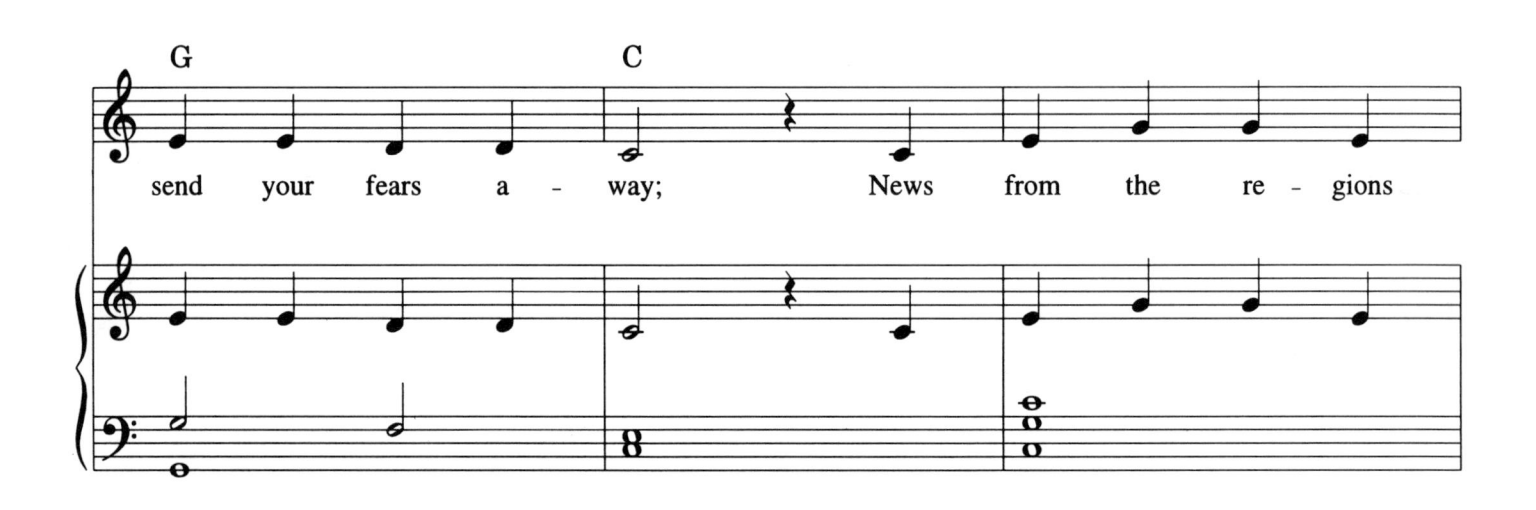

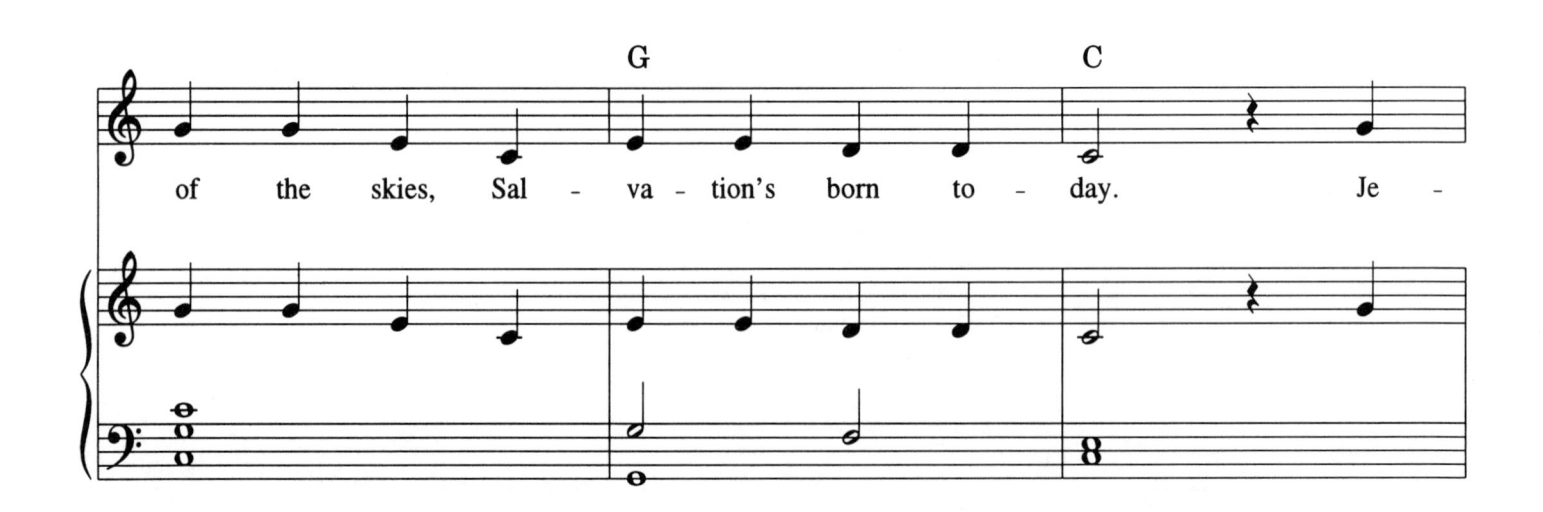

Shep-herds, re-joice, lift up your eyes, And send your fears a-way; News from the re-gions of the skies, Sal-va-tion's born to-day. Jesus, the God whom an-gels fear, Comes down to dwell with you, To-day he makes his en-trance here, But not as mon-archs do.

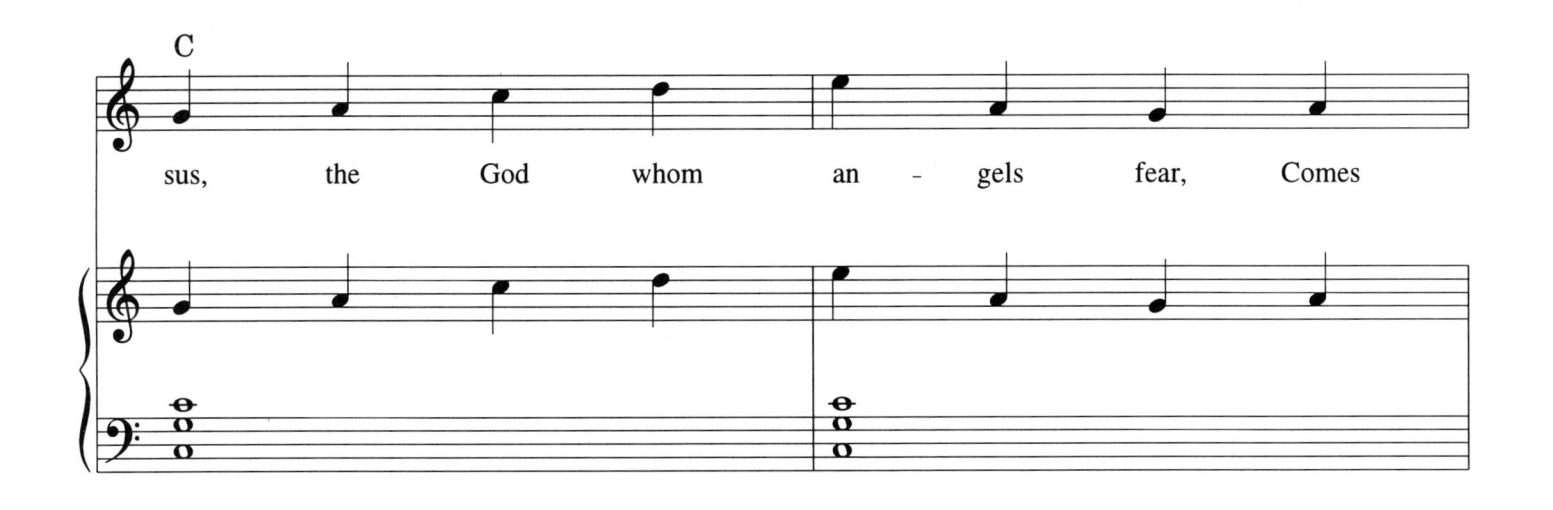

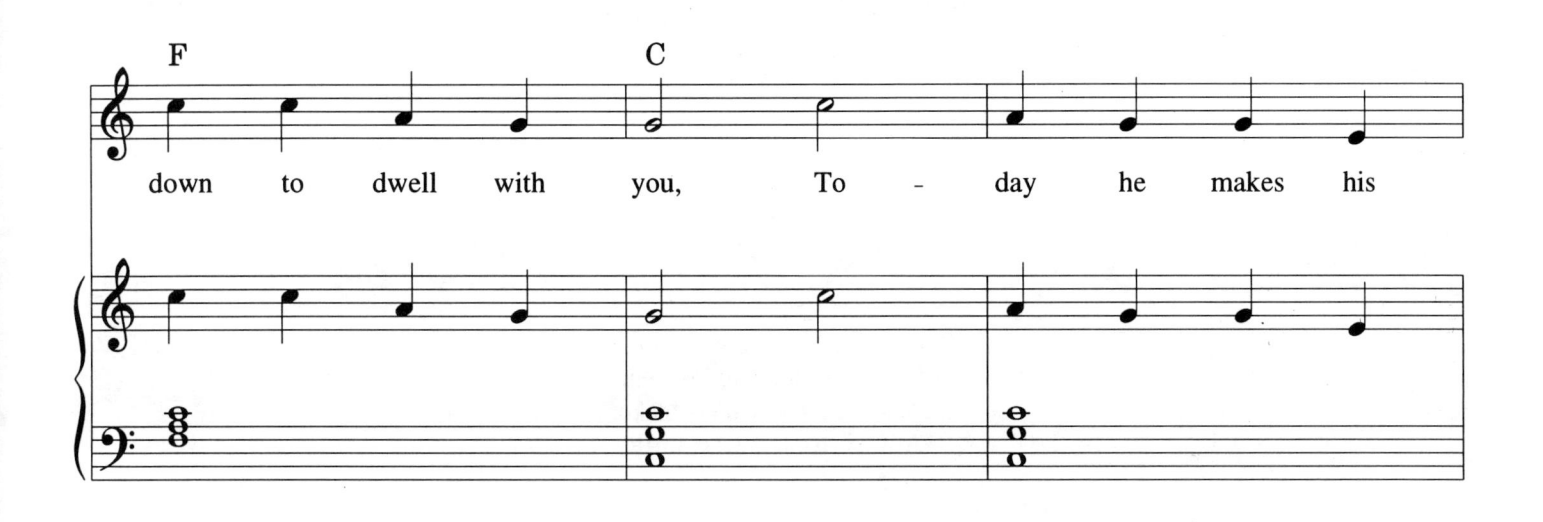

Shepherds, rejoice, lift up your eyes,
    And send your fears away;
News from the regions of the skies,
    Salvation's born today.

Jesus, the God whom angels fear,
    Comes down to dwell with you,
Today he makes His entrance here,
    But not as monarchs do.

No gold, nor purple swaddling bands,
    No royal shining things;
A manger for His cradle stands,
    And holds the King of kings.

Go, shepherds, where the infant lies,
    And see his humble throne;
With tears of joy in all your eyes,
    Go, shepherds, kiss the Son.

Thus Gabriel sang, and strait around,
    The heavenly armies throng,
They tune their harps to lofty sound,
    And thus conclude the song.

Glory to God that reigns above,
    Let peace surround the earth;
Mortals shall know their maker's love,
    At their Redeemer's birth.

Lord! and shall angels have their songs,
    And men no tunes to raise?
O may we lose these useless tongues
    When they forget to praise.

Glory to God that reigns above,
    That pities us forlorn;
We join to sing our Maker's love
    For there's a Savior born.

"The Mistletoe Seller," by Phiz. From *Illustrated London News,* Dec. 24, 1853.

SACRED DAY

Elizabeth Scott												William Tans'ur

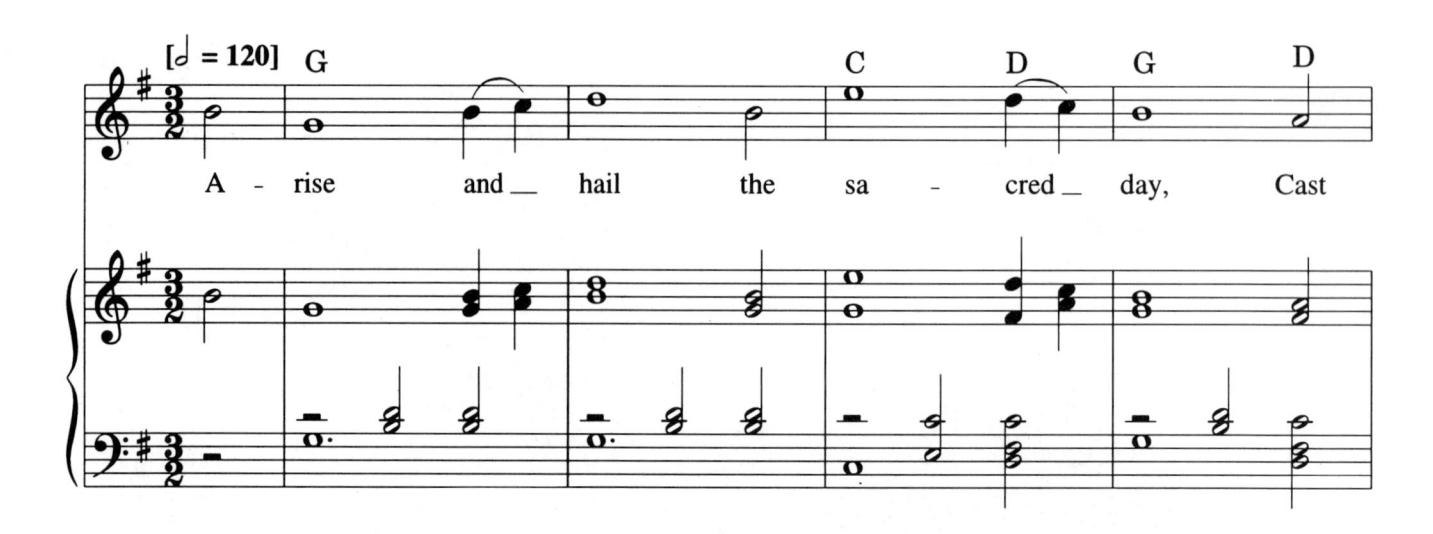

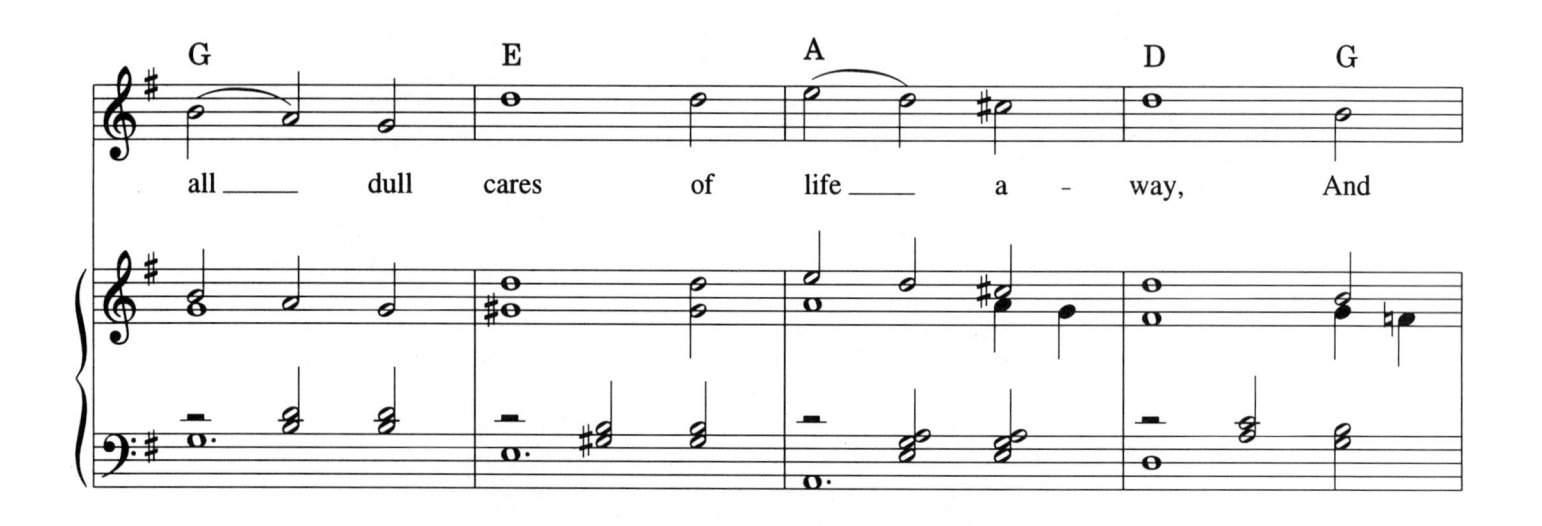

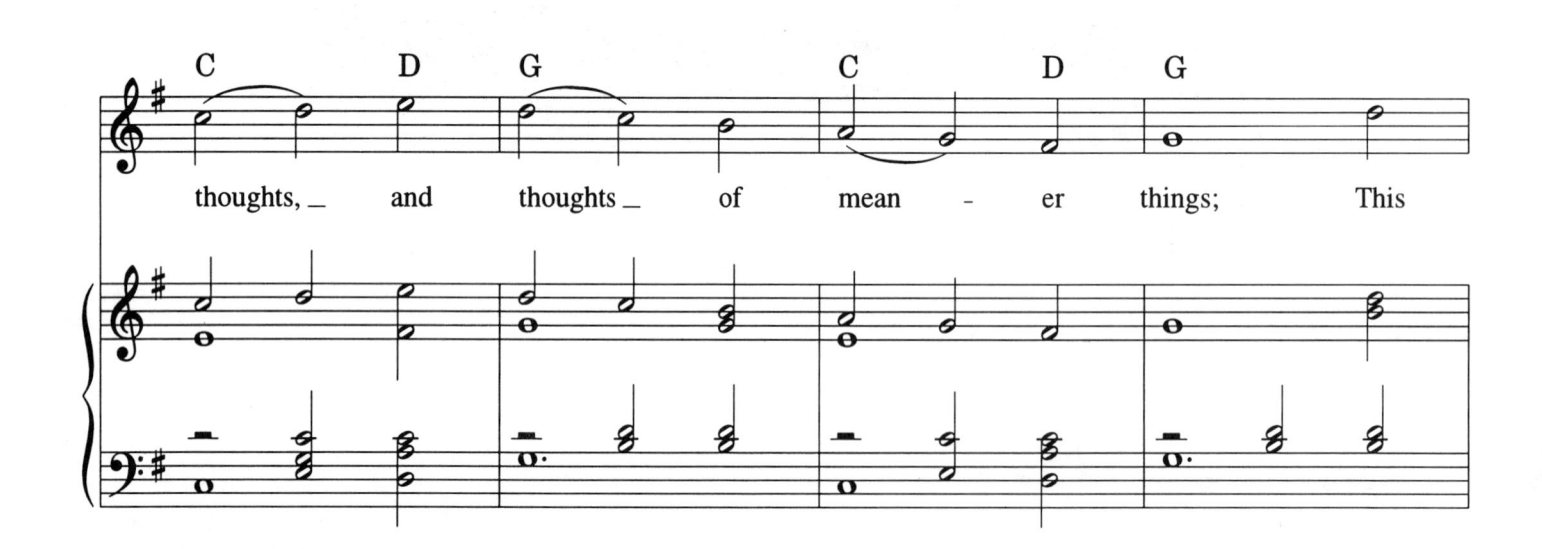

A-rise and hail the sa-cred day, Cast all dull cares of life a-way, And thoughts, and thoughts of mean-er things; This day, to __ cure thy __ dead - ly __ woes, The Son of right - eous - ness __ a - rose, With might - y heal - ing in his wings. __

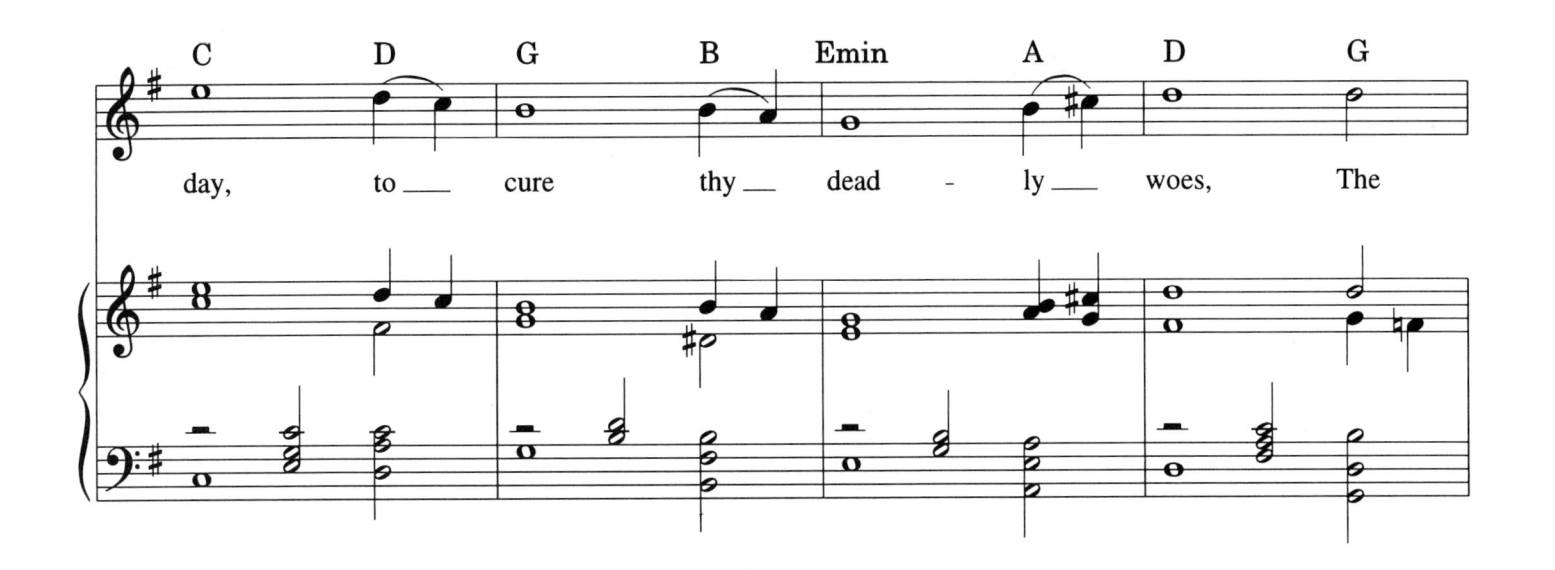

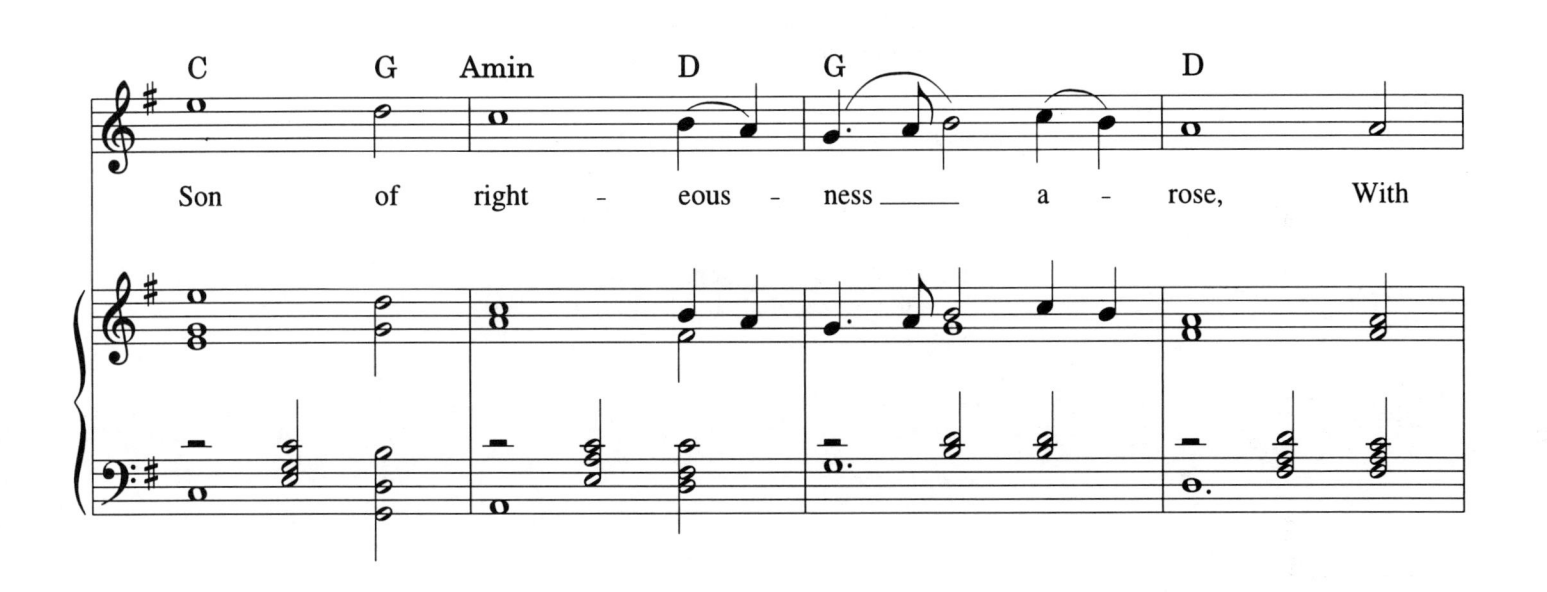

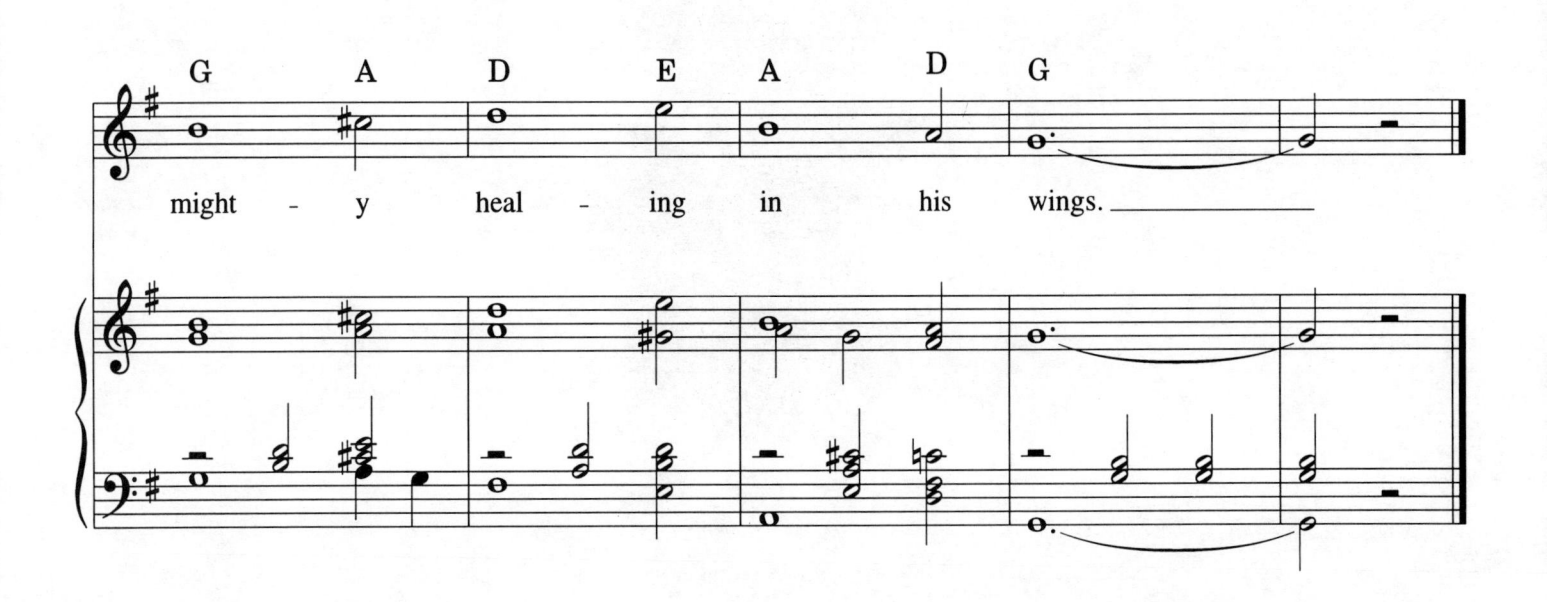

1) Arise and hail the sacred day,
   Cast all dull cares of life away,
      And thoughts, and thoughts of meaner things;
   This day, to cure thy deadly woes,
   The Son of righteousness arose,
      With mighty healing in his wings.

2) If angels, on that blessed morn,
   The Savior of the world was born,
      Poured forth, poured forth seraphic songs;
   Much more should we, of human race,
   Adore the wonders of his grace,
      To whom the mighty grace belongs.

3) How wonderful! How vast His love!
   Who left the shining realms above,
      Those happy, happy seats of rest;
   How much for lost mankind he bore!
   Their peace and pardon to restore,
      Can never rightly be expressed.

4) Whilst we adore his boundless grace,
   And pious mirth, and joy takes place
      Of sorrow, sorrow, grief and pain:
   Give glory to our God on high,
   And that among the general joy,
      Be peace and all goodwill to men.

SARK

Charles Wesley
Dr. Edward Miller

Hark, the herald angels sing Glory to the newborn King, Peace on earth and mercy mild; God and sinners reconciled, God and sinners reconciled.

1) Hark, the herald angels sing
   Glory to the new-born King,
   Peace on earth and mercy mild;
   God and sinners reconciled.

2) Christ, by highest heaven adored,
   Christ, the everlasting Lord,
   Late in time behold Him come,
   Offspring of a virgin's womb.

3) Veiled in flesh the Godhead see;
   Hail th'incarnate Deity!
   Pleased as man with men t'appear,
   Jesus our Immanuel here.

4) Hail the heaven-born Prince of Peace,
   Hail the Sun of Righteousness!
   Light and life to all he brings,
   Risen with healing in his wings.

5) Mild he lays his glory by,
   Born that man no more may die;
   Born to raise the sons of earth,
   Born to give them second birth.

6) Come, Desire of Nations, come,
   Fix in us thy humble home;
   Rise, the woman's conquering seed,
   Bruise in us the serpent's head.

7) Adam's likeness now efface,
   Stamp thine image in its place:
   Second Adam from above,
   Reinstate us in thy love.

8) Now ye saints, lift up your eyes!
   Now to glory see him rise,
   In long triumph, up the sky,
   Up to waiting worlds on high.

9) Praise him, all ye heavenly choirs!
   Praise, and sweep your golden lyres!
   Shout, O earth, in rapt'rous song,
   Let the strains be sweet and strong!

"The Watch on Christmas-Eve," by Thomas Nast. From *Harper's Weekly*, Jan. 1, 1876.

SHINING STAR

E.B. Smith E. B. Smith

A star shone in the heavens That special morn, Above the place where Jesus, The Lord, was born. O holy, holy Jesus, O

1) A star shone in the heavens
    That special morn,
   Above the place where Jesus,
    The Lord, was born.

Chorus: O holy, holy Jesus,
    O blessed, blessed Savior,
    O mighty, mighty Son of God,
    Who came to save from sin.

2) The wise men saw its brightness,
    And came from far;
   They found the way to Jesus,
    Led by the star.

3) Oh, may that star of beauty
    Still point the way,
   To lead us all to Jesus,
    Through every day.

SING ALLELUIA

Charles H. Gabriel Charles H. Gabriel

[♩. = 60]

Come, let us sing a cheerful song, Let each one join his voice; Let ev'ry heart today be glad, And ev'ry soul rejoice; For 'tis the day that Christ was born, And brought good will to

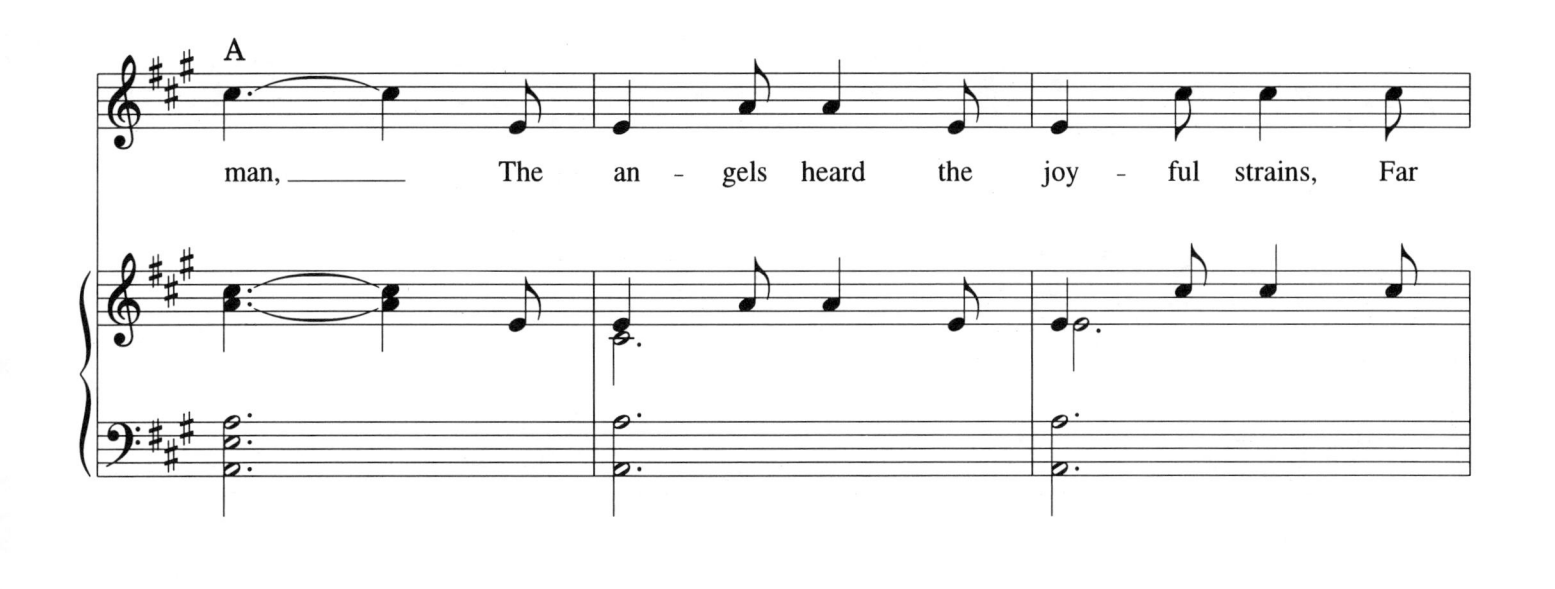

man,____ The an-gels heard the joy-ful strains, Far out of Beth-le-hem;____ The an-gels sang____ the wel-come news____ Up-on that bless-ed morn,____ In

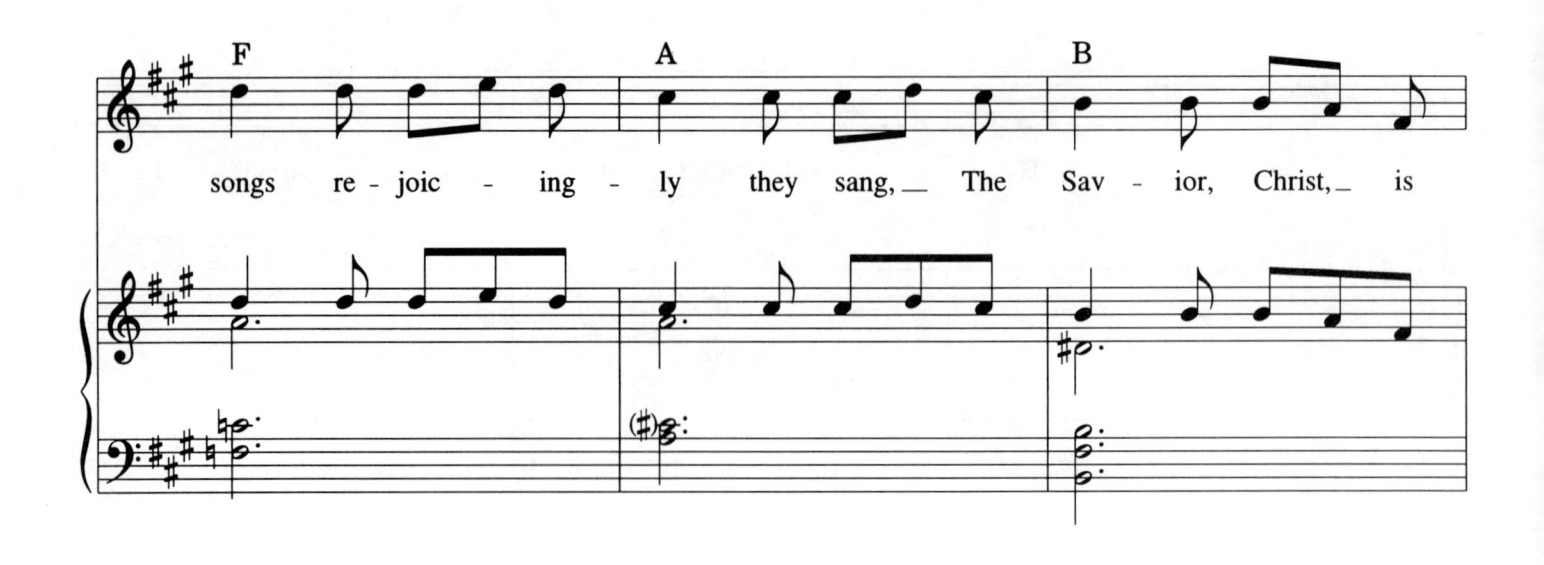

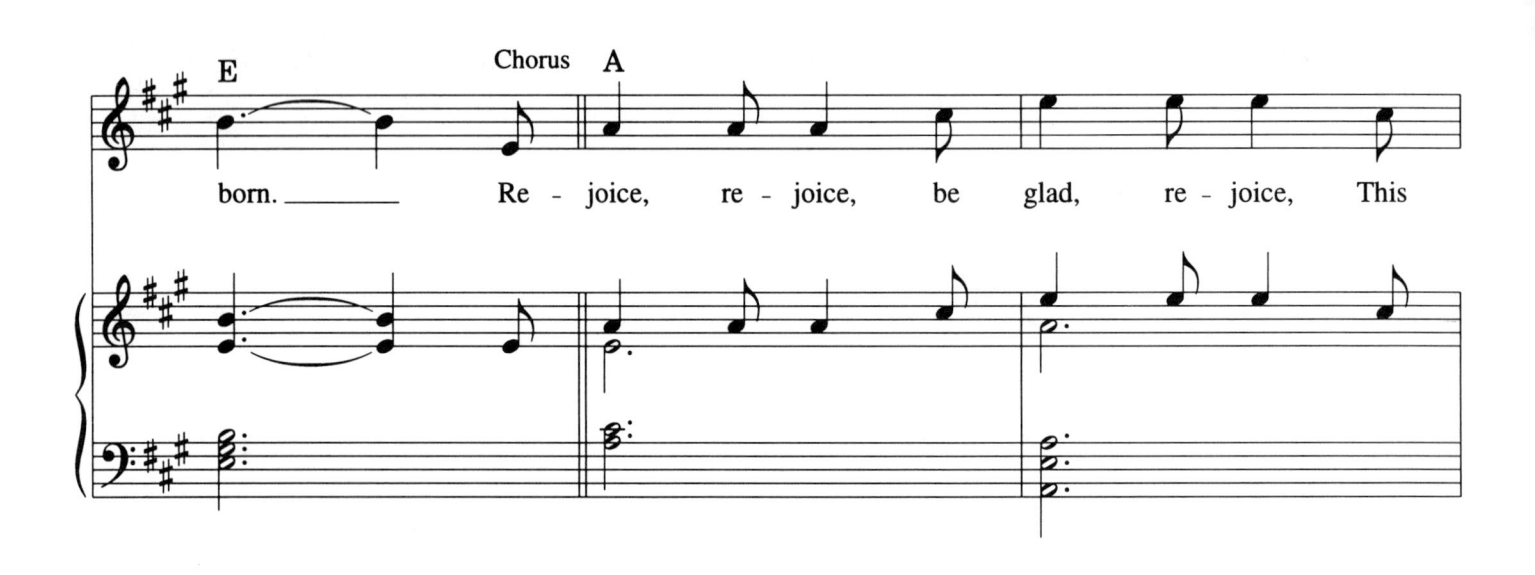

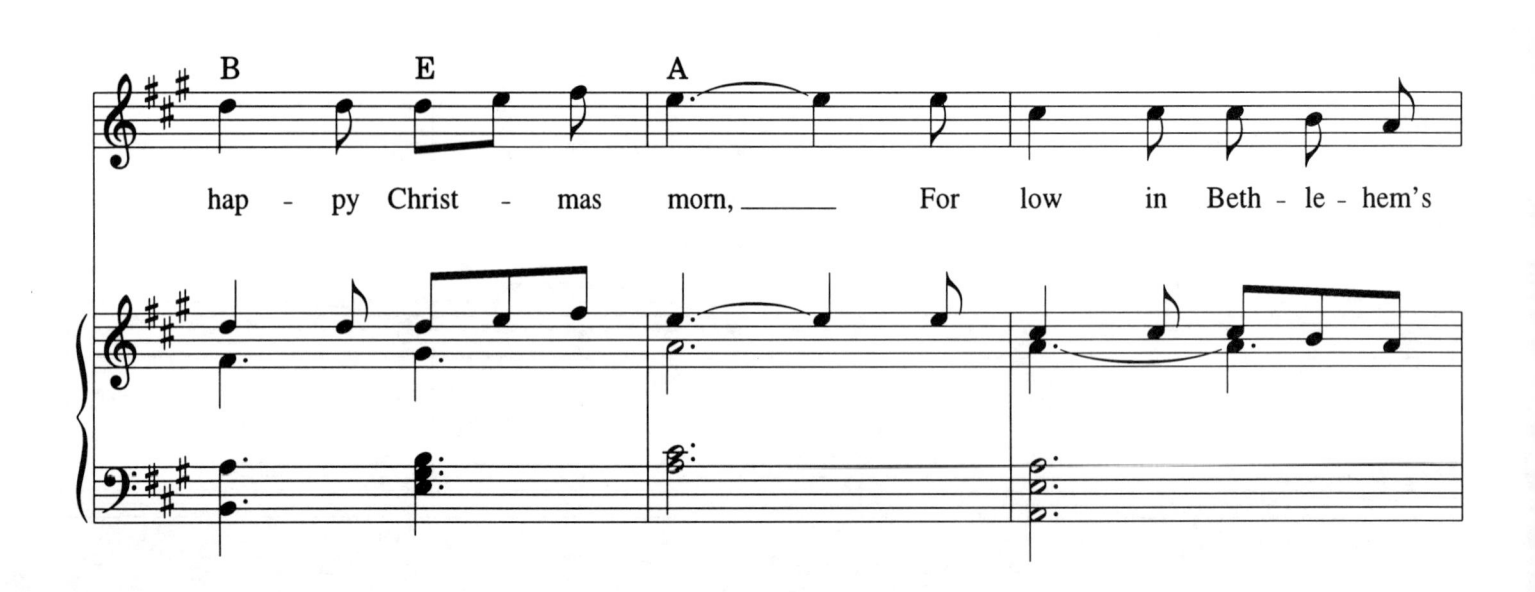

songs re-joic-ing-ly they sang, The Sav-ior, Christ, is born. Re-joice, re-joice, be glad, re-joice, This hap-py Christ-mas morn, For low in Beth-le-hem's stall to-day, A Sav-ior, Christ, is born.

Come, let us sing a cheerful song,
    Let each one join his voice;
Let ev'ry heart today be glad,
    And ev'ry soul rejoice;
For 'tis the day that Christ was born,
    And brought good will to man,
The angels heard the joyful strains,
    Far out of Bethlehem;
The angels sang the welcome news
    Upon that blessed morn,
In songs rejoicingly they sang,
    "The Savior, Christ, is born."

Chorus: Rejoice, rejoice, be glad, rejoice,
    This happy Christmas morn,
For low in Bethlehem's stall today,
    A Savior, Christ, is born.

Today in Bethlehem's stall is born
    A Savior, Christ the Lord;
"Fear not, to thee I bring great joy;"
    From Heaven, with sweet accord;
To God the glory; peace on earth;
    Goodwill to all of man;
Reechoed through the lofty sky,
    'Twas God's eternal plan.
He came to set the sinner free,
    Salvation to obtain,
For all the souls that will but come
    And wash away their stain.

SOMERSETT

Isaac Watts
Samuel Holyoke

The King of glory sends his son To make his entrance on the earth, Behold the midnight bright as noon, And heav'nly hosts declare his birth! About the young Re-deem-er's head What won-ders and what glo-ries meet! An un-known star a-rose, and led The east-ern sag-es to his feet.

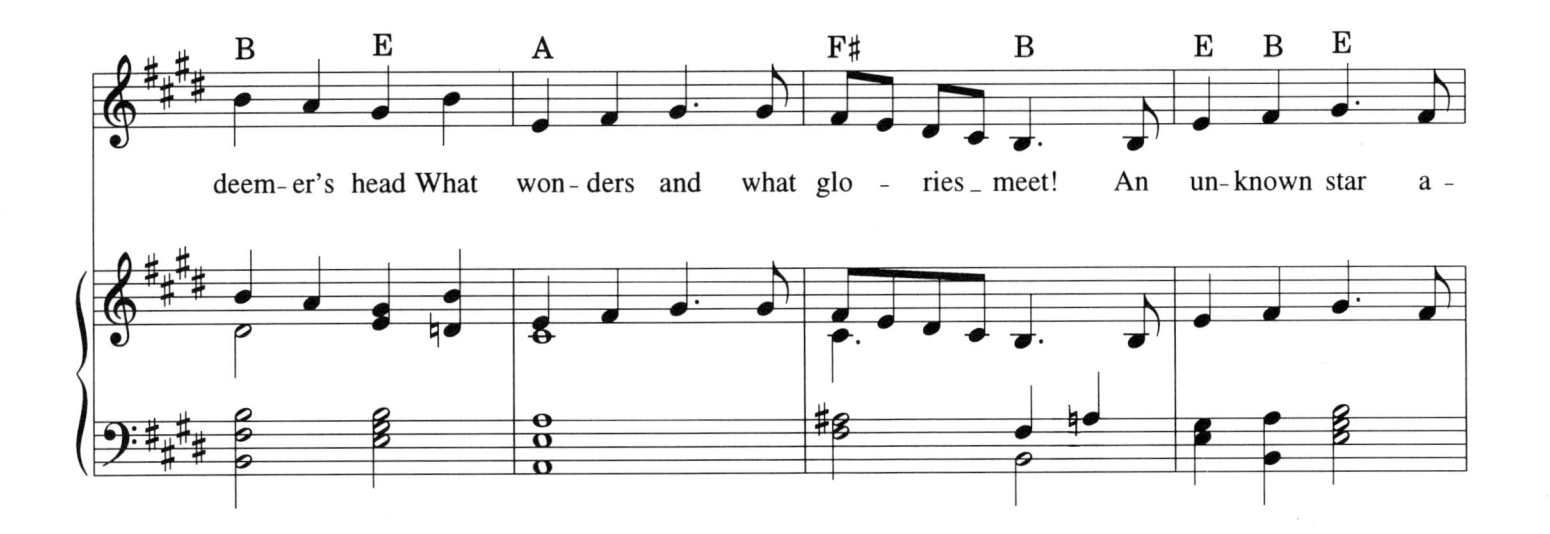

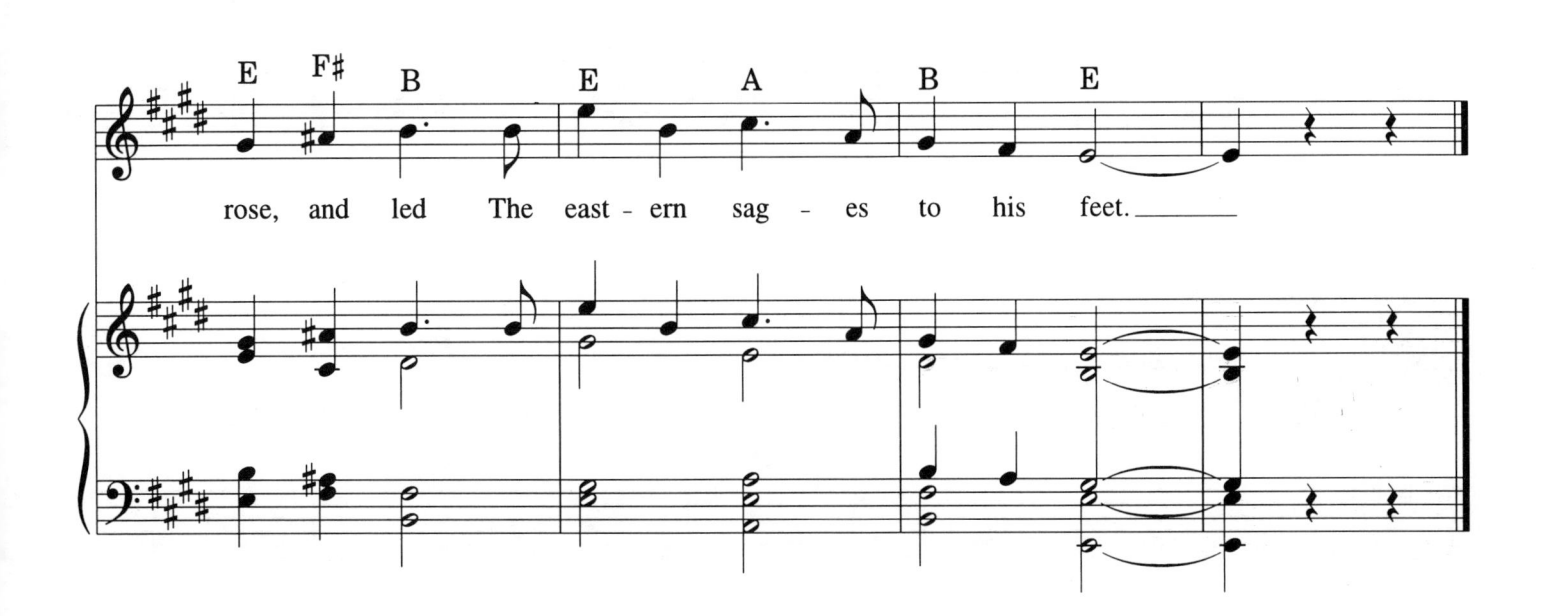

The King of Glory sends his son
To make his entrance on the earth,
Behold the midnight bright as noon,
And heav'nly hosts declare his birth!

About the young Redeemer's head
What wonders and what glories meet!
An unknown star arose, and led
The eastern sages to his feet.

Simeon and Anna both conspire
The infant Saviour to proclaim;
Inward they felt the sacred fire,
And blessed the babe, and owned his name.

Let Jews and Greeks blaspheme aloud,
And treat the holy child with scorn;
Our souls adore th'eternal God
Who condescended to be born.

STAR

Reginald Heber
Unknown

[♩ = 75]

Hail the blest morn! — see the great Mediator

Down from the regions of glory descend;

Shepherds, — go worship the Babe in the manger,

Lo! for His guard, the bright angels attend.

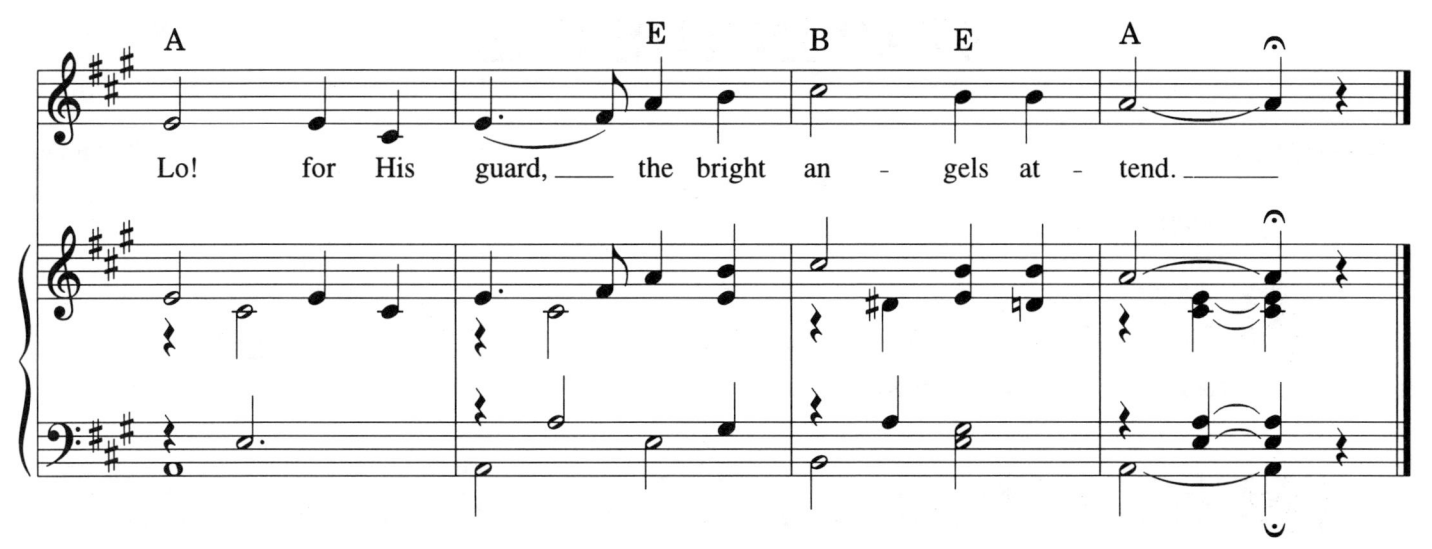

1) Hail the blest morn! see the great Mediator
  Down from the regions of glory descend;
Shepherds, go worship the Babe in the manger,
  Lo! for His guard, the bright angels attend.

Chorus: *May be used as a chorus or an additional verse:*

  Brightest and best of the sons of the morning,
    Dawn on our darkness and lend us thine aid;
  Star in the east, the horizon adorning,
    Guide where our infant Redeemer was laid.

2) Cold on His cradle the dew drops are shining,
  Low lies His bed with the beasts of the stall;
Angels adore Him, in slumbers reclining,
  Wise men and shepherds before Him do fall.

3) Say, shall we yield Him, in costly devotion,
  Odours of Eden and offerings divine;
Gems from the mountains, and pearls from the ocean,
  Myrrh from the forest and gold from the mine.

4) Vainly we offer each ample oblation,
  Vainly with gold we His favour secure;
Richer by far is the heart's adoration,
  Dearer to God are the prayers of the poor.

5) Low at His feet we in humble prostration
  Lose all our sorrow and trouble and strife;
There we receive His divine consolation,
  Flowing afresh from the fountain of life.

6) He is our friend in the midst of temptation,
  Faithful supporter whose love cannot fail;
Rock of our refuge, and hope of salvation,
  Light to direct us through death's gloomy vale.

7) Star of the morning, thy brightness, declining,
  Shortly must fade when the sun doth arise;
Beaming refulgent, his glory eternal
  Shines on the children of love in the skies.

STAR IN THE EAST

Reginald Heber / Unknown

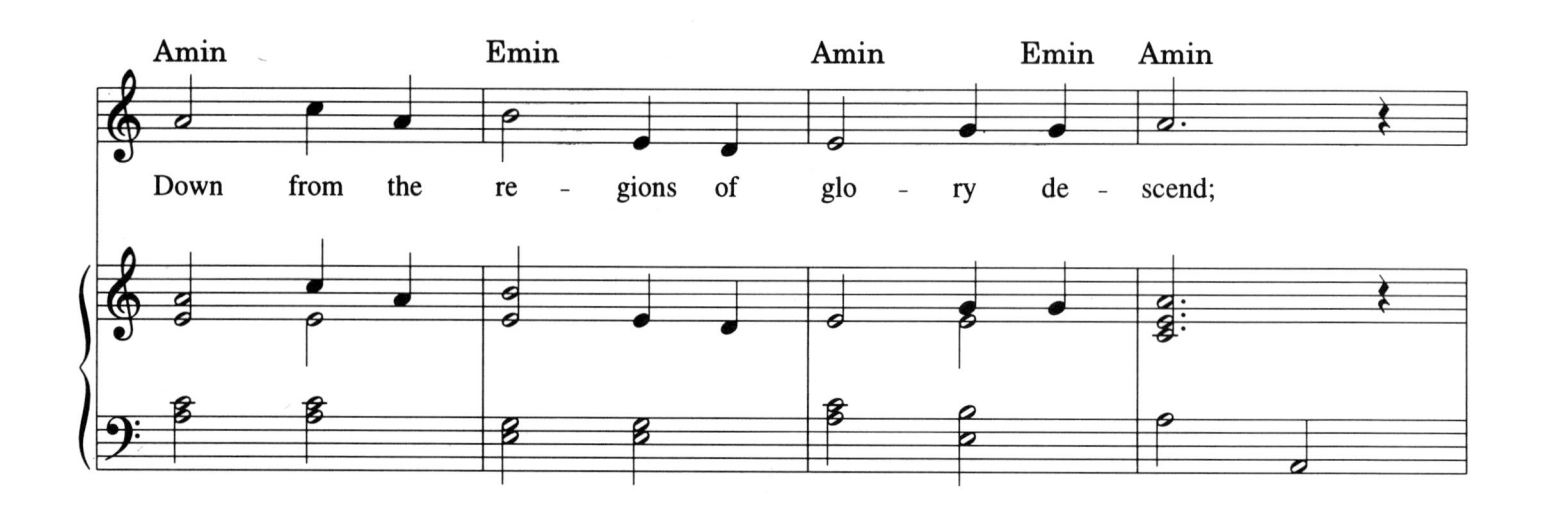

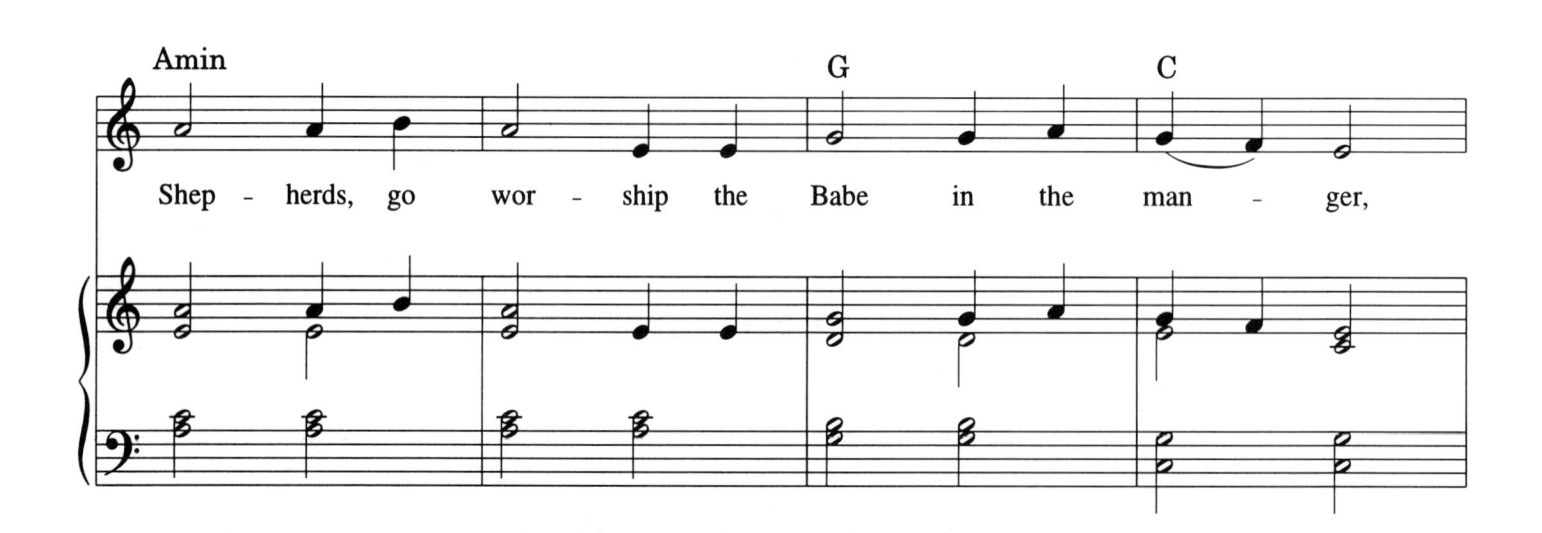

[♩ = 80]

Hail the blest morn! see the great Mediator

Down from the regions of glory descend;

Shepherds, go worship the Babe in the manger,

Lo! for His guard, the bright an-gels at-tend.

Chorus

Bright-est and best of the sons of the morn-ing,

Dawn on our dark-ness and lend us thine aid;

Star in the east, the ho-ri-zon a-dorn-ing,

181

Guide where our in-fant Re-deem-er was laid.

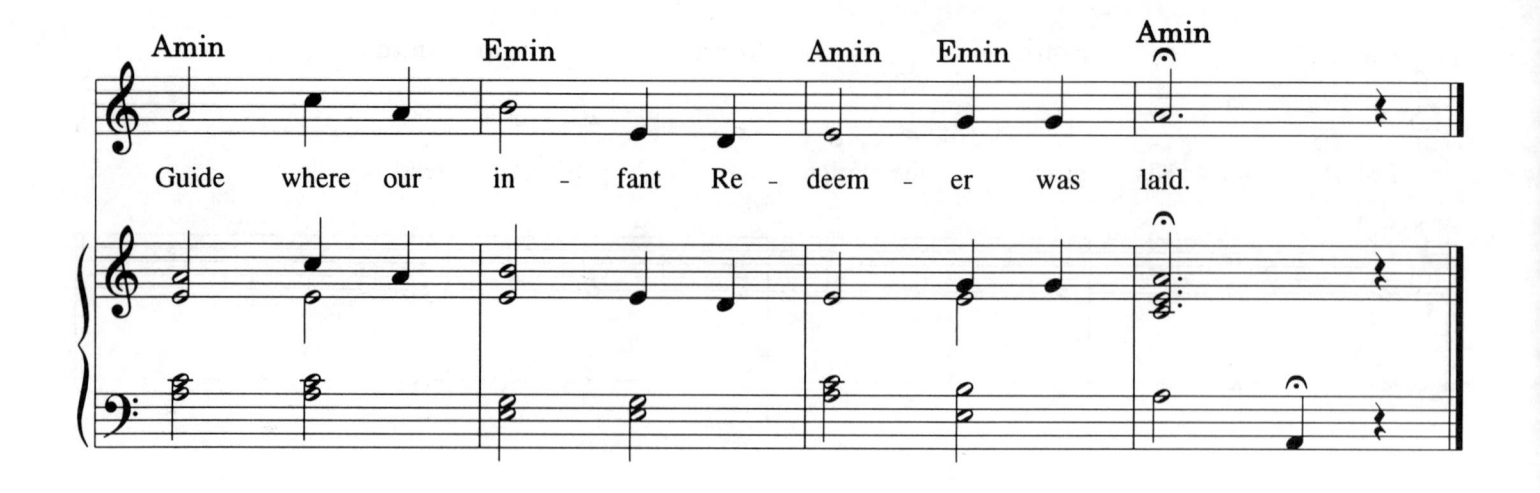

1) Hail the blest morn! see the great Mediator
    Down from the regions of glory descend;
Shepherds, go worship the Babe in the manger,
    Lo! for his guard, the bright angels attend.

Chorus: Brightest and best of the sons of the morning,
    Dawn on our darkness and lend us thine aid;
Star in the east, the horizon adorning,
    Guide where our infant Redeemer was laid.

2) Cold on his cradle the dew drops are shining,
    Low lies his bed with the beasts of the stall;
Angels adore Him, in slumbers reclining,
    Wise men and shepherds before Him do fall.

3) Say, shall we yield Him, in costly devotion,
    Odors of Eden and offerings divine;
Gems from the mountains, and pearls from the ocean,
    Myrrh from the forest and gold from the mine.

4) Vainly we offer each ample oblation,
    Vainly with gold we His favor secure;
Richer by far is the heart's adoration,
    Dearer to God are the prayers of the poor.

5) Low at His feet we in humble prostration
    Lose all our sorrow and trouble and strife;
There we receive His divine consolation,
    Flowing afresh from the fountain of life.

6) He is our friend in the midst of temptation,
    Faithful suporter whose love cannot fail;
Rock of our refuge, and hope of salvation,
    Light to direct us through death's gloomy vale.

7) Star of the morning, thy brightness, declining,
    Shortly must fade when the sun doth arise;
Beaming refulgent, his glory eternal
    Shines on the children of love in the skies.

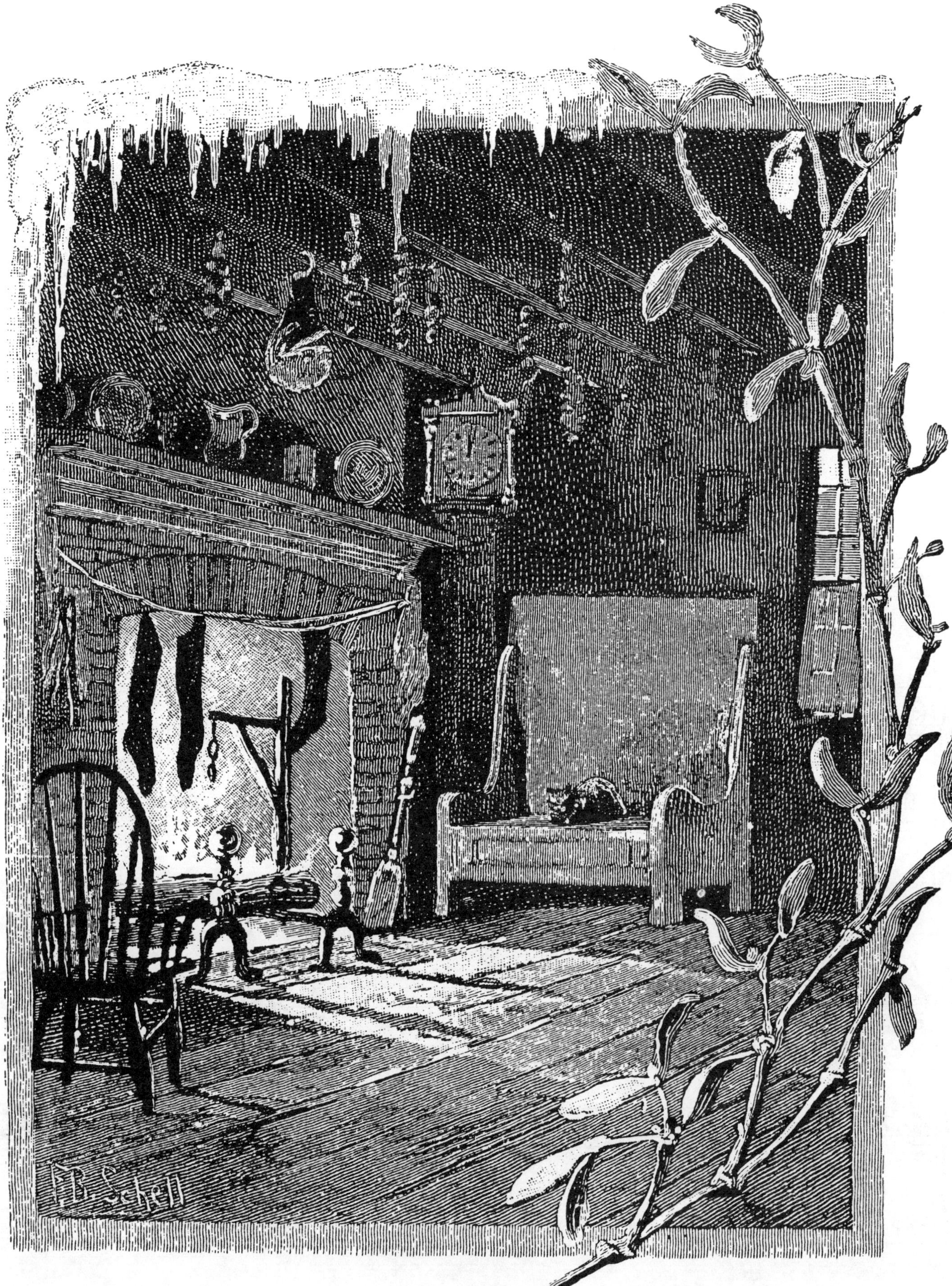
F.B. Schell

WONDER

Munson Unknown

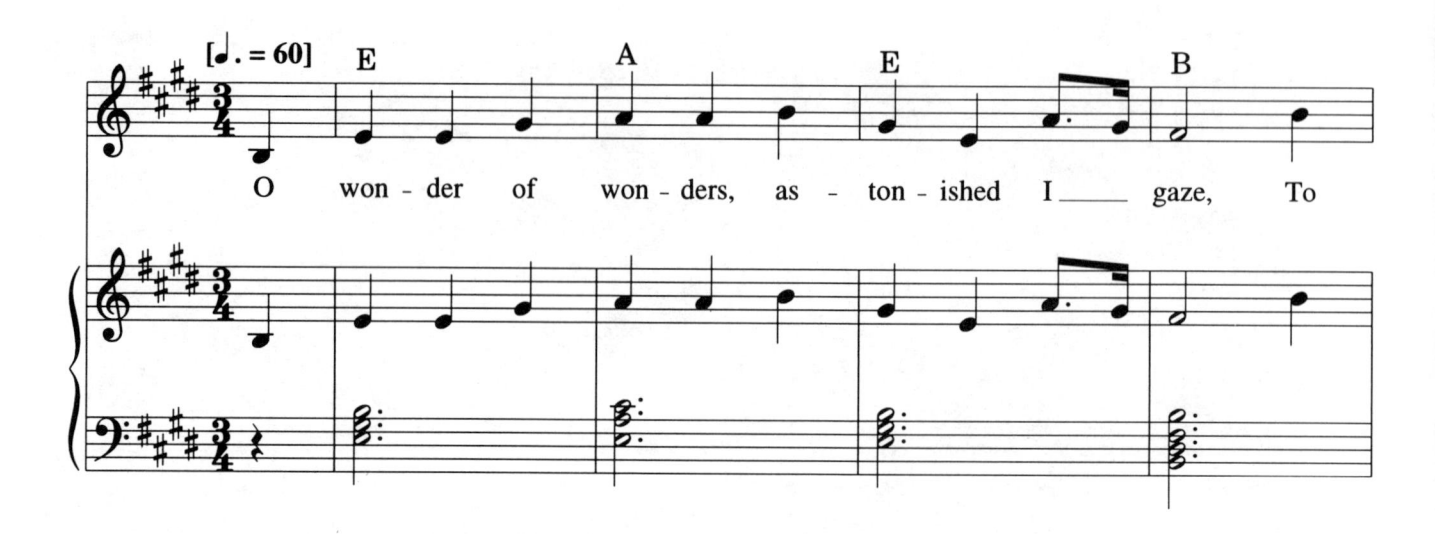

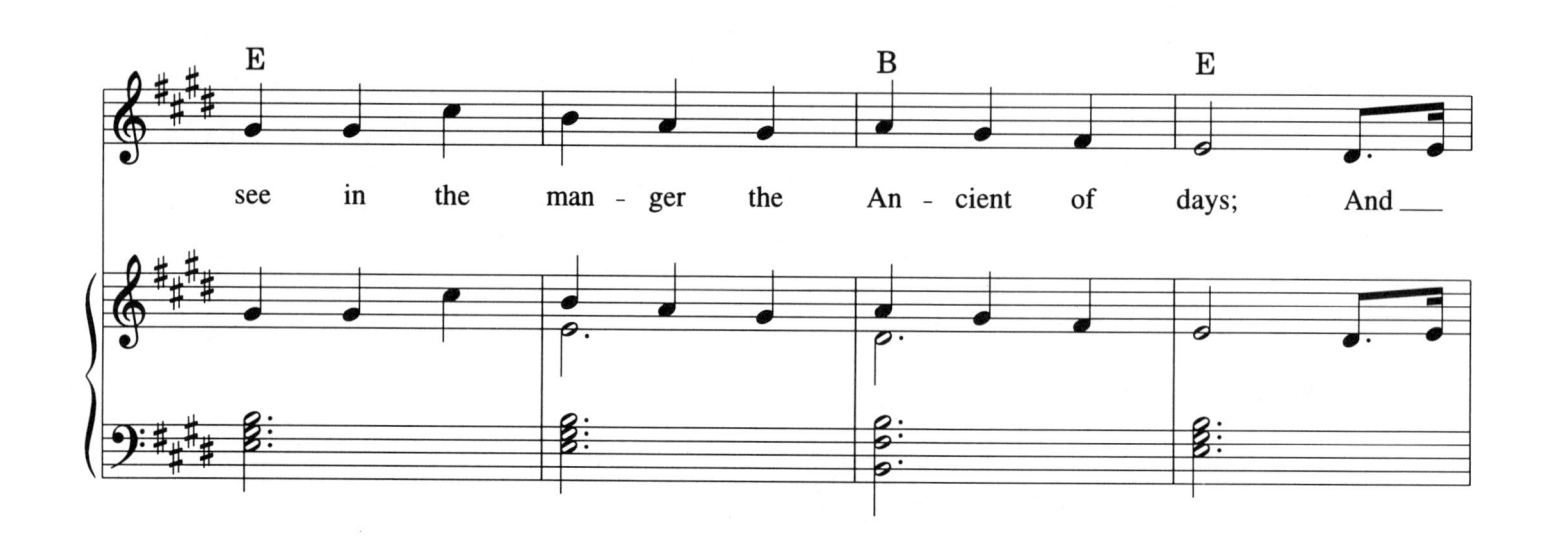

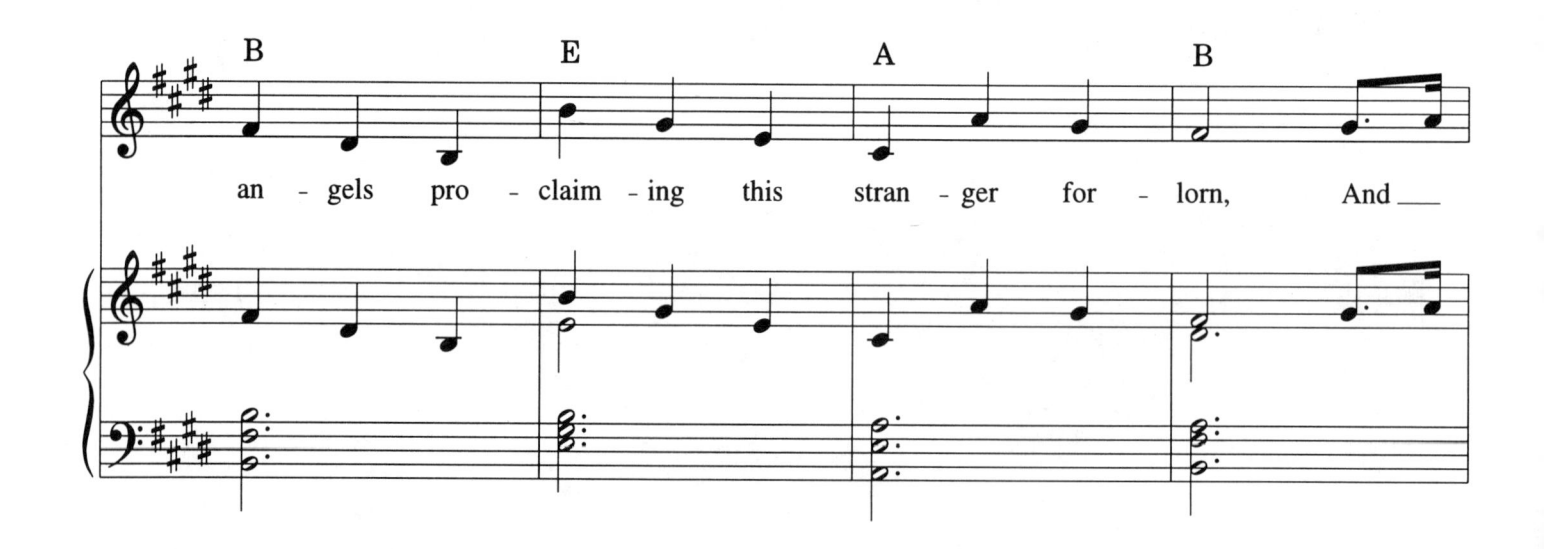

[♩. = 60]

O won-der of won-ders, as-ton-ished I gaze, To see in the man-ger the An-cient of days; And an-gels pro-claim-ing this stran-ger for-lorn, And

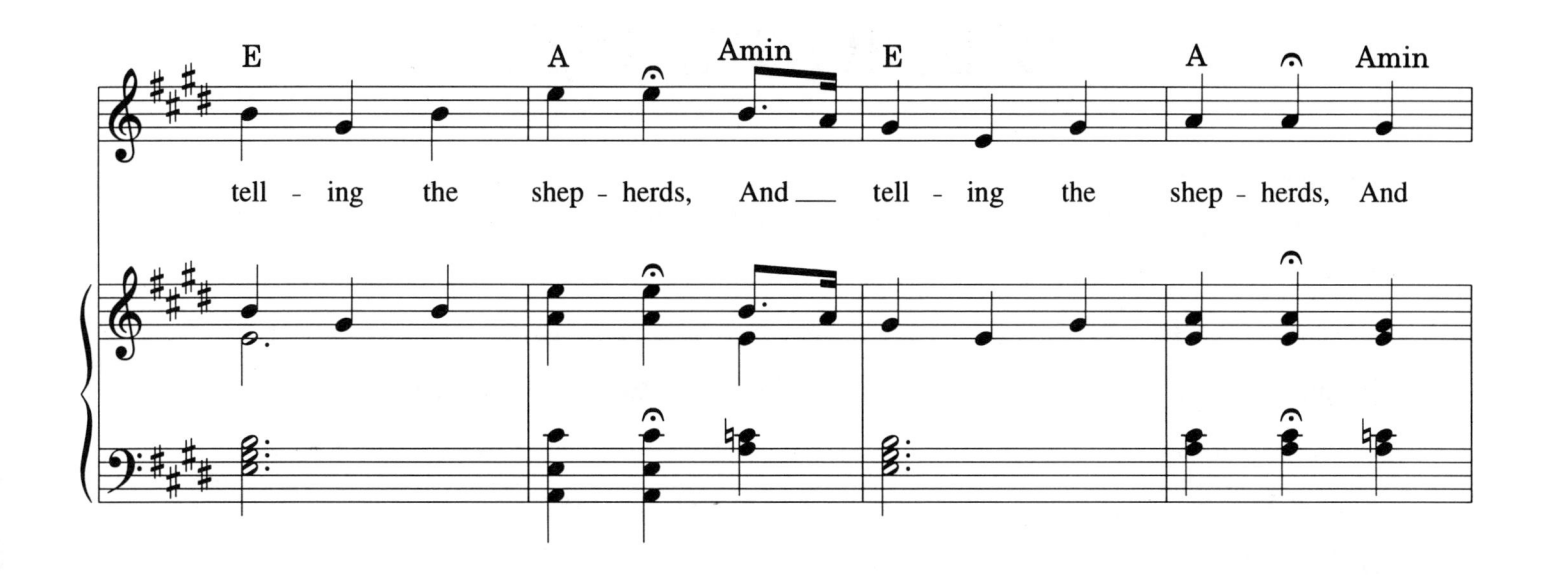

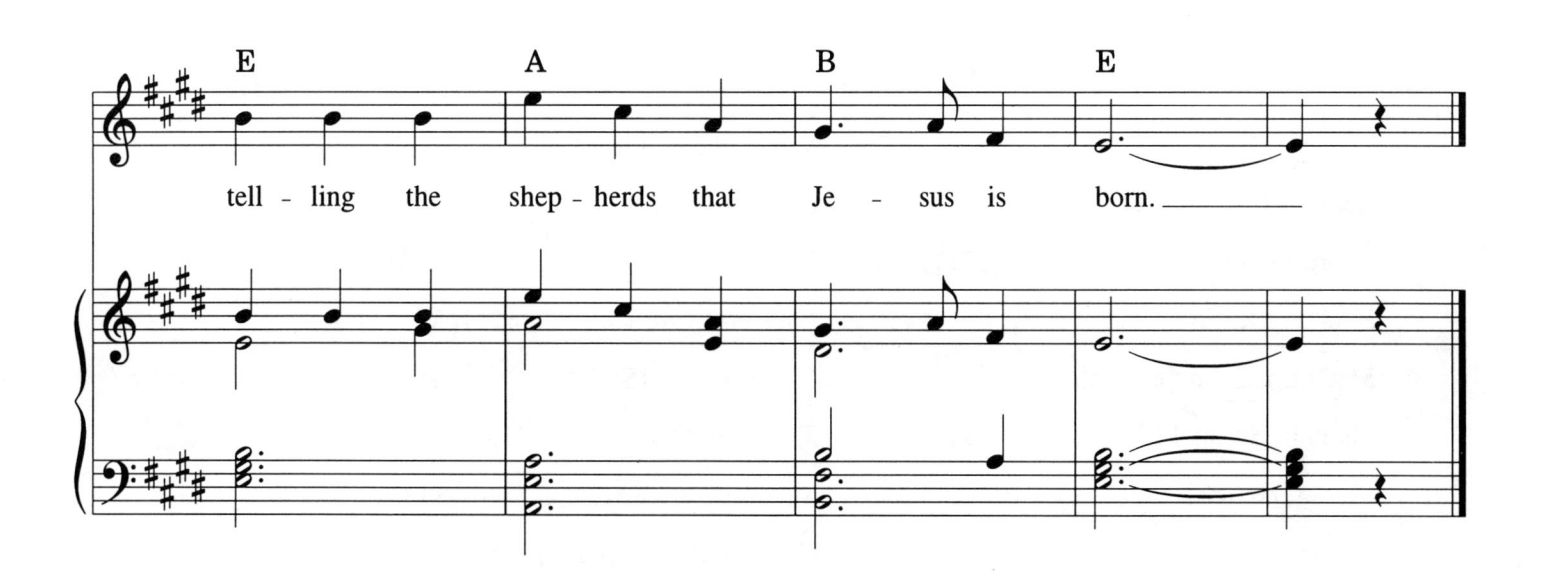

O wonder of wonders, astonished I gaze,
To see in the manger the Ancient of days;
And angels proclaiming this stranger forlorn,
And telling the shepherds that Jesus is born.

BIBLIOGRAPHY

Billings, William . . . . *Psalm Singer's Amusement,* 1781
                                                  Singing Master's Assistant, 1778

Brown, Bartholomew . . . . *Bridgewater Collection,* 1802

Davisson, Ananias . . . . *Kentucky Harmony,* 1816

Flagg, Josiah . . . . *Collection of the Best Psalm Tunes,* 1764

Gabriel, Charles H. *Sunday School Songs,* 1878

Hauser, William, M.D. . . . . *Hesperian Harp,* 1857

Holden, Oliver . . . . *Union Harmony,* 1796

Holyoke, Samuel A. . . . . *Columbian Repository,* 1802

Jackson, John B. . . . . *Knoxville Harmony,* 1840

Kimball, Jacob . . . . *Rural Harmony,* 1793

Law, Andrew . . . . *Art of Singing, Part II,* 1794
                                                  Christian Harmony, 1794
                                                  Select Harmony, 1779

Leavitt, Joshua . . . . *Christian Lyre,* 1833

Lyon, James . . . . *Urania,* 1761

Madan, Martin . . . . *Lock Hospital Collection,* 1769

McCurry, John G. . . . . *Social Harp,* 1855

Metcalf, Samuel L. *Kentucky Harmonist,* 1818

Moore, Henry E. . . . . *New Hampshire Collection,* 1833

Richards, George . . . . *Collection of Hymns,* 1801

Swan, W.H. . . . . *Harp of Columbia,* 1848

Tans'ur, William. . . . . *New Harmony of Sion,* 1760

Tate, Nahum, and Nicholas Brady . . . . *New Version of the English Metrical Psalter,* 1699

Templi Carmina, 1821

Templi Carmina, 1824

Vella, Bertha F. . . . . *Song and Study,* 1894

Walker, William . . . . *Southern Harmony,* 1854

Webb, George J. . . . . *Massachusetts Collection,* 1840

White, Benjamin F. *Sacred Harp,* 1844

Williams, Aaron . . . . *American Harmony,* 1774
                                                  Universal Psalmist, 1768

INDEX OF FIRST LINES

	Page
A star shone in the heavens	170
A virgin unspotted	112, 154
Arise and hail the sacred day	164
As I sat on a sunny bank	120
As shepherds in Jewry	70
Awake, awake, arise	88
Awake, awake the sacred song	146
Behold, the grace appears	32
Behold, the great Creator	90
Behold the lofty sky	136
Child Jesus came from heavenly height	44
Christ was born in Bethlehem	12
Come, let us sing a cheerful song	100, 172
Glory to God on high	152
Hail, hail, all glorious Lamb of God	115, 128
Hail the blest morn	178, 180
Hark! hark! glad tidings	157
Hark! hark! what news	80, 126
Hark the glad sound!	56, 82
Hark, the herald angels	58, 167
High let us swell	64
It came upon the midnight clear	150
Joy to the world	106, 122
Lift up your heads	96, 104
List to the beautiful story	24
Lo, what a glorious sight	42, 68
Methinks I see	38, 102
Mortals, awake, with angels	40
No war or battle's sound	60
O how charming are	49
O little town of Bethlehem	46, 52
O wonder of wonders	184
Ring out the glad tidings	86
Shepherds, rejoice, lift up your eyes	34, 160
Th' Almighty spake	73, 92
The heavens declare thy glory	54
The King of glory sends	176
The Lord is come	18
Unto us a child is born	138
Wake, O my soul	142
We come with joyful song	110
While shepherds watched their flocks	14, 27
Ye nations all, on you I call	132

INDEX OF AUTHORS, COMPOSERS, AND COMPILERS

	Page
Andersen, H.C. (1805-1875)	44
Arnold, Dr. Samuel (1740-1802)	122
Arnold, William (1768-1832)	56
Bayley, Daniel (1725-1799)	7, 8, 9
Belknap, Jeremy (fl. c. 1800)	6
Benham, Asahel, Sr. (1757-1815)	157
Billings, William (1746-1800)	5, 7, 8, 27, 38, 70, 102, 112
Breedlove, Leonard P. (fl. mid-19th c.)	10, 160
Brooks, Phillips (1835-1893)	46, 52
Brown, Bartholomew (1772-1854)	6, 10
Burney, Charles (1726-1814)	96
Davisson, Ananias (1780-1857)	10
Denson, James (c. 1820-after 1865)	49
Doddridge, Philip (1702-1751)	7, 56, 64, 82
Flagg, Josiah (1738-1794)	9
Gabriel, Charles H. (1856-1932)	8, 11, 100, 172
Gade, Niels W. (1817-1890)	44
Hauser, William, M.D. (1812-1880)	10
Heber, Reginald (1783-1826)	11, 178, 180
Holyoke, Samuel A. (1762-1820)	5, 6, 9, 11, 18, 176
Johnston, Julia H. (1849-1919)	24
Kimball, Jacob (1761-1826)	7, 80
Law, Andrew (1748-1821)	5, 9
Leavitt, Joshua (1794-1873)	11
Lyon, James (1735-1794)	5
Madan, Martin (1726-1790)	6, 8, 42, 96, 104
Mann, R.F. (fl. mid-19th c.)	88
Massengale, John (fl. mid-19th c.)	146
McCurry, John G. (1821-1886)	5, 34
Medley, Samuel (1738-1799)	40
Milgrove, Benjamin (c. 1731-1810)	5, 9, 32, 136
Miller, Dr. Edward (1735-1807)	10, 167
Mitchell, Nahum (1769-1853)	152
Milton, John (1608-1674)	7, 60
Moore, Henry E. (1803-1841)	6, 7
Mosher, Mrs. Julia (fl. c. 1900)	86
Needham, John (c. 1727-1786/7)	88
Palma, John (fl. c. 1760)	14
Pestel, Thomas (c. 1586-c.1660)	90

Rees, H.S. (1828-after 1911)	142
Richards, George (c. 1755-1814)	7, 8, 73, 92
Scott, Elizabeth (c. 1708-1776)	164
Sears, E.H. (1810-1876)	150
Smith, E.B. (fl. c. 1900)	11, 170
Steele, Anne (1717-1778)	10, 146
Stephenson, Joseph (1723-1810)	6, 54, 128
Tans'ur, William (1700-1783)	9, 10, 164
Tate, Nahum (1652-1715)	5, 14, 27
Towner, D.B. (1850-1919)	24
Tuckey, William (1708-1781)	106
Turner, Mrs. R.N. (fl. c. 1900)	86
Vella, Bertha F. (fl. c. 1900)	5, 6, 7, 11
Wales, E.A. (fl. c. 1900)	52
Walker, William (1809-1875)	7, 9, 132
Watts, Isaac (1674-1748)	5–11, 18, 32, 34, 42, 54, 68, 106, 122, 136, 152, 160, 176
Webb, George J. (1803-1887)	8, 9, 100, 110, 138
Wesley, Charles (1707-1788)	6, 10, 58, 167
White, Benjamin F. (1800-1879)	5, 12
Whitefield, George (1714-1770)	6
Williams, Aaron (1731-1776)	7, 8, 9, 115
Wood, Abraham (1752-1802)	46